Christ:
The Sacramental Word

Christ:
The Sacramental Word

EDITED BY
DAVID BROWN AND ANN LOADES

First published in Great Britain 1996
Society for Promoting Christian Knowledge
Holy Trinity Church
Marylebone Road
London NW1 4DU

Copyright © the editors and contributors 1996

British Library Cataloguing-in-Publication Data
A catalogue record for this book is available from
the British Library

ISBN 0-281-04849-5

Typeset by Pioneer Associates, Perthshire
Printed in Great Britain by
The Cromwell Press, Melksham, Wiltshire

Contents

Contributors

DAVID BROWN Van Mildert Professor of Divinity in the University of Durham and Canon of Durham Cathedral

JOHN CLARK Secratary of the Doctrine Commission of the Church of England

DAVID FULLER Senior Lecturer in English, University of Durham

ROBERT HAYWARD Reader in Theology, University of Durham

ANN LOADES Professor of Divinity, University of Durham and editor of *Theology*

GERARD LOUGHLIN Lecturer in Theology, University of Newcastle

JOHN MACQUARRIE formerly Lady Margaret Professor of Divinity, University of Oxford

WOLFHART PANNENBERG Emeritus Professor of Systematic Theology, Institute for Fundamental Theology and Ecumenism, University of Munich

PETER PHILLIPS Lecturer in Philosophy, Ushaw College, Durham

JOHN RICHES Professor of Divinity and Biblical Criticism, University of Glasgow

STEPHEN SYKES Bishop of Ely

ROWAN WILLIAMS Bishop of Monmouth

NICHOLAS WOLTERSTORFF Noah Porter Professor of Philosophical Theology, Yale University

FRANCES YOUNG Edward Cadbury Professor, Department of Theology, University of Birmingham

Preface

This volume of essays had its origins in a series of addresses on sacramental spirituality organized by the two editors to celebrate the nine hundredth anniversary of the present cathedral at Durham. The cathedral owes its origins to Cuthbert, a saint whose spirituality was closely bound up with nature, and thus with the sacramental in an important sense of that term. The monks of his native Lindisfarne, fleeing the invading Vikings, finally brought his body to Durham in AD 995, where it was to rest until a fresh set of invaders, the Normans, began the building of the present church in 1093. 1995 thus marked the millennium of the diocese of Durham, and it was therefore fitting that last year saw the publication of two of the volumes associated with our celebrations: *Signs of Grace: Sacraments in Poetry and Prose* (Cassell), by David Brown and David Fuller and *The Sense of the Sacramental: Movement and Measure in Art and Music, Place and Time* (SPCK), ed. David Brown and Ann Loades. It is the latter volume to which this present work is intended to be a companion piece. While the primary focus of *The Sense of the Sacramental* was visual and oral, with *Christ: The Sacramental Word* the intention is to engage the reader's interest in the way in which words (including Christ as the Word) function sacramentally, and thus to break down what we see as a false contrast between material symbol and verbal image.

Apart from our obvious indebtedness to our contributors, we would also like here to acknowledge the invaluable help, financial and otherwise, which we received from the Dean and Chapter of Durham Cathedral, the University of Durham (including its Theology Department) and the Bethune Baker Fund, Cambridge. It also gives us much pleasure to record here the many ways in which Michael Fraser, Tim Perry, Natalie Knödel, Louise Parkinson and Margaret Parkinson assisted us.

Introduction:
The Divine Poet

DAVID BROWN and ANN LOADES

To entitle a collection of essays about sacramentality *Christ: The Sacramental Word* may initially sound almost contradictory in terms. After all, it may be said, modern liturgies draw a sharp contrast between the two parts of the communion service: Rome calls the first part 'The Liturgy of the Word' and the second 'The Liturgy of the Eucharist'; the Church of England makes a similar distinction in the ASB between 'The Ministry of the Word' and 'The Ministry of the Sacrament'.[1] There is some legitimacy in the contrast, and it is certainly not the intention of what follows to reduce the sacraments to enacted preaching or scriptural proclamation.[2] Nonetheless, as these essays will illustrate, study of what might be meant by 'word' can be used as a means of entering more deeply into what it is to own a sacramental account of the world.

As the reader is already provided with introductions to each of the pieces, here we shall take the opportunity to integrate more closely some conclusions which may be drawn from the book as a whole. Each of its three sections may be seen as focusing on the relation between word and sacrament, but in three distinct ways. Each may be put in the form of a question. First, what difference does it make that Scripture has endorsed Word or Logos as one of the principal terms to be employed in describing Christ and his significance for us? Second, what impact should this have on our understanding of specific sacraments, especially as words continue to play a major role in their celebration? Finally, what comparisons can be drawn between this symbolic use of words in the sacramental context and other imaginative applications of language? We shall consider each of these questions in turn.

The poetry of incarnate Word

Hegel in his dialectical account of the origins of Christianity describes it as the perfect blend or synthesis of the extreme immanence of Greek religion and the extreme transcendence of Judaism.[3] More conventionally, it is often claimed that the Christian doctrine of the incarnation substantially modified what had hitherto been seen as the absolute necessity of stressing the radical otherness of God from the created order, so frightened were ancient Israel's theologians of the baneful influence of the surrounding nature religions.[4] It is a contrast which can be exaggerated, as Robert Hayward illustrates in his contribution. For a second century BC Jew such as the author of the book of *Jubilees* Israel's task and privilege is to mirror the worship of heaven. Sabbath and circumcision are not merely rites for this world; even the angels obey them. Hebrew too is God's language. Of course, *Jubilees* is not part of the biblical canon, but it does suggest tendencies already present towards that direction of thought.

Even so, it is important not to press the corrective too far in the opposite direction. The sense attaching to the divine word is a good case in point, inasmuch as it seems to undergo a radical transformation of meaning in John's Gospel, one which we believe has profound sacramental implications. Certainly, as in John, so also in the Old Testament word remains generally the principal mediator between God and world. But there the resemblance ends. In the Old Testament 'word' speaks of guidance and promise, and, because divine, can be assured of its result; indeed, this even guarantees it a degree of independent identity, long before the Wisdom literature's personification of Wisdom or Philo's adaptation of this to the Word, far less John's Gospel.[5] Even so, apart from notions of power or truth there is nothing to suggest that the writers envisage any intrinsic relation between God and his chosen medium. That is something which emerges with particular clarity from the opening chapter of Genesis. 'God said . . . and it was so' (Gen. 1.6–7 AV); the focus is all upon the inevitability of the divine fiat achieving its purpose, not at all upon the way God speaks. It seems to be a matter of indifference that he uses one set of words rather than another – provided of course that they both have essentially the same implication or effect. In any case what is effected bears no intrinsic relation either to the word or to God himself. In other words, it is a matter of three utterly different entities being related to one another. Divine transcendence, in this respect at least, is thus maintained with maximum rigour.

Contrast this with the use to which 'Word' is put in the Prologue to John's Gospel: 'and the Word was made flesh' (John 1.14 AV). John Macquarrie in his contribution uses this verse as a pivot for his argument which moves from creation through incarnation to sacrament. It is a logic with which we would wish to agree, but, though in the course of his discussion he has much to say about personal creativity, he makes no use of John's 'Word' as itself indicative of such an understanding. Yet it is arguable that this is John's most revolutionary contribution to Christian theology. Word has ceased to be the medium that keeps God and the world apart; instead, it has become that which binds world and God together.

Biblical scholars continue to debate whether we should look for a Palestinian or Hellenistic background for John's use, as also the extent to which wider cultural influences might be present. But, at the very least, to identify word and flesh must draw 'word' closer to the sense of 'expression' or even 'meaning' or 'explanation', as the wider meaning of the Greek *logos* does indeed permit.[6] Instead of words, God now expresses himself directly through an embodied presence. The materiality and visibility of that presence have often led theologians to switch immediately the metaphor: the 'expression' is of a divine artist rather than of a craftsman in words. In one sense the intuition is right, for it enables us to make an effective sacramental link between creation and incarnation. What God has already expressed or given of himself in the pattern of the created order reaches its culmination in the life of Christ, who fully expresses that design for humanity in the divine image of which he is such a perfect reflection.

Yet something has been lost. The Greek word from which we derive our own English word 'poet' originally meant simply 'maker' or 'creator', and that reminds us that the making of phrases and sentences is also an artistic, an expressive act. Words can of course be used purely instrumentally; they can even be used as a form of play merely to refer to one another, as deconstruction argues that we should understand all language.[7] But their power is surely at their greatest when they act neither purely referentially nor as some form of internal play. Instead, their images and metaphors are such that they too are integral in helping us to grasp whatever reality it is with which we wish to engage. One twentieth-century poet who displays a fine sensibility to this power of language is Kathleen Raine. For her our 'treasury of words' speaks 'Of heart's truth, mind's inheritance,/ From one to another told and retold',[8] and so in her poem 'Word made Flesh' it is the image of word which is retained as she speaks of all creation participating in, and reflecting, that Word:

> . . . Word that articulates the bird that speeds upon the air . . .
>
> Grammar of five-fold rose and six-fold lily . . .
>
> Hieroglyph in whose exact precision is defined
> Feather and insect wing, refraction of multiple eyes[9]

Language need not be seen as set over against our world. Instead, it can at times function as the medium precisely through which the sacramentality of the world is first or more deeply perceived. To use an image at least as old as Augustine, it is a case of one book (our language) enabling us to read another (the world), which then functions like 'a second book' (after the Bible) to speak of God to us.[10]

Let us try another way of clarifying the issue. By the sacramental is commonly understood the physical or material mediating that which is beyond itself, the spiritual; in the familiar definition, 'the outward and visible sign of an inward and spiritual grace'.[11] From that basic assumption it is easy to jump to the conclusion that only the purely physical can function sacramentally, and so in the case of the incarnation it must be Christ's 'flesh' that accomplishes such mediation, pointing to the divinity that lies behind the fleshly appearance. But the author of the Fourth Gospel by identifying word and flesh demonstrates that word can equally be conceived in sacramental terms. Words are more than sounds; they are signs or symbols pointing beyond themselves, mediating the reality into which they draw us. By calling Christ the Word John effectively declares the expressiveness, the language, the poetry of the incarnation equally sacramental. Just as the world speaks of the expressed order and pattern of intelligibility from which it draws its origin ('In the beginning was the Word', John 1.1 AV), so now 'the Word . . . made flesh' is 'full of grace and truth' (John 1.14).

Fascinating light is thrown on the sacramental character of words by the American poet Emily Dickinson in her poem 'A Word made Flesh'. There she characterizes all words as seeking to enable us to participate in something beyond themselves. However, a word 'has not the power to die' unless it succeeds in this perfectly; then:

> It may expire if He –
> 'Made Flesh and dwelt among us' –
> Could condescension be

Like this consent of language,
This loved Philology.[12]

But can even the incarnate Word succeed perfectly? Will not even divine language stumble and stutter? Clearly at one level most Christians would wish to deny this. Christ as God's Word must be the only adequate measure of truth:

Therefore these filthy rags of speech, this coil
Of statement, comment, query and response,
Tatters all too contaminate for use,
Have no renewing: He, the Truth, is, too,
The Word.[13]

Such are the sentiments of one of Robert Browning's dramatic characters, and in this case probably also the poet's own. But another poet, W. H. Auden, is perhaps nearer the truth, when he insists that though the Word brings reconciliation of opposites and restraint to Imagination's 'promiscuous fornication with her own images', it is a practical definition and intelligibility, not complete understanding: 'But here and now the Word which is implicit in the Beginning and in the End is become immediately explicit, and that which hitherto we could only passively fear as the incomprehensible I AM, henceforth we may actively love with comprehension that HE IS.'[14] God is 'the perfect poet' not in making all known to us in the Word made flesh, but all that we need know and love.[15]

Word and flesh are not then opposites: both alike are capable of functioning sacramentally; both alike participate in but do not exhaust that to which they refer. It is a mark of John's genius that such a connection is made, despite the fact that he was writing long before any explicit language of sacramentality. This is one of the main reasons why we find Bultmann's anti-sacramental reading of the Fourth Gospel so wrong-headed, irrespective of whether or not a subsequent editor made additions to the sixth chapter.[16] The argument cannot be decided simply by the question of whether explicit reference is made to the two dominical sacraments.[17] Rather, what matters is how John uses language. Not only, as we have noted, are word and flesh intimately related, it is quite likely that John's talk of the Word 'tabernacling among us' is also intentionally sacramental. This (the literal rendering of the verb at John 1.14) makes Jesus fulfil the same role in mediating the divine presence as the Tent of Meeting in the desert wanderings, while later in the gospel we regularly find him preaching in the Temple and he even speaks of himself as the new temple.[18] Moreover, again and again John has recourse to images of a sacramental kind which reinforce that opening chapter's evocation of God through enmattered reality. Thus it is surely no accident that images of water, wine and blood are used more frequently in this gospel than any other, and often intricately intertwined, as in the story of the wedding at Cana.[19]

This notion of images reinforcing or 'overlaying' one another is integral to the contribution from Frances Young. Her argument is that Paul's commitment to a doctrine of incarnation can only be fully appreciated once one realizes that his language is one of 'sacramental interpenetration', that is, an imaginative interplay of texts and images that, by being used simultaneously to speak of God and Jesus, effectively identify them as occupying the single space of him who is both God and human being. To the objection that this is still no more than an imaginative or metaphorical identification it may be responded that, just as much as the literal, the metaphorical can carry with it ontological implications.[20] It, too, can yield genuinely new knowledge that is not reducible to some more literal or analytic account.

John's Gospel provides some parallels. For example, the Lord who has declared himself the source of living water is later found on a cross, uttering the cry: 'I thirst'. Again, the same gospel that has made the taking of flesh so central can nonetheless declare: 'The flesh profiteth nothing' (John 6.63 AV). The temptation (which needs to be resisted) is to suppose that such conflicts can be resolved by reduction ('flesh' is to be rejected, 'thirst' not to be taken seriously).[21] Poetry is much more a matter of apparently conflicting images mutually enriching one another. God 'making' himself flesh – the 'poetry' of the incarnate Word – inevitably meant a plurality of images and metaphors as language struggled to capture the mystery of what had happened. The words, like the flesh itself, function sacramentally in both pointing to a divine reality beyond themselves, while at the same time mediating, however inadequately, something of that reality.

Language and sacrament

One place where the danger of a reductionist approach to religion's symbolic language is seen at its clearest is in discussion of the sacraments themselves. So convinced is the theologian or philosopher that a certain image has only one particular and definite meaning that, however illuminating his or her account is from that chosen perspective, instead of the brilliant hues of the multi-faceted original symbol we are left with a flat monochrome. This is illustrated by one of the major themes with which Part II is concerned, the personal and social identity that is given to us, particularly through baptism and the eucharist. For Pannenberg and Williams it is in fact their principal concern.

For the Christian one obvious way in which that social identity is mediated is through the Pauline imagery of the body: we can become part of Christ's body, and it is one principal function of the sacraments to make this a living reality. Eating Christ's body means becoming part of him. If we likewise allow the images of the Fourth Gospel mutually to enrich one another, then to drink his blood must mean becoming part of the vine that is Christ, and by implication eating his flesh must mean becoming part of the flesh in which the Word tabernacled. But what are we to take as the meaning of this? The temptation is to speak of powerful metaphors and leave the matter there, or else suppose that no more is meant than two individuals (Christ and the believer) relating to one another.

But is not mutual interdependence thereby implied? Admittedly, in the Captivity Epistles Christ is distinguished as part of the body – the head; but elsewhere the language is consistently of him being synonymous with the whole body and not part of it.[22] Likewise, a vine ceases to be a vine if it loses all its branches! Yet again and again through history the ontological implications of the imagery have been discounted. Certainly our dependence on Christ has been fully acknowledged, but seldom with the same force has his dependence upon us.

Consider two very different examples: the nineteenth-century Roman Catholic poet and priest, Gerard Manley Hopkins, and the twentieth-century Protestant theologian, Eberhard Jüngel. In a powerful sermon Hopkins avers: 'for myself I make no secret I look forward to seeing the matchless beauty of Christ's body in the heavenly light'. Here we have no reference to his body the Church; instead, Hopkins seems to mean it quite literally. It will be a beauty of body that matches Christ's beauty of mind and beauty of character. In itself that might be no bad sentiment, but with Hopkins it is developed in such a way as to suggest that it is beauty born of isolation, a beauty that has no need of others. Thus Christ's mind is that of 'genius', while his body must have had 'neither disease nor the seeds of any' since, even on earth, it was 'framed directly from heaven': 'picture him . . . in his bearing how majestic, how strong and yet how lovely and lissome in his limbs'.[23] Again, for Jüngel, though he happily endorses Luther's talk of Christ as sacrament, it is, as one might expect of someone so concerned to defend the absolute priority of divine grace, wholly of Christ as giver, never as receiver. Even the sacraments themselves can only be enacted parables of Christ preached, lest there be any hint of us taking an initiative or ourselves offering something to God.[24]

It is an aspect of Jüngel's theology for which Geoffrey Wainwright has taken him severely to task. For Jüngel, both the Church as a whole and individual Christians remain purely passive before the grace of God. But, Wainwright asks, is this really consistent with the incorporationist language of the New Testament? 'How far may, and indeed must, the church be viewed as the continuing body of Christ in which the Holy Spirit dwells transformatively in such a way that in its very being, as well as in its words and its gestures, the church becomes an *active bearer* of the gospel by which it is itself constituted?'[25] To our mind the willingness of Paul and John to speak indifferently of Christ indwelling us or us indwelling him hints at such a reciprocity. Similarly, the identification of Christ with the whole of the body implies a willed dependency upon the effectiveness of individual limbs, an idea that Teresa of Avila powerfully captures in her well-known lines: 'Christ has no body now on earth but yours; no hands but yours, no feet but yours; yours are the eyes through which his love looks out to the world; yours are the feet with which he goes about doing good; yours are the hands with which he blesses men now'.[26]

But it is reflection upon Hopkins' remarks that demands of us the stronger response. For, had the incarnation been as Hopkins supposes it, major questions are surely raised regarding the extent to which it could even be described as a full entering into our humanity. Whether it be in mind or in body, human beings are dependent creatures: our minds in large part the creation of the society in which we are set, and the health of our bodies heavily dependent on the environment in which we find ourselves. Thus, for example, Christ's physiognomy must surely have reflected the typical diet of a peasant culture. We might ask whether his teeth could conceivably have been perfect when he died? But, more importantly, there must also have been various forms of psychological dependence. Like all of us, he would have needed the support of family and friends to carry him through, and that is surely what the gospels tell us. Mark in particular tells of his longing for the support of his disciples in his agony in the Garden of Gethsemane, as also of his inability to perform any miracle in his home town (Mark 6.5), so overwhelmed was he by its hostility. Significantly, both passages are softened in Matthew and Luke, as is also Mark's recording of how 'power had gone forth from him' (Mark 5.30 RSV) when he healed the woman with a haemorrhage. Whether plausible in this incident or not, Mark seems to imply that physical exhaustion was a normal consequence of Jesus' bodily care of others.

In drawing attention to these features of the use of the image of body, it is certainly no part of our intention to suggest that this exhausts the term's meaning. That would be only to repeat the mistake which we have been criticizing. Rather, our point is that body is an intense or focused symbol, and this is what precludes its reduction to any one literal or analytic account.[27] The symbolism of the metaphor reinforces the symbolism of the sacramental reality, enriching it such that word, far from simplifying the act, actually adds further layers of intensity of reference to whatever is enacted during the course of the sacrament's celebration.

This point can be made clearer if we consider another, related issue raised by Part II, namely the way in which particular words are held to effect or bring about the sacramental reality. It is an issue that has been more sharply focused in the Western than in the Eastern tradition, and indeed the last three essays in Part II are really only intelligible against the backdrop of Western rather than Orthodox assumptions. Thus, John Clark records the narrowing of focus within the rite of sacramental confession upon the formula of absolution (*ego te absolvo* – the priest's 'I absolve you'), while Gerard Loughlin's modern defence of transubstantiation and Nicholas Wolterstorff's substitution of action language in its place alike find their centre within the same narrow compass of the words of institution at the Lord's Supper.

At one level such a narrow focus has its appropriate justification. In the case of the eucharist, it would be odd, to say the very least, if no reference were made to the words uttered by our Lord at the Last Supper, and so, even if some of our earliest liturgies make no such reference,[28] the Church was right subsequently so to insist. But to go on from that admission and suppose everything else incidental to Christ's sacramental presence would be equally to err in the opposite direction. Two quite different questions need to be addressed: when, objectively, Christ may be said to be present; and when, subjectively, that presence is most likely to become a personal reality for the communicant. In the former case we need to ask about which formulae best reflect the intentions of the Church and under what circumstances they may appropriately be said to be realized. Here the notion of the sacraments functioning *ex opere operato* has its legitimate place; the activity of God cannot be made to depend either on the holiness

or otherwise of the priest or on the recipient's degree of attentive-
ness but only on 'the rite properly executed'. But, quite different
and of more relevance here, is the subjective question.

So long as we think of the body and blood as things, it is very
easy to think that the words of institution might be enough. But
as soon as we conceive of Christ's presence in more personalist
terms, as with all personal relations it becomes a cluster of images
that mediate the 'other' rather than one particular thing. So, for
instance, if we walk into an empty room, it is seldom one thing
that tells us that it belongs to a close relation or friend, but
numerous small indicators – the way the cushions are strewn, the
newspapers in the magazine rack, the half-drunk cup of tea with
the biscuit on the saucer and so forth. The images reinforce one
another in generating a sense of the 'other's' presence.[29] Nor does
this change should the 'other' appear. The 'other' is seen as other
in gesture, intonation, twinkle of the eye, all of which help us
draw upon memories of the 'other' as having the identity and
history which in fact they have.[30]

Similarly with the eucharist. Words, even the words of institution, can do little of themselves to evoke a sense of presence.
What matters is how they resonate, their ability to build image
upon image in a way that brings to life that sense of presence. In
some respects this is a lesson modern liturgy has learnt. For
instance, instead of a narrow focus on Christ's death, the ana-
phora or consecration prayer now seeks to encapsulate the entire
history of our salvation: the Christ of the infancy narratives, of
the ministry and of the resurrection is thus brought to remembrance no less than the Jesus of the passion. Yet, on the other
hand, there remains a fear of the allusive, as though what may not
be immediately understood must therefore be misunderstood.
Consider for instance the retreat of both the Church of England
and Rome from the image of Christ not only tabernacling within
us but coming to a home in need[31] in the words: 'Lord I am not
worthy that thou shouldst come under my roof', now replaced by
the prosaic: 'Lord, I am not worthy to receive you', where the
image of food is merely repeated. Thereby is lost all the wonderful resonances of the analogy, however remote, of Christ now
deigning to tabernacle in our flesh as once he did at the incarnation. Or consider the way in which David Frost's lively image
of us like shipwrecked sailors 'grasping' at a hope was in the ASB
reduced to the flat 'a hope set before us'.[32]

Just as the application of the term 'Word' to the incarnate
Christ did not leave things as they were but changed how the
term was understood, so sacramental words cannot be said to

achieve their purpose simply as mediating words, quite distinct from what they are intending to convey. It matters deeply that they should resonate and interact with as wide a range of ways of perceiving Christ as possible, but at the same time in a manner which grounds each allusion as part of the identity of what it is to be the incarnate Lord who is also Lord of the Church. The fact that that qualification necessitates conservatism in the choice of imagery should not mislead us into supposing that the imagery does not matter, or that it cannot be used in new or even startling ways.

Both in the history of the Bible and in subsequent church history unexpected and innovative use of traditional language is to be observed, as is the enriching interplay of allusions across textual references.[33] Yet in marked contrast to sixteenth- and seventeenth-century translators of the Bible, our modern preoccupation equates accuracy with the elimination of ambiguity, with narrowing (no doubt, sometimes rightly) the possible range of meanings.[34] It suggests a less meditative, less engaged way of reading the text. Because of their hostility to visual imagery, Judaism and Islam are usually deemed to be anti-sacramental religions. Though this is largely true, their treatment of their sacred texts suggests another perspective. For Orthodox Judaism each word, and indeed sometimes each letter, is taken to have the power to convey the sense of the presence of God,[35] and the ritual chanting that takes place in the mosque can be similarly interpreted. The words must not be chained down, for they are the vehicle through which God speaks to the believer. That sense of Scripture as sacrament, as the vehicle of God's presence, occasionally finds twentieth-century parallels within Christianity, as in the extraordinary effect upon Simone Weil of frequent recital of the Lord's Prayer in Greek as she went about her work in the fields.[36] But, on the whole, current Western practice assumes one meaning in the text, and that, when found, constitutes the end of our quest.

Western theology has paid a high price in its constant temptation towards such reductionism. If the imagery of baptism can be reduced to remission of sins, the whole rite becomes problematic in a world in which we have ceased to believe that babies are deeply infected by original sin. If penance is no more than the receiving of absolution, the penitent's recurring sins will remain as problematic as ever. If the eucharist is only about Christ's death or his presence, then it too becomes difficult when belief in substitutionary atonement no longer seems plausible, or if the presence is isolated from any sense of transforming relationship.

Likewise, doctrines get undermined if we define resurrection by empty tomb, or ascension as an event forty days later. For it is precisely as focused images bearing more than one meaning that they can maintain their power, with resurrection, for instance, about new life generally, or ascension about humanity's permanent place in the divine scheme of things. Words that allude to sacraments or doctrine burst out beyond any attempt to contain them by some strict literal definition. It is precisely because of this that they not only exercise their power, but move us towards thinking in a manner transcendent to the words, of God himself. All imagery forces us beyond containment, and though this may sometimes only make us move laterally or sideways to think of another earthly matter, the process has thus begun of thinking analogically, and analogy is of course of the essence of religion: the words induce us to move beyond their literal meaning towards thinking of a new order of reality.

The religion in poetry

If the argument of the preceding paragraph is correct, then this explains why poetry and religion are often thought to be closely allied. Certainly it is an assumption shared by all four writers in the concluding section of this book, as they discuss poets as varied as Spenser, Wordsworth and Hopkins. It is also a theme taken up a number of times by the contemporary Australian poet, Les Murray. For him:

Full religion is the large poem in loving repetition; . . .

. . . and God is the poetry caught in any religion,
caught, not imprisoned. Caught as in a mirror
that he attracted, being in the world as poetry
is in the poem, a law against closure.[37]

That resistance to closure, the refusal to accept that any word or deed has fully expressed all that need be said, the persistence of transcendence as a point of contact between the two, is a theme which he reiterates elsewhere:

Art is what can't be summarised:
it has joined creation from our side,
entered Nature, become a fact
and acquired presence, . . .

Art's best is a standing miracle . . .
an anomaly, finite but inexhaustible, . . .

. . . a passage, a whole pattern
that has shifted the immeasurable
first step into Heaven.[38]

That notion of both poetry and religion conveying an 'inexhaustible presence' is of course not a new one. As already noted, Christianity has a long tradition of viewing God as author of two books – Scripture and nature; and in seeing both as artistic creations it endorsed what had already become a pagan commonplace.[39] Augustine even applies the analogy to God's providential ordering of history; for him it is 'a beautiful poem' in which 'the beauty of the world's history is constituted through the clash of contraries as a kind of eloquence in events, instead of in words'.[40] Again, in the Middle Ages we find Boccaccio so stressing the extent to which God uses poetic devices in Scripture, that poetry and Bible can even be identified as the same thing.[41]

It is perhaps Coleridge with whom we most strongly associate this claim. In *Confessions of an Inquiring Spirit* he launches a tirade against the deadening hand of biblical literalism, which he sees as effectively destroying the power of biblical imagery: it 'plants the vineyard of the Word with thorns for me'.[42] Earlier in his *Lectures on Literature* he had sought to define what it is that makes 'religion . . . the poetry of all mankind'. Like poetry, religion 'bids us while we are sitting in the dark round our little fire still look at the mountain tops'.[43] Either by generalizing or by distancing us from our immediate concerns, he suggests that both pull us on to an altogether different plain, but for that to be possible a certain type of use of language – imagery – is indispensable.

Inevitably such imagery comes from the natural, created world, and so the question of the relation between divine and human poetry or 'making' is raised. For Plato art stood at two removes from reality; it imitated nature, itself an imitation of the ideal world of the Forms. But also in Plato one finds the inspiration of the poet compared to a form of madness, and, though this was intended as a strategy for demoting the artist's status,[44] Renaissance Neoplatonism turned it into a compliment. Coupled with that was the possibility of analogy with the mystic inspiration of the Old Testament prophet.[45] Milton, for instance, talks of poetic inspiration coming 'by devout prayer to that eternall Spirit who can enrich with all utterance and knowledge, and sends out his Seraphim with the hallow'd fire of his Altar to touch and purify the lips of whom he pleases'.[46] The allusion to Isaiah 6.6–7 is repeated in his poem 'On the Morning of Christ's Nativity' when he speaks of the Muse 'From out his secret Altar toucht with hallow'd fire' (28), while in *Paradise Lost* (3, 1–55) he opts instead for an analogy with classical poets and seers blind like himself – Homer and Teiresias.

Such analogies which bypassed nature made poetry less derivative, and even allowed for the possibility that the poet's creation could surpass the natural order. This is the view advocated by Sir Philip Sidney: 'Nature never set forth the earth in so rich tapestry as divers poets have done . . . Her world is brazen, the poets only deliver a golden.' Yet, though such a claim could easily have been used to denigrate the divine, that is no part of his intention:

> Neither let it be deemed too saucy a comparison to balance the highest point of man's wit with the efficacy of Nature; but rather give right honour to the heavenly Maker of that maker, who having made man to his own likeness, set him beyond and over all his works of that second nature: which in nothing he showeth so much as in poetry, when with the force of a divine breath he bringeth things forth surpassing her doings.[47]

Nor is it a contention of which we should fight shy. Nature has its focused symbols which find their appropriate place in the Christian religion, such as water, bread and blood, but that focus surely gains added intensity and power by the use to which these symbols have been put, not only in the Bible as a literary creation but also in the Christian tradition of liturgy and poetry. In John Keble we find the sacramental character of this relation made quite explicit: 'Poetry lends religion her wealth of symbols and similies; religion restores them again to poetry, clothed with so splendid a radiance that they appear to be no longer symbols, but to partake (I might almost say) of the nature of sacraments.'[48]

Such an exaltation of the role of the artist may seem to have taken us far from Platonism, but the position of Platonism is much more complex than is usually acknowledged. It is all too easy to take the dying Socrates' longing for release from the body as normative, and certainly in the Neoplatonism of Plotinus a strongly ascetical side was developed. But against that must be set the positive estimate of the world given by Plato in dialogues like *Timaeus* or *Symposium*; likewise, Plotinus not only conceives of the world as emanating from God but also has a long tract against the Gnostics defending the inherent goodness of the world.[49] Plato's Theory of Forms can in fact be read in two different ways: as suggesting that anything really worthwhile exists elsewhere, because the world is always pointing to something other than itself; or as claiming that precisely because this world imitates or participates in that other world necessarily it has an inherent, transcendent value. Clearly, the more closely one follows the latter account the nearer one comes to a sacramental position.

But increasingly we live in a world where both accounts are under threat. Matthew Arnold might be taken as the most obvious case of a nineteenth-century literary figure who denied that religious imagery pointed beyond itself, while in the twentieth century we have philosophers like Derrida denying that any texts, religious or otherwise, have any life outside of themselves. This is a huge issue, and can only be briefly addressed here, but it is still important to address it.

In a famous essay Matthew Arnold wrote:

> Our religion has materialised itself in the fact, in the supposed fact; it has attached its emotion to the fact, and now the fact is failing it. But for poetry the idea is everything; the rest is a world of illusion, of divine illusion. Poetry attaches its emotion to the idea; the idea *is* the fact. The strongest part of our religion today is its unconscious poetry.[50]

Arnold writes as the son of a famous cleric, determined to save something of Christianity from the ravages of the nineteenth-century undermining of belief through biblical criticism and scientific discoveries (and he is quite clear about the inadequacy of science by itself to save). Nonetheless, one may question his solution. We may illustrate some of the difficulties by considering someone in our own day – John Drury – who finds his position entirely congenial.

For Drury, though the historical achievements of his own discipline of biblical studies have been considerable, this has been bought at the cost of a real engagement of the imagination with the text. With that part of his analysis we cannot but agree. But he goes on to develop a 'nothing but . . .' or reductionist approach. He wants to 'tie the poet and the sacred Scriptures so fast together as to invite glossing the clause about Christ in the Nicene Creed, "he rose again according to the Scriptures"', as 'he rose again according to poetry'.[51] There follows a comparative analysis of two poems on the resurrection (one by Hopkins and one by Herbert), with the Herbert poem judged superior because of its this-worldly reference. The estimate has become moral and metaphysical, rather than allowing the poems of themselves to pull us out of ourselves into fresh perceptions of how things might be. The language traps us where we are, rather than taking us where we might be. Significantly, we can be well-nigh certain that, unlike Drury, the two poets would have endorsed one another's poems.[52]

In other words, the transcendent dimension is an essential element in the imagery's power, whether it be pointing to an unfamiliar or totally other world. To clarify matters, consider the use of pagan mythology in the history of European poetry. It has of course sometimes functioned simply as adornment, but where more was intended it is significant that it then never survived in its own right. It became of vital importance that the nature of allegory be clear, either as pointing to a personified pattern in nature, or as reinforcement of reference to another kind of reality, even more transcendent to the poem itself, namely the Christian dispensation. So, for instance, Boccaccio takes the story of Saturn devouring his children as an allegory for the destructive power of the passage of time, whereas in Virgil's talk of 'Jupiter omnipotens' he detected a reference to the Christian God.

Milton provides a fascinating illustration of the tensions such an approach could create in a Christian poet. When writing *Comus* (512–18) he was still of the view that the traditional method was the right one, and that a Christian allegorical interpretation of references to pagan gods could find its appropriate justification. However, in *Paradise Lost* (7, 1–12) he displays a more critical attitude. Gone are the nine Muses of pagan mythology, and in their place has come 'Urania' ('the heavenly One') whom many commentators identify with Christ the Logos. Ironically, this is combined with a fresh commitment to pagan thought, in a view of the origin of the world that bears some analogies with Plotinus' emanationist account (cf. 7, 163–71). But more important for our purposes here is to note the recurring issue of whether poetry can truly succeed without some kind of transcendent reference,[53] whether it is a matter of pagan mythology, or, more recently, the adaptation of Christian imagery for secular purposes.

Such a transcendent reference is one which is even more fiercely resisted by modern Deconstructionism. For Derrida there is nothing outside the text: *il n'y a pas de hors texte*.[54] It is a position which is strongly challenged by George Steiner in *Real Presences*, where, in an argument similar to that defended here, he maintains that literature gains its power precisely through the sense of presence within it of something beyond itself, or, putting matters the other way around, through its ability to disclose a transcendence beyond itself. More recently, the argument has been taken up by Valentine Cunningham in his book *in the Reading Gaol*, a title which is a play upon both Oscar Wilde's famous poem and the jail or prison into which modern accounts of reading have thrown us. He insists upon the inescapably theological character of the success of literature, should it indeed succeed:

> The question of presence, of what is made really present or not, in writing and reading, is, as Eliot knew and George Steiner keeps insisting, of course theological and biblical . . . The issue is, in the end, sacramental; the table at which the literary parasite sits looks oddly akin to a eucharistic one.[55]

It was to a different sort of parasite that George Steiner drew attention in the address he gave at Durham in the series of which these essays were also part. Comparing the two suppers described in Plato's *Symposium* and in John's Gospel, he observed that the latter gained its power in part as an anti-supper. Here too the theme of love was prominent, but even as the beloved disciple reclined on Jesus' breast, the one to betray Jesus is identified as he to whom Jesus personally gives the bread, and 'as soon as Judas had received the bread he went out. It was night' (John 13.30 NEB).

It is a point which we may develop in our own way to bring out more fully the type of sacramentalism which we have been concerned to articulate throughout this essay. Many commentators, if they detect a sacramental reference at all, assume that it must be anti-sacramental: that it is John's way of saying that what really matters is faith, and not participation in a church's celebration of the Lord's Supper. But on our view this is to ignore the more poetic way in which John is writing. Literalism requires an 'either/ or' (one reading or another), whereas imagery and metaphor legitimate a 'both-and'. Before applying this directly to John, we may illustrate the latter approach from three poets who tackle closely related issues.

First, consider what is in fact the longest episode in Dante's *Inferno*. Canto 32 ends with Ugolino eating the marrow of his enemy's head 'as starved men tear bread' (127), while in the following canto we hear the reason for this. His enemy, Archbishop Roger of Pisa, had locked him and his 'children' in a tower, to die of starvation. Though this did indeed happen, while Ugolino gnawed his hands in desperation, his 'boys' cry out:

> O Father, it will give us much less pain
> If thou wilt feed on us; thy gift at birth
> Was this sad flesh, strip thou it off again (61–3).[56]

Here too we have a supper and an anti-supper, an eating out of hate, and the offer of an eating out of love. Each, however, reinforces and interprets the other to say something about the possibility of sacramental incorporation into another human being. Ugolino eats with hate, and so remains in hell; yet another eating had been available to him in life, one based on love. The parallel with John becomes even closer if those commentators are right who suggest that Dante intended a eucharistic reference at this point.[57]

Now consider another famous poem, this time from the eighteenth century, Hölderlin's 'Brod und Wein' (Bread and Wine). It sees our own world as 'night', with the 'day' of classical Greece in the long distant past. For most of the poem it looks as though 'the god who is to come' is Dionysus or Bacchus and that it is he who will bring recovery: 'a wine-cup more full, a life more intense and more daring'. But then comes the surprise of the ending:

> Meanwhile, though, to us shadows comes the Son of the
>   Highest,
> Comes the Syrian and down into our gloom bears his torch.
> Blissful, the wise men see it; in souls that were captive there
>   gleams a
> Smile, and their eyes shall yet thaw in response to the light.[58]

The identification of Christ and Bacchus is startling, but all the more effective as a result. Our night is not total blackness; the bread and wine continue to speak of a divine presence, and so give hope.[59] Put more prosaically, classicism and Christianity are in the end not set against each other as day against night: both are enlarged. The night of the anti-supper has become part of the day.

Finally, as a twentieth-century example, we might take another German poet, Paul Celan. His 'Die Winzer' (The Vintagers) was written shortly after reading Heidegger's essay on Hölderlin's 'Brod und Wein'. Celan admired both men. In Heidegger's case the admiration was ironical in view of the philosopher's ambivalent attitude towards the Nazis. For having lost both parents in the Holocaust, Celan found it difficult to commit himself to the German language; yet it was Heidegger who in his view gave back to German its 'limpidité' (lucidity).[60] The poem opens:

> They harvest the wine of their eyes,
> they crush out all of the weeping, this also:
> thus willed by the night.[61]

At one level the positive biblical images of the wine are subverted and turned into night.[62] Yet at another level the very fact that Celan expresses himself in German at all speaks of hope: that what we have here is a negative theology, rather than no theology at all. The surface meaning is all about anti-supper; but the use of the language (German) and of the imagery (biblical) hints after all at a supper, and so qualifies it.

Similarly then in John, we would suggest not a final anti-supper reading, but one in which supper and anti-supper mutually complement and interpret one another. Admittedly, at one level that particular chapter (13) could easily be read as anti-sacramental or even world-denying. One could, for instance, argue that because Christ is portrayed as knowing everything, including that 'he had come from God and was going back to God' (John 13.3 NEB), the intention is to demonstrate that even the traitor doing his worst cannot shake Christ's confidence. But John, the master with words, achieves so much more.

Already in chapter 6 Christ's discussion of the eucharist (35–59) had concluded with no less than two references to the traitor (60–71). There the reference had been secondary to the main point of the discussion; here in chapter 13 it becomes primary. Even so the dialectic continues: of feet washed and hand betrayed, of sharing and non-sharing, of hospitality and treason, of darkness and light. Only excessive literalism would read the conclusion of the passage, 'It was night', as intended simply to report fact. The Light of the World is already there in the night of darkness and betrayal. The fact that human nature means that every supper will inevitably also partake of the quality of an anti-supper does not imply that there is no supper after all, no presence of Christ. In this world the two go together, and so, while the anti-supper reminds us of how badly things can go wrong, the dialectic also speaks of a promise, that Christ will never let us down: there will also be a supper of presence.

In the history of Christian theology some theologians have been suspicious of words, arguing that, if used at all, they should always point beyond themselves.[63] Certainly, reference beyond the text ought to be part of their purpose. But, if our argument here is correct, equally important is another strand of the Christian tradition that sees the words as themselves 'comestible', to be 'chewed and digested'.[64] As Anselm enjoins, 'taste the goodness of your Redeemer . . . chew his words as a honey-comb . . . chew by thinking, suck by understanding, swallow by loving and rejoicing. Rejoice in chewing, be glad in sucking, delight in swallowing'.[65] Only by such lingering delight over words will their full richness be discovered.

Whether within the biblical text or beyond, words can and do thus function sacramentally, despite all their apparent clash and dissonance. For it is precisely through meditation upon such images that our participation in the Word made flesh is most effectively deepened. Chewing the eucharistic elements and chewing the words should thus not be seen as opposed activities. Words, no less than the Word himself, can be fully sacramental. The divine Poet whose Word shaped the language of creation also thereby made possible the words – the human poetry – that describe that creation, and it is these words that enable us to participate in the Word as their source and ours. If Dorothy Sayers is right,[66] Dante combined the incarnate Christ with the books of the Bible in a single eucharistic procession: Word, words and sacrament all as one. Whether a correct account or not, it was a wise intuition.[67]

Notes

1. English Methodism makes a similar distinction; cf. the headings 'The Ministry of the Word' and 'The Lord's Supper' in *The Methodist Service Book* (1975).

2. This is a criticism sometimes made (unfairly) of Calvin, who insists upon the inseparability of sacramental sign from proclaimed word, e.g. 'A sacrament is never without a preceding promise but is joined to it as a sort of appendix'; 'the sacrament requires preaching to beget faith', *Institutes of the Christian Religion*, ed. J. T. McNeill and F. L. Battles (Philadelphia: Westminster Press, 1960) 4, 14, 3 & 4, pp. 1278, 1279. But such insistence is combined with a full recognition of the Holy Spirit working through this medium. A better example of reductionism comes from Eberhard Jüngel for whom the sacraments only 'display' or 'proclaim' salvation rather than mediate it; cf. 'The Church as Sacrament?' in *Theological Essays I* (Edinburgh: T. & T. Clark, 1989), pp. 189–213.

3. For his contrast between Greek and Jewish religion, cf. G. W. F. Hegel, *Lectures on the Philosophy of Religion*, ed. P. C. Hodgson (Los Angeles: University of California Press, 1988), pp. 328–75.

4. For an extended argument against the view that Judaism had as transcendent and monotheistic view of God as is usually claimed, cf. M. Barker, *The Great Angel: A Study of Israel's Second God* (London: SPCK, 1992).

5. The theology of the semi-independent divine word is seen clearly in Isaiah 55.10–11. It probably reflects a more general view that all words have an inherent power of their own, as can be seen in the impossibility of revoking a blessing, even though given unintentionally (e.g. Gen. 27). The treatment of Wisdom in Proverbs 8.22–31 and Wisdom 7.22ff. is eventually adapted by Philo (d. AD 50) to speak of the divine Word (e.g. *De Agricultura* 31; *De Confusione Linguarum* 146–7); in this he is to some small extent

anticipated by Ben Sira's identification of Wisdom with Torah or Law (Ecclus. 24.23).

6. Thus the usual Greek for to give an account or explanation of something is *didonai logon*.

7. Or at least the most common version of deconstructionism as it is applied in the theological writings of Don Cupitt or in Mark Taylor's seminal work *Erring* (University of Chicago Press, 1984). But more positive interpretations have been proposed: cf. K. Hart, *The Trespass of the Sign* (Cambridge: Cambridge University Press, 1989).

8. From 'Words: For Wendell Berry', in K. Raine, *Living with Mystery: Poems 1987–91* (Ipswich: Golgonooza Press, 1992), p. 39.

9. From 'Word made Flesh', in K. Raine, *The Pythoness* (1948); reprinted in *Selected Poems* (Ipswich: Golgonooza Press, 1988), p. 24.

10. For some parallels in Augustine, cf. C. Harrison, *Beauty and Revelation in the Thought of St Augustine* (Oxford: Clarendon Press, 1992), pp. 118–21; for its use in English literature, cf. S. Prickett, *Words and the Word* (Cambridge: Cambridge University Press, 1986), pp. 123–48.

11. As in the definition of a sacrament in the Catechism of the Book of Common Prayer (1662).

12. Our punctuation; Dickinson's original idiosyncratic punctuation can be found in *The Complete Poems of Emily Dickinson*, ed. T. H. Johnson (London: Faber & Faber, 1975), pp. 675–6. Another of her poems that reflects on the power of words in an interesting way is 'A word is dead' (*Poems*, pp. 534–5).

13. R. Browning, *The Ring and the Book*, X, 373–7; ed. R. D. Altick (Harmondsworth: Penguin, 1971), p. 487.

14. W. H. Auden's reflection on the Word is to be found in his 'Meditation of Simeon' in *For the Time Being* (London: Faber & Faber, 1953), pp. 105–11, esp. pp. 109, 108.

15. The phrase is Browning's in *Paracelsus* II, 648; in *The Poetical Works of Robert Browning*, ed. I. Jack and M. Smith (Oxford: Clarendon Press, 1983), I, p. 265. An excellent study of Browning's reflections on the incarnate Word is to be found in W. Whitla, *The Central Truth: The Incarnation in Robert Browning's Poetry* (Toronto: University of Toronto Press, 1963).

16. While in his *Theology of the New Testament* (London: SCM, 1955, Vol. 2, p. 59) Bultmann finds John's attitude towards sacraments as 'critical' or at least 'reserved', his position in *The Gospel of John* (Oxford: Blackwell, 1971, p. 472) is, if anything, strengthened: 'The truth is that the sacraments are superfluous for him'. Though C. K. Barrett (*Essays on John*, London: SPCK, 1982, pp. 37–49) offers strong arguments in favour of John 6.51–58 being part of the original text, he too sees John's attitude to the sacraments as at most that of 'critical acceptance' (p. 97).

17. John, it should be noted, is unique among the four gospels in recording Jesus as himself baptizing (3.22), while, though there is

no institution narrative, not only are there the allusions to the eucharist in chapter 6, for some commentators at least (e.g. B. Lindars, *Essays on John*, Louvain: Leuven University Press, 1992, p. 53), the foot-washing in chapter 13 that is recorded in its place at the Last Supper 'certainly describes a sacramental act'. That is also how it has been frequently understood in liturgical practice well into the twentieth century (cf. E. C. Hoskyns, *The Fourth Gospel*, ed. F. N. Davey, London: Faber & Faber, 1947, pp. 443–6).

18. For a recent presentation of such an argument, cf. R. F. Collins, *These Things Have Been Written: Studies on the Fourth Gospel* (Grand Rapids, Michigan: Eerdmans, 1990), pp. 198–216.

19. For an interpretation of the miracle along these lines, cf. D. Brown, *The Word To Set You Free* (London: SPCK, 1995), pp. 128–31.

20. For a detailed argument to this effect, cf. J. M. Soskice, *Metaphor and Religious Language* (Oxford: Clarendon Press, 1985).

21. Some commentators talk of an 'irony' that 'suspends meaning' and induces 'uncertainty' (W. H. Kelber, 'The Birth of a Beginning', in *The Gospel of John as Literature*, ed. M. W. G. Stibbe, Leiden: E. J. Brill, 1993, pp. 225–6). But that applies only if we refuse to allow the apparently opposed assertions to complement one another.

22. Contrast e.g. 1 Cor. 12.12–27 with Col. 2.8–19. For a discussion of the use of the image in Paul, cf. D. E. H. Whiteley, *The Theology of St Paul* (Oxford: Blackwell, 1970), pp. 190–9.

23. Sermon for 23 November 1879; e.g. in *Gerard Manley Hopkins: A Selection of his Poetry and Prose*, ed. W. H. Gardner (Harmondsworth: Penguin, 1953), pp. 137–9.

24. e.g. E. Jüngel, *Theological Essays II* (Edinburgh: T. & T. Clark, 1995), pp. 163–90.

25. G. Wainwright, 'Church and Sacrament(s)', in *The Possibilities of Theology*, ed. J. Webster (Edinburgh: T. & T. Clark, 1994), pp. 90–105, esp. p. 103.

26. This prayer of Teresa of Avila, though quoted in several prayer anthologies, is almost certainly like St Francis' prayer 'Lord make me an instrument of thy peace' without secure historical attribution.

27. There have been a number of recent major studies of body as a focused or concentrated image. Cf. e.g. M. Rubin, *Corpus Christi* (Cambridge: Cambridge University Press, 1991); C. W. Bynum, *Fragmentation and Redemption* (New York: Zone Books, 1992); C. W. Bynum, *The Resurrection of the Body* (New York: Columbia University Press, 1995).

28. The most natural interpretation of the second century *Didache*, chapters 9–10 is that it offers us a eucharistic prayer, although there is no mention of the words of institution.

29. Even negative judgements can sometimes take this form, as in Sartre's comment about the unexpected absence of his friend Pierre from a café; cf. *Being and Nothingness* (London: Methuen, 1958), pp. 9–11.

30. E. Levinas is the philosopher most associated with meditations on the significance of the other as other, as in his comments on 'The Face' in Sections III–IV of *Totality and Infinity* (The Hague: Nijhoff, 1979).

31. The original remark is attributed to the pagan centurion at Capernaum (Matt. 8.8).

32. The so-called 'Prodigal Son' prayer in the ASB Communion Service, no. 52; 'corrected' by vote of General Synod.

33. For illustrations, G. B. Caird, *The Language and Imagery of the Bible* (London: Duckworth, 1980); S. Prickett, *Words and the Word* (Cambridge: Cambridge University Press, 1986).

34. cf. Prickett, *Words and the Word*, ch. 1.

35. For a Jewish poem that meditates on each word of the first verse of Genesis, as well as meditating on words and the Word, cf. Anne Winters' poem 'The First Verse', in *Modern Poems on the Bible*, ed. D. Curzon (Philadelphia: Jewish Publication Society, 1994), pp. 33–6.

36. Simone Weil, *Waiting on God* (London: Routledge & Kegan Paul, 1951), pp. 23–4.

37. From 'Poetry and Religion', in Les Murray, *Collected Poems* (Manchester: Carcanet, 1991), pp. 272–3.

38. From 'Satis Passio' in Murray, *Collected Poems*, pp. 222–4.

39. cf. the argument of Plotinus in *Enneads* V, 8.

40. Augustine, *City of God* 11:18; our translation.

41. Boccaccio, *Life of Dante* in *The Early Lives of Dante*, trans. P. H. Wicksteed (London: Chatto & Windus, 1907), p. 72. Boccaccio actually writes: 'Theology and Poesy may be considered to be almost one and the same thing'; but earlier (p. 67) he has already informed us that by theology he understands 'divine Scripture'.

42. S. T. Coleridge, *Confessions of an Inquiring Spirit* (Philadelphia: Fortress, 1988), Letter II, p. 28.

43. *Lectures 1808–19 on Literature*, ed. R. A. Foakes (London: Routledge & Kegan Paul, 1987), vol. I, Lecture 8, pp. 325, 326.

44. In both the *Ion* (534) and in the *Phaedrus* (245) Plato compares poetry to an attack of madness. Though poets are thereby explicitly placed in good company with divine seers such as the prophetess at Delphi, Plato's intention is negative, to undermine the poet's claim to be practising a skill. The account is thus closer to his view of art as imitation in the *Republic* (595ff.) than may initially appear.

45. For early development of the parallel between poet and prophet, cf. *Poetry and Prophecy: The Beginnings of a Literary Tradition*, ed. J. L. Kugel (Ithaca: Cornell University Press, 1990); the parallel was also adopted by Lowth in his influential *Lectures on the Sacred Poetry of the Hebrews* of 1787.

46. Milton, 'The Reason of Church Government', in *The Works of John Milton* (New York: Columbia University Press, 1931), vol. III. 1, p. 241.

47. Sir Philip Sidney, *An Apology for Poetry* (Manchester: Manchester University Press, 1965), p. 101.
48. J. Keble, *Lectures on Poetry* (Oxford: Clarendon Press, 1912), vol. II, 480.
49. Plotinus, *Enneads* II, 9. For a fascinating study of the influence of Platonism on English literature, cf. *Platonism and the English Imagination*, ed. A. Baldwin and S. Hutton (Cambridge: Cambridge University Press, 1994).
50. M. Arnold, 'The Study of Poetry', in *Essays in Criticism: Second series* (London: Macmillan, 1888), p. 663. Arnold was in part anticipated in his approach by Shelley's 'A Defence of Poetry' where he talks of 'the poetry in the doctrines of Jesus Christ': *The Complete Works of Percy Bysshe Shelley*, ed. R. Ingpen and W. E. Peck (London: Ernest Benn, 1965), vol. VII, p. 126.
51. J. Drury, 'According to Poetry', in *Resurrection*, ed. S. Barton and G. Stanton (London: SPCK, 1994), p. 202.
52. Drury speaks approvingly of Herbert's poem 'The Flower', but another of his poems 'Death' in fact expresses very similar sentiments to those which Drury condemns in Hopkins' 'That Nature is a Heraclitean Fire and of the Comfort of the Resurrection'.
53. In her book *Eucharistic Poetry* (Lewisburg: Bucknell University Press, 1992), Eleanor McNees significantly finds herself forced to ask just such a question. Contrasting the use of eucharistic imagery in Dylan Thomas and Geoffrey Hill with that in Donne and Hopkins, she comments: 'One is finally tempted to ask if poetic language can really achieve any kind of real presence without a grounded metaphysical belief' (p. 109).
54. French version, 1967; tr. G. C. Spivak in *Of Grammatology* (Baltimore: Johns Hopkins University Press, 1976), p. 158.
55. V. Cunningham, *in the Reading Gaol* (Oxford: Blackwell, 1994), p. 393. We are grateful to Brian Horne for drawing our attention to the appearance and importance of this book.
56. Using Dorothy Sayers' translation in *The Divine Comedy: Hell* (Harmondsworth: Penguin, 1949). For dramatic effect Dante makes them 'children', though in fact they were all young men, Ugolino's sons and grandsons.
57. cf. J. Freccero, 'Bestial Sign and Bread of Angels', in *Dante's Divine Comedy: Modern Critical Interpretations*, ed. H. Bloom (New York: Chelsea House, 1987), pp. 121–34.
58. *Friedrich Hölderlin: Poems and Fragments*, tr. M. Hamburger (London: Routledge & Kegan Paul, 1966), pp. 242–53.
59. Here we follow the interpretation of the poem offered by D. Constantine in *Hölderlin* (Oxford: Clarendon Press, 1988), pp. 199–206.
60. cf. D. J. Schmidt, 'Between Meridians and Other Lines: Between Heidegger and Celan', in *The Poetry of Paul Celan*, ed. H. M. Block (New York: Peter Lang, 1991), pp. 30–7.
61. Tr. in J. Felstiner, *Paul Celan: Poet, Survivor, Jew* (New Haven: Yale

University Press, 1995), p. 84. Copyright © 1995 by Yale University. There is a very helpful discussion of the whole poem, pp. 83–91.

62. Intensified in the German by the play on *herbsten*, to 'harvest'. *Herbst* (autumn) and *herbe* (bitter, acrid) also lie in the background, according to G. Steiner in *Times Literary Supplement* (2 June 1995), p. 4.

63. Augustine's *De Doctrina Christiana* exhibits some of these suspicions e.g. I, 13; III, 9. Cf. also R. Williams, 'Language, Reality and Desire in Augustine's *De Doctrina*'; A. Louth, 'Augustine on Language', in *Journal of Literature and Theology*, 3:2 (1989), pp. 138–58.

64. Cunningham, *in the Reading Gaol* (in part quoting Bacon), p. 203.

65. Opening of 'A Meditation on Human Redemption', in *Anselm of Canterbury*, ed. J. Hopkins and H. W. Richardson (London: SCM, 1974), I, p. 137.

66. In *Dante: The Divine Comedy 2 Purgatory*, ed. D. L. Sayers (Harmondsworth: Penguin, 1955), Canto 29 with commentary, pp. 298–306. For a different view, cf. P. Armour, *Dante's Griffin and the History of the World* (Oxford: Clarendon Press, 1989), pp. 1–14.

67. We are very grateful to David Fuller for his detailed comments on two previous drafts of this essay, and to Ronald Coppin for embarking us upon one fruitful line of thought.

PART ONE
THE EMBODIED WORD: INCARNATION AS SACRAMENT

'In the beginning was the Word . . . and the Word became flesh and dwelt among us, full of grace and truth . . .' (John 1.1, 14 RSV). In searching for the origins of Christian sacramentalism (God mediating himself through the material world), it is natural to begin with the incarnation. Here we have God taking human form and thus through a specific, physical body disclosing himself to those willing to watch, or touch, or listen. It is a form of mediation no longer available to us in our own day, since that specific, physical body is no longer part of our world. But from that one should not deduce that such sacramentalism is at an end. For, at Christ's own command, in place of his temporal body there has come a new material mediation, that of bread and wine. It is thus this notion of incarnation as primary sacrament that rightly legitimates all other ways in which we conceive of the divine being mediated through our material world.

John Macquarrie in his essay seeks to reinforce that connection on two fronts: first, by widening its framework in placing incarnation in the context of creation, as in the opening chapter of John's Gospel; secondly, by anticipating the objection that the move from body to bread represents a degeneration from personal categories to 'things'. For him we live in a universe which is shot through and through with the sacramental: God as artist is everywhere inherent within the expression of himself which is our world.

Frances Young was for a time happy to identify herself with those who spoke of *The Myth of God Incarnate* (the title of a book

27

to which she contributed two essays in 1977). Now, however, she argues that this was to concede altogether too much to rationalism. The apparent logical contradictions in traditional formulations of Christology need to be balanced by a more imaginative approach: one which acknowledges the possibility of the sacramental coincidence of divine and material in the same place or person.

This is an approach which, she suggests, was not only congenial to Paul but also had its roots in the earliest form of Jewish mysticism, called 'Merkavah'. Literally this means 'chariot', and refers to visions of the divine Throne of Glory surrounded by heavenly creatures, as in Ezekiel's opening vision (1.15–28). The angels who played such a central role in this mysticism are the theme of Robert Hayward's essay. In contrast to the common assumption that Judaism had too transcendent a conception of God to allow of a sacramental view, he draws attention to the way in which human beings were seen to bring heaven to earth when they reduplicated the life of the angels in heaven. Incarnation and sacrament could thus be viewed as a legitimate culmination of Judaism rather than its perversion.

1

Incarnation as Root of the Sacramental Principle

JOHN MACQUARRIE

In contrast to the early heresies which were matter denying and theologians such as Calvin who overstressed the transcendent, John Macquarrie insists that Christianity is a religion that combines equally immanent and transcendent in what he calls 'dialectical theism' or 'panentheism' ('God in all things'). God's relation to his creation is like that of an artist, achieving maximum expression when he puts most of himself into it – in the incarnation. To answer the objection that the sacramental use of things is a regrettable degeneration away from such personal use of imagery, Martin Heidegger's two discussions of the notion of a thing are then brought into play. Both advocate a strongly personalist understanding, which enables the sacraments to be seen as the culmination of a consistent dynamic that stretches from creation through incarnation to a 'transfigured' future.

Transcendent distortions

In many religions of the world, matter has been suspect. It has been regarded as the opposite of spirit, and so it has been shunned by those who have dedicated their lives to the pursuit of spiritual ends. However, in the case of the three great religions which look back to the revelation contained in the Hebrew Scriptures, I mean Judaism, Christianity and Islam, there is or ought to be an affirmative attitude to matter. For the material world, in the belief of these three faiths, is the creation of God and was pronounced by him to be good; and in Christianity this affirmative attitude is reinforced by the doctrine of incarnation, the claim that the Word became flesh.

But in the history of Christianity, there have been moments when the high status of the material creation has been obscured. This was often due to the influence of Greek philosophical ideas, though these may in turn have come from the east, where in some important religions matter has always been despised, as morally destructive of the best human aspirations and as metaphysically belonging to a lower level of reality than spirit.

Thus very early in Christian history the Church was threatened by the rise of various gnostic and docetic sects. Sometimes these denied that the creation is the work of God and assigned it to demons; or in the case of Marcion, it was even claimed that the God of the Hebrew Scriptures is himself a demonic power. Likewise, the doctrine of incarnation had to be denied. The humanity of Jesus was explained away as mere appearance.

Even in much later times, when the cruder mythological aspects of the early heresies had been left behind, there still appeared tendencies which might very broadly be called manichaean and which showed themselves – and still to some extent continue to show themselves – in puritanical ethics and in the marginalizing of the sacraments. In Protestantism generally, the Word and the activity of preaching are exalted as the primary functions of the Church, to the neglect of the sacraments. Certainly, the Word and the preaching of the Word should be exalted, and sacraments without the Word tend to degenerate into superstition. But perhaps even greater violence is done to our essential human nature if the Word and the hearing of the Word, that is to say, verbal communication, is isolated from sacramental action. Calvin went so far as to claim that the sacraments are simply *verbum visibile* (a visual aid to the Word)[1] and though he himself is said to have favoured a celebration of the Lord's Supper at least once a week, in Calvinist churches such celebrations, even today, take place usually at three-monthly or even six-monthly intervals.

Calvin, of course, strongly believed both in creation and incarnation as central Christian doctrines. How then did the imbalance between Word and sacrament arise? I think it may be a reflection of another imbalance in his theology, that between the transcendence and the immanence of God. It is true that in the Bible itself, God is primarily a transcendent God, especially in the Old Testament. Even there, of course, God remains close to his chosen people. But in the New Testament, the ties between God and the creation are given a new expression and a new prominence. This is due above all to the emerging doctrine of the Trinity, not fully worked out until about three centuries later. In this revised conception of God, one has to take account of Jesus Christ as

Emmanuel, 'God with us', and increasingly also of the Holy Spirit, as 'God in us'. With the rise of the trinitarian, or, better expressed, triunitarian conception of God, Christianity had moved from the transcendent theism of Judaism to a form of panentheism, or, as I prefer to call it, of dialectical theism, in which the transcendence and immanence of God are combined to accord with the incarnation.

Mainline Christian theologians have usually taken care in their teaching to say something about the immanence of God in the world, but there can be little doubt that this has usually been made very subordinate to the idea of the divine transcendence. St Thomas Aquinas, for instance, tells us that 'God is everywhere, in substance, power and presence',[2] and if we go on to unpack these three terms, 'substance', 'power' and 'presence', we can arrive at a very strong doctrine of divine immanence. But within the total framework of St Thomas' classical theism, the weight given to immanence is not great. But surely there is some correlation between a stress on divine immanence and the doctrine of incarnation. Islam took a different direction from Christianity in increasing the transcendence of God in comparison with the Old Testament, and because of this it is hard to imagine how Islam could accommodate the idea of incarnation.

Creation, immanence and incarnation

Post-Reformation Christianity has, on the whole, stressed God's transcendence at the expense of his immanence. There were exceptions to this general tendency at some points in the nineteenth century, but in the early part of the twentieth century, transcendence was again the dominant idea, especially in the theology of Karl Barth. But this brought a reaction, which I think is still with us. William Temple, in his Gifford Lectures, claimed that 'Christianity is the most avowedly materialistic of all the great religions.'[3] He tried hard in these lectures to find ways of expressing God's closeness to the material world. One of his analogies was that of the artist to his work of art, a relation in which the artist in an important sense puts himself or herself into that art work. But this analogy, Temple says, does not go far enough in expressing the intimacy of the relation. Meanwhile, John Baillie, in a criticism of the phrase 'wholly other' which had been used of God by Otto, Barth, Brunner and others, asked for a renewed appreciation of the divine immanence.[4]

But the theologian who went furthest in this direction was probably Teilhard de Chardin. 'By virtue of the creation,' he wrote, 'and still more of the incarnation, nothing here below is profane for those who have eyes to see.' Again, 'In the life which wells up in me and in the matter which sustains me, I find much more than your gifts. It is you yourself whom I find, you who make me participate in your being, you who mould me.'[5] Teilhard's language tends to be extravagant, almost pantheistic, when he celebrates the dignity and the mysteries of matter. I think it almost certain that Baillie, who has a much more cautious approach in these matters, would have objected to some of the expressions that Teilhard used.

Perhaps to do justice to Teilhard, we should remember the key place that the idea of evolution had in all his thinking. This meant that he was always considering things not just as they are at any given time, but in the light of their potentialities. He followed Aristotle's principle: One does not simply ask what something is (*ti estin*), but what it has in it to become (*ti en einai*). In former times (and the idea still lingers on in our minds) matter was seen as something lifeless and inert, without any distinguishable characteristics. There still remains in our minds the idea that matter is such a degenerate form of being that it is next to nothing. But nowadays we recognize that matter, even in its humblest form, is highly organized and highly active and capable of many transformations and transmutations. Matter, perhaps owing to characteristics already immanent in it and conferred on it in creation, has brought forth the living creatures that today inhabit this planet. In the course of evolution and then of human history, intelligent, moral, spiritual beings have lived on the planet's surface and aspired toward that God from whom, as they believe, all things have had their origin. Jesus Christ himself has come to be in this history. In him is gathered up the whole of this history, including those important centuries which constitute the history of Israel, and from there we come to that moment when the divine life can enter the creation in an event which we call 'incarnation'. This word, of course, has a variety of meanings. We need not in this context try to define it too closely. Perhaps one or the other of the New Testament phrases is enough – Paul's 'God was in Christ' or John's 'The Word was made flesh' or some other expression. Whatever we say must be, at least in part, metaphorical or symbolic, but what we try to express is the Christian conviction that in this man, Jesus of Nazareth, God, who, theologians tell us, is everywhere by substance, power and presence, is here encountering us with a special, it may even be a unique, luminosity.

Let us pause for a moment and recall the course of the

argument so far. We have been considering what might be called a hierarchy of truths. The broadest one, which serves as a foundation for the others, is the doctrine of creation. The universe is not just something that has come about by chance, but has been brought into being by God, the ultimate source of being. But God has not created it as something quite external to himself. His creation is an act of love, and in his love he has, like an artist, put himself into his works. This is where the doctrine of immanence becomes important. Not all of God's works are on the same level. A human being, made according to the Bible in the image and likeness of God, is obviously 'receptive' to God in a way not possible for some subhuman creature. William of Ockham, who emphasized God's transcendence and the arbitrary power of the divine will, claimed that God might have incarnated himself in a stone or an ass or an object of wood. This view has usually been regarded as absurd. 'Incarnation' may well, as I said, have several meanings, but it could hardly have been reduced as far as this and yet retain any theological or religious significance!

The human being is the only creature on this planet and, as far as we know, anywhere, who has the spiritual nature that is necessary for that intimate union with God which we call 'incarnation'. So Schleiermacher was, I think, correct in saying that Jesus Christ is the completion of the creation of humanity.[6] If the human race is made in the image and likeness of God, then its completion in Christ would mean that in him the image had achieved its full expression, that, in Paul's words, 'he is the image of the invisible God' (Col. 1.15 AV). The hierarchy of truths then consists first, in the doctrine of creation, second, in the doctrine of a divine immanence in the creation, third, in the emergence of human beings as bearers within creation of the divine image, and fourth, in the coming to birth of Jesus of Nazareth as the completion of the process so far. I say, 'so far', for no one can lay down what the future holds. To come back for a moment to Teilhard de Chardin, he visualized a 'christification' going on in ages to come until all things are united or gathered up in Christ (cf. Eph. 1.10). This is very much a visionary or even, some would say, a wildly speculative point of view, but how one judges it will depend on how seriously one takes the Christian revelation.

The foregoing remarks constitute something like a *rationale* for incarnation, that is to say, for the idea of incarnation. Even if one accepted the idea of an incarnation, there would still be needed a specific act of faith, namely, the acceptance of Jesus Christ as the fulfillment of the idea.

Christ as personal subject of the sacraments

Such is the argument so far, but it has not yet reached the sacraments of the Church. I think the next link in the chain is to
acknowledge Jesus Christ himself as the basic or primordial
sacrament. This way of speaking has become very common in
Roman Catholic circles since Vatican II. We hear it said, both that
Christ is the basic sacrament and that this description applies
also to the Church. I must confess, I am not altogether happy
with this manner of speaking. The word 'sacrament' usually refers
to a rite or ceremony in which some visible symbolic actions take
place and which has also an inner or spiritual significance. To
extend the word to Christ (a person) or to the Church (a community) does not make for clarity or for a careful use of language.
It would be better to say that Christ is the subject of the sacraments and that the Church is the bearer and dispenser of the
sacraments. But I suppose that the language I have criticized may
be excused as a kind of shorthand. It does draw attention to the
fact that the sacraments are rooted in Christ and the Church, and
that they continue in a different way God's drawing near to the
creation which took place in Christ and in the community he
gathered around him. The sacraments constitute, as it were, a new
stage in that hierarchy of presencing, which we have already
traced through the steps of creation, immanence, the gift of the
divine image to the human family, and the realization of this gift
in Jesus Christ.

The connection of the sacraments with the incarnation in
Christ has been very clearly expounded in a book of the Belgian
Dominican, Edward Schillebeeckx. The book is entitled *Christ the
Sacrament*,[7] and was written partly to correct a defect which,
Schillebeeckx believed, had characterized much of the sacramental theology taught in Catholic seminaries. In his own words, 'the
theology of the manuals does not always make a careful distinction between that unique manner of existence which is peculiar
to man, and the mode of being, mere objective "being there,"
which is proper to the things of nature. The absence of this distinction, particularly in treating of grace or of the sacraments,
occasionally obscures the simple fact of encounter with God.'[8]
His aim in rooting the sacraments in the personal existence of the
incarnate Lord was then to ensure that we do not lose sight of the
essentially personal nature of the action of God in the sacraments. If God's approach to his creation attained its climax in the
human personal existence of Jesus Christ, then is it not a step
back to move into a situation in which Christ is mediated to us
through things? That might be the case if Schillebeeckx' fear that

things sacramental were regarded in a quite impersonal objective context was justified. Perhaps this was never quite the case, because the sacraments have always been celebrated within a community of faith. Nevertheless, his fears are sufficiently well founded to cause us to look very seriously at the problem of how things can function in such a way as to become the vehicles for a personal encounter.

Heidegger and the impersonal objection

We have to ask a somewhat fundamental question: 'What is a thing?' This is not an easy question to answer, for the word 'thing' is a word of such generality that it is difficult to find any distinguishing characteristic that could define it. Nevertheless, we can make some distinctions that would mark off things from other kinds of beings. We do not normally use the word 'thing' about a person, perhaps not even about an animal. Again, we usually draw a distinction between a thing, as having real existence in space and time, from an idea that is merely in someone's mind. We do, however, sometimes use the word 'thing' for an action or an event, as when we say, 'That was a fine thing that you did!' But this would seem to be a derived usage. The typical meaning of the word 'thing' refers to a real, solid material object located in space and time. Likewise, the concept of 'thinghood' is the state of existing typified by the solid enduring physical object.

It may help us if, at this point, we turn to the views of a philosopher who, both in his earlier and his later work, spent considerable effort in seeking an understanding of thinghood. I mean Martin Heidegger. He believes that, at least in the west, we think of a thing primarily as an object standing over against us. But he believes also that this is a somewhat artificial attitude to take up towards things, and that it has been derived from more primordial and more intimate relations. He reminds us that the Greek word for a thing was *pragma*, that is to say, something with which we have to do, not so much something that we observe as something we encounter in our concernful dealings (*praxis*).[9] Actually the Greeks too, like ourselves, came to think of things as just lying around – to think of them 'objectively' as we would say – but this way of relating to the world of things is an abstraction from an originally more active and pragmatic way. The world itself, in Heidegger's view, was conceived as more than a mere collection of things. The world, as human beings see and understand it, is a unity in which every item is related to every other item and each has a place in the practical concerns of human beings. This is true not only of artefacts, those things made by men and women for their own purposes, but even of natural things which they press into service. A river becomes a means of transport, a mountain becomes a quarry for building material, even the sun is used for time-reckoning.

Think, for example, of a hammer. It can be considered simply as a physical object, and we can learn about the nature of the metal and the wood of which that object is made. But we would entirely miss the being of the hammer, so to speak, what makes it a hammer rather than, say, a musical instrument. We only know what a hammer is when we see someone actually using it in the act of hammering.

Heidegger, of course, is not denying that there is an objective scientific view of the world, a view that abstracts from all human interests and tries to show us bare things, apart from our concerns. But this is derivative, it is not the fundamental human way of perceiving the world. We always perceive things *as* something or other – we perceive the hammer as a tool, we perceive the nails and the wood *as* likewise instrumental to the activity of hammering, which may itself be related to any number of projects on which human beings may be engaged in the world. There is nothing 'subjective' about this view of the world and the things found in it. It is not unlike the 'anthropic' view of which cosmologists talk – it means simply that, as human beings, we are bound to see things through human eyes. If there is a God's-eye view or if there is a 'view from nowhere', it is not our way of seeing things.

This view of the world and things is not irrelevant to the sacramental problem, because the notion of 'seeing as' which Heidegger was expounding in 1929 argues that when we perceive anything, it already bears a meaning. We do not first have a bare sensation and then attach a meaning to it. We do not see just a patch of colour – we see a field, let us say; we do not hear just a noise, we hear an automobile. Meaning is not something like a label that we stick on to some bare objective datum. Meaning has already been conferred within the context of relations, the 'world', in which we encounter the datum. But the trouble with Heidegger's early view of thinghood is that it is too closely tied to the everyday routines of life – like hammering – to have any obvious significance for the problem of sacramental meaning. In fact, Heidegger himself became dissatisfied with that early view of the world of things set forth in *Being and Time*. He saw that it was too utilitarian and needed broadening to take in other dimensions of human experience. Also, it was too closely tied to an exploitative view of nature as existing solely or chiefly for human use, a view which allows no room for the dignity and beauty of things in themselves.

Heidegger's mature view of thinghood has to be sought in an essay, 'The Thing',[10] written more than twenty years after *Being and Time*. He now tells us that a thing is not only more than a bare object, it is more even than that which human beings have produced or composed out of the natural material. Heidegger's new theory of the thing is expressed in terms of the fourfold or the quadrate (*das Geviert*). Each thing has, so to speak, four dimensions all of which give it its meaning. The four dimensions or relations are: earth and sky, mortals and gods. The example which he uses to explain his theory is no longer a hammer, but a wine-pitcher. This pitcher is made of material from the earth. It is used for wine, which has come from grapes warmed and ripened by the sun. The pitcher has been made by a skilled potter, and is used for human purposes. Finally, the pitcher may be used to pour a libation to the gods. One may feel that it is only by straining matters somewhat that Heidegger fits the pitcher into the fourfold scheme, and one may also think that this language of earth and sky, mortals and gods, has moved over from philosophy into the realm of myth or poetry. This would not in itself worry Heidegger very much, because for him poetry is by no means merely emotional or non-cognitive. The poet too sets forth truth, and truth at the deepest level. So Heidegger would claim that the philosopher can learn more from poetry than from science. As in the case of the hammer which is revealed by the act of hammering, so with the pitcher it is the act of pouring the wine that reveals what we might call its 'pitcherhood', its being or meaning as a pitcher.

Although I said that this notion of the fourfold seems to come from poetry rather than philosophy, it is not difficult to recognize in it a new version of Aristotle's doctrine of the four causes. According to Aristotle, every thing has a material cause, the stuff out of which it is made, in the case of the pitcher, some kind of clay; then there is the formal cause, the idea of the thing, for before anyone can make anything, he or she must have an idea of that thing, as a kind of pattern which shows how it is to be made; the efficient cause is some already existing state of affairs, in this case, the craftsman or artist himself, who brings the pitcher into being; lastly, there is the final cause, the end for which the pitcher exists, and this is where the gods come in, since the pitcher that will pour out the libation is for their glory.

Heidegger himself and some of those who are interested in this part of his philosophy seem to suggest in places that the fourfold could be reduced to a threefold. This would in some ways make a better fit with his analysis of the thing. The dimension to be dropped would be heaven or the sky, and its contribution divided between earth and mortals. Talk of earth and sky is very ancient – we find it already in Genesis, 'In the beginning God created the heavens and the earth' (Gen. 1.1 RSV), and for centuries heaven and earth were two contrasted realms. Now we see them as parts of a single vast universe. We are told that most of the elements in the earth's crust were formed originally in the stars, while the formal cause of the pitcher can be assigned to the human maker, rather than to the heavens. Then the four become three – earth, the human race, the gods.[11]

This in turn allows us to apply these ideas to the eucharist and complete the chain that has led from incarnation to the sacraments. In many Christian churches nowadays, one hears at the offertory prayers, borrowed, I believe, from Judaism: 'Blessed are you, Lord God of all creation; through your goodness we have this bread to offer, which earth has given and human hands have made. It will become for us the bread of life.' And then, over the chalice: 'Blessed are you, Lord God of all creation; through your goodness we have this wine to offer, fruit of the vine and work of human hands. It will become our spiritual drink.'

The wheat and the grapes come from the earth, through human labour they have been transformed into bread and wine: then, looking forward to the consecration, it is declared that they will become for us the bread of life and our spiritual drink. All this may be considered one form of the doctrine of transignification, a change in the meaning of things, within the rich understanding of a thing in threefold or fourfold relations, and in continuity with and ultimately derived from the doctrine of incarnation.

In days when the Aristotelian philosophy was still in the ascendant, the doctrine of transubstantiation was a very good attempt to elucidate the eucharistic mystery, though perhaps only a relatively few people were able to understand it. In our own time, when the old philosophy has lost its influence, transubstantiation has become little more than a name, as is evident in the mention of it in the 'agreed statement' on the eucharist, issued by the Anglican-Roman Catholic International Commission. Heidegger's philosophy of thinghood seems to me to offer the possibility of a contemporary statement that will preserve the truths of the traditional doctrine and will also escape the criticism of Schillebeeckx that the traditional language was possibly too objective and impersonal.

Notes

1. J. Calvin, *Institutes of the Christian Religion*, Library of Christian Classics XX–XXI (Philadelphia: Westminster, 1960), 4, 14, 4, p. 1279.
2. Thomas Aquinas, *Summa Theologiae*, tr. Timothy McDermott (London: Eyre & Spottiswoode, 1964), 1a, 8, 3.
3. W. Temple, *Nature, Man and God* (London: Macmillan, 1934), p. 478. See also A. M. Suggate, *William Temple and Christian Social Ethics Today* (Edinburgh: T. & T. Clark, 1987).
4. J. Baillie, *The Idea of Revelation in Recent Thought* (London: Oxford University Press, 1956). See also D. Fergusson (ed.), *Christ, Church and Society: Essays on John Baillie and Donald Baillie* (Edinburgh: T. & T. Clark, 1993).
5. P. Teilhard de Chardin, *Le Milieu Divin* (London: Fontana, 1967), p. 78.
6. F. Schleiermacher, *The Christian Faith* (Edinburgh: T. & T. Clark, 1976), p. 374.
7. E. Schillebeeckx, *Christ the Sacrament* (London: Sheed & Ward, 1963).
8. Schillebeeckx, *Christ the Sacrament*, p. 1.
9. M. Heidegger, *Being and Time* (Oxford: Blackwell, 1983), pp. 96–7.
10. M. Heidegger, *Vorträge und Aufsätze* (Pfullingen: Neske, 1954), pp. 163–81. See also J. Macquarrie, *Heidegger and Christianity* (London: SCM, 1994).
11. See W. J. Richardson, *Heidegger: Through Phenomenology to Thought* (The Hague: Nijhoff, 1974), p. 572.

2

From Analysis to Overlay: A Sacramental Approach to Christology[1]

FRANCES YOUNG

The analytic or logical and synthetic or imaginative are frequently seen as opposed, with some giving the palm to one, some to the other. But Frances Young argues that we need both, not least in our understanding of the significance of Christ. The analytic Chalcedonian definition is rightly premised (in contrast to Greek assumptions) upon the utter distinctiveness of divine and human nature, but with that must be joined the synthetic approach of Paul under which, paralleling Merkavah Jewish Mysticism and Julian of Norwich, we find him (as in 2 Cor. 3) 'overlaying' images in a way which speaks of the divine and human Christ occupying the same space. Such a sacramental meeting or coincidence of both identities enables us to transcend the apparent logical contradictions of the analytic approach.

The complementarity of analysis and imagination

Come with me in imagination to Pembrokeshire. We are walking the coast path. Impressive cliffs break off the end of a great ridge ahead. We pause at a stile and lean over, contemplating the awesome sight in front of us. One of our party is a geologist. She begins to talk about the layers of soft sedimentary rocks, the hard limestone above, the long process of weathering which has exposed the history of that bit of earth, the reason why there is an overhang there, with the lower softer rocks crumbling first. Her friend points out the twisting of the strata, a sudden fault-line, a dyke, all of which create the characteristic shapes in the headland.

But his main interest is in the action of the sea, and it is the way the sea gouges out the weak points in the geological structure, and the motion of the tides and waves that he is able to expound. Our wonder is growing deeper, and the artist with us is enabled to grasp the whole and capture shapes and proportions with a fresh vitality, precisely because those so-called analytical scientists have both enhanced perception and communicated a deep sense of enthusiasm for the reality which in our different ways we are all contemplating. We begin to 'know' that cliff through the integration of analysis and synthesis.

Wisdom is reached when synthesis and analysis work together. Despite the science fiction dreams of creating artificial intelligence, the human mind does not work in algorithms like a computer. Arthur Koestler told the story of the development of science under the title *The Sleepwalkers;*[2] for great scientific breakthroughs have never come simply by one logical statement leading to another, but through insight, brilliant and unexpected correlations, intuitions, one might say. My husband used to say in his scientific research days, 'I've had an idea.' That heralded weeks of work testing it out, but the point is made. Poets, musicians, artists, sculptors, all know that creativity involves much more than feeling or intuition – they too have to engage the intellect in hard work, working out the 'idea' that has come to them through careful technical or analytical engagement with their medium. There are profound analogies in the way all creative thought, artistic and scientific, is both 'inspired' and the outcome of conscious mental discipline.

One of the many tragic breakdowns in the way we twentieth-century people apprehend things is the perceived split between what we might call analytical and synthetic thinking, a split related to but not identical with that between fact and value to which Lesslie Newbigin and the 'Gospel and our Culture' movement has drawn attention. As many react against our supposedly analytical culture, heart is contrasted with head, feeling with rationality, intuition with the intellectual, and the difference is sometimes even genderized, analysis being associated with science and masculinity, femininity with intuition, emotion, mysticism, poetry, synthesis. It has become fashionable to decry the dominance and oppression of the so-called 'cerebral', to reject objective analysis in favour of subjective and holistic apprehension.

It is, of course, true that this kind of thing has fuelled the welcome renewal of interest in spirituality – not just in the churches, however, but in the New Age movement as well, and unfortunately it has also fostered an anti-intellectualism which will ultimately, I suggest, be very damaging for the defence of Christian truth. It has become associated with what one might almost dare to call the myth of the two halves of the brain: there certainly is scientific evidence that one side of the brain handles mathematics, logic, analysis, and the other, perception, artistic appreciation, intuition, and so on, but the reality is that if the two halves of the brain are not connected, the person is profoundly handicapped.

In this climate, theology is often treated as cold, critical, objective, rational, analytical, distanced, even irrelevant. There is perhaps a little truth in the notion that theology is so-called 'second order discourse', a rational account of prior faith or experience. But this distinction is based on another unfortunate split in modern apprehension. There is a very real sense in which theology at some level, so far from being second order discourse, is a prerequisite for faith. No specifically Christian experience is possible without prior knowledge of Christian doctrine – or, perhaps we might say, prior awareness of the Christian story which provides the narrative into which we are drawn, and through which we apprehend the meaning of our own stories, as we become believers. Experience is never discrete from the categories we use to understand or articulate what has happened to us. A good example is provided by Mother Julian of Norwich. Her visionary experience presupposes a search for understanding of the love of God through assimilation to the passion of Christ. In other words, it presupposes the Christian story, indeed the doctrines of the Trinity and of incarnation.

Theology cannot, then, be dismissed as an ivory tower, rational, objective, critical endeavour more likely to destroy faith than anything else. Rather it is the lifeblood of the Christian life. My inaugural lecture in Birmingham was entitled, 'The Critic and the Visionary'.[3] Both are required. Only a reintegration of paths presently perceived as split will enable us to find renewed confidence in the truth by which we live as Christians. The Christian life needs theology, and theology involves both analytical and synthetic thinking.

In my lecture in honour of Charles Gore I wanted to celebrate the life and work of one who, despite being a bishop, remained a theologian. He knew that loving God with mind and heart meant being prepared to engage in tough thinking – in each generation it meant, to quote one of his titles, *The Reconstruction of Belief*; for there is a necessary doctrinal task to be performed in every context, including each intellectual culture. It is impossible simply to repeat the past. For the language of the past, whether scriptural or credal, has to become intelligible in the present through a process of interpretation, exegesis, re-statement, even re-conception. So in honouring Gore I took up one of the central doctrinal issues which exercised, not only his mind, but that of most serious reflective Christians of every century, not least our own, namely, the doctrine of incarnation. In exploring this, my preliminary remarks about analytical and synthetic thinking will become crucial to the argument.

Analysis and the Chalcedonian definition

The classic Chalcedonian definition of the person of Christ was arrived at by a process of debate and controversy leading up to, and settled at, the Council of the same name in AD 451, though with some significant dissenters. The agreed statement (then, as now, an agreed statement was the fruit of such a synod!) affirmed that Jesus Christ was truly God and truly Man. This was the true meaning of Scripture and creed. It has been claimed, notably by John Hick, that the Chalcedonian definition is incoherent, a logical impossibility like the square circle. In his recent book, *The Metaphor of God Incarnate*,[4] his position is a little more nuanced, but his essential charge remains: no one has ever satisfactorily given an account of what this statement means in practice.

In this essay I want to hazard an account of Christian claims about Jesus which might go some way to making sense of them, at least for those of us who take seriously the notion that theology is faith seeking understanding and there are some 'givens' with which we need to work. The classic definition is not, in my view, unthinkable or irrational, and furthermore it makes the right connections, because what we call Christology, the doctrine of Christ's person, is inextricably bound up with all other doctrines, with Christian understanding of human nature, of creation and redemption, of God's nature, of worship and spirituality. My suggestion will be that, while the traditional definition of the person of Christ belongs to the realm of analytical thinking, synthetic thinking is required to make sense of it. On the other hand, without the analytical definition, synthetic thinking would easily sink into pagan myth. So the dialectic between the two is vital for Christian understanding of Christ. It is when there is a divorce between spirituality and theology that the definition becomes apparently unintelligible and vulnerable to the attacks of those who claim either common sense or rationality.

First then a few words about the definition and its important analytical thrust:

Things or persons are necessarily defined over against other things or persons. To define is to determine boundaries. Like Adam naming the animals, a child points and names the things and persons in its environment. The way of differentiation, which is the beginning of analysis, is the only way to get to know things, to know others – even to know oneself. Until one learns a few names, it is hard to identify different birds or flowers. To see similarities and differences requires classification according to types, and the process of trying to identify by name leads to a much finer perception of the particular detailed characteristics of each one, as well as enabling recognition.

Now ancient philosophy was dominated by the issue: What exactly is this? Is it to be defined in terms of the matter out of which it is composed? Or the particular characteristics that make it what it is and not something else? If the latter, is it the features it has in common with other examples of the same thing, or those which it distinctively has itself, in its particularity? This meant the question of a thing's 'being' or 'substance' was the prime analytical question.

There are those who have dismissed Chalcedon because it is framed in so-called out-dated 'substance' language, or in static ontological terms. But early in my theological formation, I learned from Donald MacKinnon that that suggestion fails to grasp what 'substance' is about. It is, as I have noted, a question about what exactly a thing is. I suppose we would put the same issues in terms of identity. It is naive to think that modern believers have never wondered about the identity of Jesus Christ, or been puzzled about the claim that he is to be identified as God and as Man. Could a particular living creature be identified as both gnat and elephant? Chalcedon was about specifying the identity of Jesus Christ.

The analytical argument reached what many have treated as impossible paradox for a number of reasons which I do not intend to go into or I should find myself offering a potted history of the formation of doctrine. What we do need to realize, however, is why the analytical process was so important. Ancient religion and philosophy did not make a clear distinction between Creator and creature, between the divine and the human. Nature was filled with mysterious divinities, and places felt to be holy were natural wonders, grottoes and woods, mountaintops, promontories. The gods were conceived and depicted in anthropomorphic terms – they were made in the image of humankind, male and female – and in mythology the boundaries were quite slippery. The gods were manifested in human form in many popular stories, and a common theory about the origin of the gods was that they were divinized supermen or heroes.

More sophisticated philosophy also blurred the distinction between the divine and the universe. Stoicism was essentially pantheistic, the divine being identified as the rational order, the mind or spirit (Logos) which was fire, the basic element, the stuff at the heart of the universe. Platonism found reality not in material being, but in the 'ideas' or 'ideals' which shape the world; so Platonists could conceive of transcendent divine being, and their conceptuality became the natural ally of Christian theology, but they thought the human soul belonged to that transcendent spiritual world. My point is: everybody tended to assume in one way or another a kinship between the divine and the human, and confused created things with the divinity.

For Christians, with their philosophical ideas radicalized by their Jewish heritage, the distinction between God the Creator and everything else became more and more important. Already in the epistles of St Paul we find attacks on those who 'claiming to be wise, . . . became fools, and . . . exchanged the glory of the immortal God for images resembling a mortal human being or birds or four-footed animals or reptiles . . . and served the creature rather than the Creator, who is blessed forever! Amen' (Rom. 1.22–25 NRSV). Such remained a key apologetic argument against idolatry and anthropomorphism. Pagan myths and idols were mocked.

In more theoretical terms, the second century was crucial. Then explicit differentiation of the Christian position from pagan philosophies and gnostic heresies generated the following argument: God did not create the world out of the divine self by a process of emanation, otherwise everything would be God; nor did God create out of a pre-existent matter, because such a medium would have to be co-eternal with God and would therefore effectively be a second divine Being; therefore God must have created everything out of nothing. This was the initial move which was bound to lead to a radical distinction between God and every other existent thing, with every other existent thing being wholly dependent upon God's will for its existence.

So the grounding analytical principle was this: God was not to be confused with any other existent thing. God's identity and the identity of everything else were defined by contrast with one another, by differentiation. No wonder critics of Christianity like Celsus could accuse the Christians of inconsistency when they worshipped as God a man who had recently lived and died in Palestine. But in the end it was not external pressure that led to Chalcedon's definition. Rather it was the result of prolonged internal struggles which involved the exclusion of a number of so-called heretics, struggles arising from the tendency in Christian thought itself to confuse that fundamental distinction when it came to Jesus Christ. In the debates immediately preceding the Council, more than anything else it was concern to preserve the Godness of God, the 'otherness' of the divine, that fuelled controversy.

There was, then, a fundamental analytical distinction which was characteristic of Christianity over against the mythologies and religious assumptions of the ancient world which required the exclusion of inadequate accounts of the identity of Jesus Christ as either some kind of mediating being – neither fish nor fowl we might say – or as a confusion between God and humanity. I believe that that distinction remains vital for Christian theology. I believe also that the genuine humanness of Jesus needs preserving against the persistent tendency of popular Christianity to divinize him in a way analogous to pagan mythology – to that extent I cannot ever go back on what I argued in the recently re-published book, *The Myth of God Incarnate*.[5] The analytical process remains essential. To put it in the language of Chalcedon, there are two distinct Natures, divine and human, which we dare not confuse, yet we find, perhaps to our embarrassment, that we have to assert that Jesus Christ has to be identified as being wholly both.

Synthesis and imagination in Paul

So much for analysis – now what about synthesis? Let us return to the New Testament, and particularly the writings of St Paul. As we have seen, Paul the Jew takes the distinction I have mentioned for granted at one level, but at another level, I suggest, he thinks synthetically rather than analytically. There is a tendency for this to appear to lead to confusion if we press the logic of what we find. But I want to explore the idea that it is in the ambiguities produced by overlaying images and concepts that creative perceptions arise.

For Paul, Christ is the image of God (2 Cor. 4.4; Col. 1.15). But the thrust of this is curiously double-edged. Certainly in the Colossians passage, the term is linked with divinity: although wisdom is not mentioned, most exegetes believe that scriptural depictions of God's wisdom underlie this picture of the cosmic Christ, and there are other hints (e.g. 1 Cor. 1.24; 8.6) that Paul saw Christ as embodying God's own wisdom, as did the author of Hebrews and other New Testament writers such as the author of John's Gospel. The divine Sonship of Christ is linked with this; for in this tradition, 'wisdom' is God's offspring, her nature is conceived as a reflection of God's glory, as the imprint of God's very being (Heb. 1.3) – not 'mere likeness' but 'faithful representation' – rather as we might say, 'That child is the splitting image of its father.'

But Paul is also acutely aware of the biblical understanding of humanity as made in the image of God. In fact, in 1 Cor. 11.7, he almost casually uses the, for him unquestioned, fact that 'man is the image and glory of God' as a premise in what has become a rather controversial discussion about gender relations. More often he understands Christ in terms of renewed humanity or re-created Adam, and as the means whereby the image of God is formed anew in those who are baptized into Christ and, whether male or female, take on Christ's name and identity.

Some obvious passages may be cited (using NRSV):

> For those whom he foreknew he also predestined to be conformed to the image of his Son, in order that he might be the firstborn within a large family. (Rom. 8.29)

> Just as we have borne the image of the man of dust, we will also bear the image of the man of heaven. (1 Cor. 15.49)

> . . . you have stripped off the old self with its practices and have clothed yourselves with the new self, which is being renewed in knowledge according to the image of its creator. (Col. 3.9–10)

These provide the clues to understand that awkward but key verse at the end of 2 Cor. 3:

> All of us, with unveiled faces, seeing the glory of the Lord as though reflected in a mirror, are being transformed into *the self-same image* (my trans. and emphasis) from one degree of glory to another . . . (2 Cor. 3.18)

So the notion that Jesus Christ is the image of God cannot be logically pinned down. It is a statement about the perfect humanity, which God intended and Adam spoiled, being realized in Jesus. It is a statement about the possibility of our humanity being transformed so that it too becomes God's image – the 'self-same

image' as Christ. But it is also a statement about the immanence
of the divine wisdom in all creation, about God's self-revelation,
about the presence of God's own glory. The notion of God's
image is, we might say, a 'synthetic' way of thinking. It involves
metaphors about mirrors and reflections, about the imprint of a
seal in wax – for it is by giving us the Spirit of Jesus in our hearts
as a first instalment that God has anointed us and 'sealed' us (2
Cor. 1.21–2; Eph. 1.13 speaks of being stamped with the seal of
the promised Holy Spirit). If we take this metaphorical way of
speaking seriously, we could say that Paul understood human
nature to be stamped with the divine imprint, through and in
Christ. The divine imprint is as real as the human wax.

This is not by any means the only idea which is deeply ambiguous in Paul's treatment of Christ, which is why discussion of how
to interpret his Christology is never ending. It is hard sometimes
to distinguish the Risen Christ and the Spirit, yet the notion that
they are simply different ways of speaking about the same thing
is not, I think, sustainable if we take what Paul says overall and in
context. It is hard to know what is implied by the apparent trans-
fer of God's title, 'Lord' (*kyrios*), to Jesus. It seems that for Paul,
Christ stands for God, yet is a kind of archetypal Man, envisaged
at God's right hand. We could go on. But let me rather attempt to
find ways of characterizing and illuminating this way of thinking
more precisely.

An overlay of texts and images

What I suggest is that Paul adopts a method of 'overlay'. This is
deeply rooted in his use of Scripture. We may take 2 Cor. 3 by
way of example. We cannot deal here with every element in this
complex passage; so despite the importance of this extraordinary
accumulation of image and allusion for our purposes, we will
have to content ourselves with the major lines of argument. Much
ink has been spilled trying to trace Paul's logic here – it scarcely
follows the kind of logic we are used to. The key, I suggest, lies in
a method of 'overlaying' texts and images.

The opening words and the preceding context indicate that
Paul is on the spot. He begins by insisting that he does not need
letters of recommendation – references or testimonials, if you like
– because the Corinthians themselves are his testimonial. They
constitute Christ's letter, the letter prepared and delivered by
Paul, who was the slave or servant charged with conveying the
message on the master's behalf (the conventional translations
using 'minister' carry all kinds of connotations these days which

obscure what Paul must have had in mind). This document is written not with ink but with the Spirit of the living God, not on tablets of stone but on tablets of human hearts.

The 'tablets of stone' alert us immediately to a complex biblical allusion. Paul refers to the two tablets of the covenant, tablets of stone, written with the finger of God (Exod. 31.18; 32.15–16; Deut. 9.10), and given on Sinai to Moses. He implies a quite audacious contrast between this and Christ's letter written on hearts, which he has just identified with the Corinthians, and claimed as his testimonial. This he implicitly justifies by allusion to the prophecies of Ezekiel: 11.19 (NRSV) reads 'I will give them one heart, and put a new spirit within them; I will remove the heart of stone from their flesh and give them a heart of flesh', and the words are essentially repeated in 36.26. But altogether the contrast also implies an allusion to Jer. 31.31ff., the prophecy of a new covenant, when the law will be written on the heart and everybody will know the Lord. Already we can see texts being compounded and interpenetrated by Paul's own situation. But we have hardly begun yet.

In verse 5 Paul draws out the conclusion: his competence is not his own but God's. God has made Paul the servant who delivers the new covenant, just as God made Moses the servant who delivered the covenant on tablets of stone. Now when Moses returned from Sinai, he had such 'glory' on his face that the people could not look at it, and he had to veil it. According to Exod. 34.29 NRSV, 'the skin of his face shone because he had been talking with God'. The people were afraid. He delivered the word of the Lord, and then put a veil over his face, which he removed each time 'he went in before the Lord to speak with him' (Exod. 34.34 NRSV) until he came out again. Once he had told the Israelites the word of the Lord, he would put on the veil again.

Using this story, Paul compares and contrasts the 'veiled glory' of Moses with the openness and freedom of the gospel. He suggests that the veil was put on to conceal the fact that the glory of the old written covenant, with which Moses was identified, was to be abrogated. He then shifts the metaphor; the veil prevented the people from seeing the glory, and so Paul suggests that the veil is over the minds of everyone who reads the old covenant, and that that remains the case. The veil is only removed when one 'turns to the Lord', Paul's phrase for Moses going in to speak with God. This phrase 'turning to the Lord', according to general usage in the Scriptures, means repenting and returning to God and his covenant; Paul treats it as meaning much more particularly 'turning to Christ', so that Moses becomes the archetype of the

Christian believer.[6] In Christ, then, the veil is removed: the Scriptures are read with new eyes, the fulfilment is discerned. So in the course of Paul's argument, not only are scriptural allusions compounded, but the reference of Scripture becomes complex: the 'Lord' somehow means the Lord who is God, the one and only God who revealed the divine self to Moses, and also the Lord Jesus Christ.

But now another puzzling shift: 'the Lord is the Spirit,' says Paul, 'and where the Spirit of the Lord is, there is freedom' (2 Cor. 3.17 NRSV). Exegetes used to worry about whether Paul really identified the Spirit with the Risen Christ, referred to here as 'the Lord'. But it would seem that what the Greek rather cryptically expresses is something like this: when you read 'the Lord', you should understand that 'turning to the Lord' means 'receiving the new covenant in the Spirit'. In other words Paul is tying up the whole argument, and the whole argument depends on seeing his key texts not just as a collage, but as a synthetic whole in which they all penetrate and illuminate one another. And so the climax is the assertion that 'we all' (presumably both Paul, the Moses-like servant who delivers the new covenant, and the Corinthians, the recipients of this new covenant in the Spirit), with faces that are unveiled, and therefore able not only to behold the glory of the Lord, but also to reflect it as Moses did, are being transformed from one degree of glory to another – for this is what the Lord effects through the Spirit, through the gift of the new covenant.

That does not exhaust all the meaning in that final verse, to which we will return, but let me just underline the point of that fairly detailed exploration of a highly complex passage. Clearly what we have here is not analytical exegesis of written texts in their discrete integrity. It is like overlaying images so that they are all seen at once and so are seen differently. At the heart of this process is a kind of overlaying the God of the Scriptures with Jesus Christ, so that Jesus Christ becomes the manifestation of that God, and an overlaying of Jesus Christ with the experience of the Spirit so that that experience becomes, not merely the continuing presence, but the transformative power of Jesus Christ, or indeed of God, in the lives of Christians. The 'synthesis' means that distinctions are not removed, but a union which is a sort of coinherence is perceived.

Synthesis and mysticism

Now to penetrate that 'overlay' we need to turn to the world of Jewish mysticism. When I was doing the research for *The Myth of God Incarnate*, Gershom Scholem had already demonstrated that the Hekhaloth texts were much earlier than had been supposed, and had linked the development of Jewish mystical reflection on the Creation and the Merkavah, the chariot-throne of God in Ezekiel 1, with apocalyptic literature and gnostic influences. In the last twenty years these researches have been taken much further by Jewish scholars such as Ithamar Gruenwald and Alan Segal.[7] In a particularly significant book published in 1990, the latter argued that Paul provides our best evidence that already in the first century AD these mystical traditions were flourishing. From our point of view the important thing is that aspects of this mystical tradition illuminate Paul's ambiguous or synthetic Christology.

Clearly in these Jewish traditions meditation on certain key passages in Scripture was the generator of mystical experience. Segal writes:

> In the Hebrew Bible, God is sometimes described in human form. Exod. 23.21 mentions an angel who has the form of a man and who carries within him or represents 'the name of God.' A human figure on the divine throne is described in Ezekiel 1, Daniel 7, and Exodus 24, among other places, and was blended into a consistent picture of a principal mediator figure who, like the angel of the Lord in Exodus 23, embodied, personified, or carried the name of God, YHWH, the tetragrammaton . . .
>
> Several Jewish traditions discuss the *eikón* or image of God as . . . an especially glorious and splendid form that humanity lost when Adam sinned. The lost 'image and form of God' (Gen. 1.26) is thereafter associated with God's human appearance in the Bible or with the description of the principal angel of God who carries God's name. The human figure on the merkabah described by Ezekiel is called 'the appearance of the likeness of the Glory of the Lord.' Thus God's Glory or *Kavod* can be a technical term for God's human appearances . . .[8]

Later mystical writings speculated in extraordinary detail about the *Shiur Komah*, the 'body of God', but speculation about the human figure on God's throne can be traced already in Hellenistic Jewish writings. What is clear is that such mystical writings presuppose God's transcendence and 'otherness' – even

Moses could not see God for 'no-one can see God and live' (cf.
Exod. 33.18–23). But in mystical thinking, God's manifestation
of his Glory in human or angelic form is accepted and meditated
upon. 'We do not know God himself, who is beyond our figura-
tion,' writes Segal. 'We only know his Glory, the form in which he
chooses to reveal himself.'[9] So the language of 'image' and 'likeness' conveys two important strands: the 'visionary' nature of the
experience and the fact that what is seen is an 'appearance' of
God's Glory, not the divine self.

Segal believes that Paul's conversion-experience may well have
been analogous to this. Ecstatic experience (whether in the body
or out of the body Paul is not at all sure) is claimed in 2 Cor.
12.1–9. In 1 Cor. 15, Paul adds himself to a list of those to whom
the Risen Christ granted an appearance. In Galatians Paul states
'God revealed his Son in me', (literal trans. Gal. 1.16) and Acts 9.3
speaks of the blinding light that represents glory in theophanies.
Paul claims to have gazed on the Glory, suggests Segal, and thus
to have seen God's self-manifestation as the angel or heavenly
Man on God's throne or at God's right hand, and he identifies
this vision of God's Glory in human form with the person of Jesus
Christ. Associated with such visions was the idea of transformation, and as we have seen, transformation of human beings into
God's image through Christ is central to Paul's expectations. The
notion of 'seeing the glory of the Lord as though reflected in a
mirror', and so being 'transformed into the same image from one
degree of glory to another' (2 Cor. 3.18 NRSV) fits strikingly well
with these visionary traditions.

So Paul's way of appropriating his experience of Christ may
well have been in the language and categories of Jewish mystical
exegesis of biblical theophanies, but this does not explain away
his Christology. His visionary understanding was anchored to a
particular human being, and its ethical consequences worked out
in the life of the Christian communities. It had its own particularity. As we saw earlier, it also had its own key scriptures giving
it a distinct basis. All I am suggesting is that Jewish mystical texts
help us to see how Paul could operate with what appear to be
ambiguities, even inconsistencies, from an analytical point of
view.

I do not think it is an accident that Evelyn Underhill could
describe the mystical sense in terms of the 'synthetic'.[10] Earlier I
made a passing reference to Mother Julian of Norwich. She
provides a wonderful illustration of the kind of synthesis or 'overlay' I have been trying to describe. In one of her visions,[11] Julian

'saw' two people, a lord and his servant. The lord sent the servant off on an errand. The servant rushed off to do his master's will, and without warning falls headlong into a deep ditch, and injures himself very badly. Though he groans and moans and cries and struggles he is quite unable to get up or help himself in any way. Julian notes that basically the servant wanted to do his master's will, and has difficulty in finding fault with him. Meanwhile the lord was thinking of the well-earned rest and reward he would give the servant; his fall and subsequent suffering were to be transformed into great and superlative honour and everlasting joy. Julian spells out the obvious meaning: the servant stands for Adam or everyman. But then she sees other details, and realizes that the servant also represents the Son of God, the second person of the Trinity. When Adam fell, God's Son fell too. Christ was united with Adam. The interpretation is detailed and allegorical, but at its root is this same process of 'overlay'.

It is the ability to discern the union-cum-distinction of all things, the potential for the created order to be overlayed or interpenetrated by what is other and so become its medium, that is characteristic of the mystic. To penetrate 'synthetically' to the sacramental value of the creation as the vehicle of the divine is not ultimately to confuse Creator and created, but to hold in union two distinct identities.

From less than a century before Chalcedon comes a Christian sermon (the first of the Pseudo-Macarian Homilies) which is based on Ezekiel 1, and takes a route similar to Merkavah mysticism. Ezekiel is described as having seen on God's throne what appeared to be the likeness of a man, but this vision is a foreshadowing of a mystery only understood later, when Christ appeared. Another synthesis mystically perceived as the chariot-throne is overlayed by Plato's chariot-image of the soul, Christ becoming the Rider in the Chariot, the Christian the throne of God:

> The soul is completely illumined with the unspeakable beauty of the light of the face of Christ and is perfectly made a participator of the Holy Spirit. It is privileged to be the dwelling-place and the throne of God, all eye, all light, all face, all glory, all spirit, made so by Christ who drives, guides, carries and supports the soul about and adorns and decorates the soul with his spiritual beauty.[12]

Sacramental interpenetration

Much early Christian exegesis evidences the kind of synthetic overlaying of texts and experiences we have noted in Paul, together with spiritual reflection which is often described as mystical. This synthetic thinking co-existed with the analytical thrust that led to the Chalcedonian definition. Indeed, it presupposed sharp differentiation, as did the Jewish mystical traditions. It nevertheless envisaged the possibility of a sacramental interpenetration of those differentiated entities.

Chalcedon worked in the end, I suggest, because the differentiation of Creator from creature meant that the divine nature was defined by contrast with created entities. So it did not suffer from the same limitations as the created entities we know. Place and shape, time and structure, and most certainly gender, were regarded as irrelevant to the nature of the divine Being which is totally 'other', and therefore there was no contradiction in the divine, as it were, occupying the same space as another entity. Divine being could be both differentiated from and mystically identified with another being. God could be envisaged as transcending human nature, but even so human nature could mirror God, receive God's impress, while God could accommodate the divine self to human form, and express the divine communication in human terms. Through overlaying texts and visions, through the metaphor of the divine imprint, through a sense of interpenetration, mediation could be understood, not in terms of a 'semi-divine' being, or a 'mixture', but in terms of the whole character of God being 'imaged' in a wholly human medium.

The structure of Christian belief, I suggest, demands such an account of the person of Christ, not least because, as I hinted at the beginning, it makes the right connections. Christ's uniqueness is constituted by the fact that this 'overlay' of divine and human was not in any sense 'accidental': here was not the 'adoption' of 'a' good man, or the mere inspiration of a prophet, but God's will to stamp the divine imprint on human nature, to re-create the divine image in humanity. Christ is therefore unique, but not disconnected. Rather he is the 'type' or 'model' of human salvation through re-creation. The apparent paradox of two natures which coinhere without confusion, a natural impossibility which cannot be conceived either by the analogy of mixing wine and water or by combining sugar and flour, is the only way of expressing the identity and significance of Jesus Christ. An oscillation between the critic and the visionary, the analytic and synthetic mode of comprehension can alone do justice to the peculiar truth to which we as Christians bear testimony.

The contemporary contemplative, Thomas Merton, writes:

> As a magnifying glass concentrates the rays of the sun into a little burning knot of heat that can set fire to a dry leaf or a piece of paper, so the mystery of Christ in the Gospel concentrates the rays of God's light and fire to a point that sets fire to the spirit of man . . . Through the glass of His incarnation He concentrates the rays of His divine Truth and Love upon us so that we feel the burn, and all mystical experience is communicated to men through the Man Christ.[13]

For Merton, the dogma of the unity without confusion of two natures is essential, but the outcome even more so: 'it is the Spirit of God that must teach us who Christ is and transform us into other Christs'.[14]

Notes

1. The piece which follows was originally delivered as the Gore Memorial Lecture at St Margaret's, Westminster and Birmingham Cathedral, November 1993, under the title 'Visions, Mirrors and Imprints: the Image of God in Human Form'; it was repeated as an address in Durham.
2. Arthur Koestler, *The Sleepwalkers* (London: Hutchinson, 1959); cf. also, *The Act of Creation* (London: Hutchinson, 1964).
3. 'The Critic and the Visionary', *Scottish Journal of Theology*, 41 (1988), pp. 297–312.
4. John Hick, *The Metaphor of God Incarnate* (London: SCM, 1993).
5. John Hick (ed.), *The Myth of God Incarnate* (London: SCM, 1977, 1993).
6. This observation I owe to Richard B. Hays, *Echoes of Scripture in the Letters of Paul* (New Haven: Yale University Press, 1989). Chapter 4 of his book addresses itself to 2 Cor. 3.1—4.6 with the issue of Paul's hermeneutics to the fore. His understanding of the passage coheres with mine in almost every disputed point, so for a fuller treatment of the textual details I refer the reader to his chapter.
7. See Gershom Scholem, *Major Trends in Jewish Mysticism* (New York: Schocken Books, 1960); *Jewish Mysticism, Merkabah Mysticism, and Talmudic Tradition* (New York: Jewish Theological Seminary of America, 1960). Ithamar Gruenwald, *Apocalyptic and Merkavah Mysticism* (Leiden: E. J. Brill, 1980); also Christopher Rowland, *The Open Heaven: A Study of Apocalyptic in Judaism and Early Christianity* (London: SPCK, 1982); Alan F. Segal, *Two*

Powers in Heaven: Rabbinic Reports About Christianity and Gnosticism (Leiden: E. J. Brill, 1977); *Paul the Convert: The Apostolate and Apostasy of Saul the Pharisee* (New Haven: Yale University Press, 1990).

8. Segal, *Paul the Convert*, pp. 40–1.
9. Segal, *Paul the Convert*, pp.52–3.
10. Evelyn Underhill, in her classic study, *Mysticism* (London: Methuen, 1911).
11. Julian of Norwich, *Revelations of Divine Love*, tr. Clifton Walters (Harmondsworth: Penguin, 1966), ch. 51, pp. 141–51.
12. Eng. tr. G. A. Moloney, SJ, *Macarius*, in the Classics of Western Spirituality (London: SPCK, 1989).
13. Thomas Merton, *Seeds of Contemplation* (paperback edn Wheathampstead, Hertfordshire: Anthony Clarke Books, 1972 [copyright 1961]), ch. 21, p. 117.
14. Merton, *Seeds of Contemplation*, p. 122.

3

Heaven and Earth in Parallel: The Key Role of Angels in Ancient Judaism

ROBERT HAYWARD

Angels as mediators between the spiritual and the material, between God and ourselves, already have a clear sacramental role, but in this essay Robert Hayward argues for a much deeper connection. The book of Tobit treats them as revealers of the heavenly 'secret' or 'mystery' ('sacramentum' in Jerome's Latin), and what this means in particular for the book of Jubilees is an elaborate paralleling of life and worship between heaven and earth, with sabbath, festival and even circumcision all finding their echo in the actions of the angels in heaven. 'Echo', however, is the wrong word since, as Robert Hayward's discussion of the treatment accorded Jacob well illustrates, it was earth that was seen as required to echo heaven: this was the nation's responsibility, and it was as guardian of this mystery that Jacob was understood as having received his new name of 'Israel' (Gen. 32).

Angels as sacramental presences and revealers

Although angels are intelligent beings of pure spirit, their place in a scheme of things which may be called 'sacramental' is not difficult to discern or justify. Belonging by nature to the supernatural, spiritual word of heaven, they nonetheless may have contact with the physical, created order, and communicate with human beings. The Hebrew Bible itself records many such encounters, of varying kinds and degrees, between angels and the physical world;[1] indeed, an occasion no less momentous than the revelation of God's Name to Moses in the burning bush presupposes the presence of an angelic being (Exod. 3.2). It is not surprising, then, that Jews of the post-biblical period developed a highly sophisticated and intricate understanding of the angels, and of their role in the relationship between Israel and God. The well-known story of Tobit, which dates probably from the third century BC, will serve to illustrate some of the basic principles taken for granted by Jews as they considered the angels and their part in God's plan.[2]

Tobias and his son Tobit are presented as pious Jews, faithful to the Jerusalem Temple (Tobit 1.3–4): their conduct is true and just (1.3; 4.5; 14.2), not least with regard to the worship of God. Thus Tobias declares:

> I alone went often to Jerusalem at the feasts, as it hath been ordained unto all Israel by an everlasting decree, having the firstfruits and the tithes of my increase, and that which was first shorn; and I gave them at the altar to the priests, the sons of Aaron. The tithe of all my increase I gave to the sons of Levi, who ministered at Jerusalem: and the second tithe I sold, and went, and spent it each year at Jerusalem: and the third I gave to whom it was fitting . . . (Tobit 1.6–8)

Tobias is thus faithful to God's *everlasting decree* about the festivals, firstfruits, and tithes. Not only this: he lays great stress on the giving of alms, and goes to some lengths to ensure that Tobit gives also (1.3; 4.7–11); and he is scrupulous in burying the dead (1.18–19; 2.3–8). It is because of this piety and justice that no less an authority than the Archangel Raphael assumes human form, to accompany and assist Tobit on his perilous journey to rescue his father's money. Raphael also delivers Tobit's wife from an evil demon, and restores sight to the blind Tobias; but his true identity is not revealed until Tobias seeks to reward him. Then, Raphael uses the occasion to assert that it is good to bless God, to exalt his Name, and show forth his deeds: twice he declares that 'it is good to keep close the secret of a king, but to reveal gloriously the works of God' (12.7, 11). He endorses Tobit's concern for justice and prayer (12.8; cf. 4.5), and especially commends Tobit's view of almsgiving as a means of delivery from death and of purging sin (12.9; cf. 4.10). Only then does he say:

> When thou didst pray, and Sarah thy daughter-in-law, I brought the memorial of your prayer before the Holy One: and when thou didst bury the dead, *I was with thee* likewise. And when thou didst not delay to rise up, and leave thy dinner, that thou mightest go and cover the dead, thy good deed was not

hid from me: but *I was with thee* . . . I am Raphael, one of the seven holy angels, which present the prayers of the saints, and go in before the glory of the Holy One. (12.12–13, 15)

The full significance of what we have set out here can be appreciated only when we recall that, however strange it may seem, almsgiving and the burial of the dead are nowhere in the Torah of Moses commanded as binding upon Jews. Indeed, in a period later than Tobit, the Rabbis found it necessary to explain how God had commended these acts of piety not with a verbal command, but by his own deeds.[3] Thus burial of the dead is prescribed by the Torah, not through an uttered command of God, but by his action in burying Moses in the land of Moab (Deut. 34.5–6). For the author of Tobit, however, these righteous deeds are revealed as being completely in accordance with God's will through the agency of Raphael, not simply because the archangel says so, but because Raphael himself makes it clear that *he was present* with Tobias, albeit invisibly, as he buried the dead. The presence of an angel who 'goes in before the glory of the Holy One' at the burial of the dead indicates an alliance between things earthly and heavenly which goes beyond the mere instruction of a mortal by a member of the heavenly court.

Yet Raphael's role as instructor should not be underestimated. As we have seen, at the very moment he explains that he was present when Tobias buried the dead, he twice contrasts the 'secret' of an earthly king, which should be kept close, with God's works, which are to be revealed. God, of course, is the supreme King, and Tobit's prayer of thanksgiving makes no fewer than six references to his kingship in the course of eighteen verses (Tobit 13.1, 6, 7, 10, 11, 15). God's deeds, which Raphael says are to be revealed, therefore correspond, *mutatis mutandis*, to the 'secret' of an earthly monarch (12.7); and Jerome's Vulgate represents this notion with the word *sacramentum*. The Septuagint of Tobit 12.7, 11 use *mustêrion*, which Jerome often renders as *sacramentum* elsewhere.[4] These are the words usually employed by the Septuagint and Jerome respectively to render the Aramaic word *râz*, which occurs some nine times in the book of Daniel.[5] Its primary meaning is 'a secret'; but it most particularly designates *heavenly* mysteries which may, by God's favour, be revealed to human beings.[6] And the 'secret', Greek *mustêrion* and Latin *mysterium*, is most often the prerogative of a king, as Judith 2.2 testifies.

The function of the angels as revealers of heavenly secrets is, of course, well attested in both biblical and non-biblical writings. In one particularly influential work of Second Temple times,

however, the presence of angels with just Israelites who worship
according to the commandments of the Torah (rightly interpreted)
is combined with belief in angels as revealers of heavenly mysteries, in such a way that the heavenly and earthly realms should
exactly coincide. The natural and the super-natural, the physical
and the spiritual, Israel and the angels are intended by the
Almighty as separate parts of one single, harmonious continuum
whose function is the perfect fulfilment of the will of God, the
eternal King. Such an ideal is given full expression in the book of
Jubilees, whose understanding of the angels and their relationship
with Israel forms the substance for discussion in this essay.

Replicating heaven on earth:
Sabbath and circumcision

Jubilees probably dates from the mid-second century BC. It seems
to have been widely known, and was certainly used by the Jews
who formed the group at Qumran, for whom it had a special
status.[7] In form, it is a re-written account of the biblical narrative
Gen. 1.1—Exod. 15.22, given as a speech delivered to Moses by
an 'Angel of the Presence'. Foremost among its many concerns is
the calendar: *Jubilees* powerfully advocates a solar calendar, in
which a 364-day year of exactly fifty-two weeks precisely and
regularly recurs annually, in such a way that the Sabbaths, New
Moons, and Festivals always fall on the same date, and the same
day of the week, each year.[8] This calendar is itself a heavenly
mystery communicated by the angel to Moses: it is engraved for
ever 'on the heavenly tablets' (*Jub*. 6.29–38), the repositories of
supernatural knowledge which may, from time to time, be made
available to Israel or to individuals by the angels.[9] From the out-
set, *Jubilees* seeks to make known and promote order, God's order
of things, in the daily life of the Jewish people; and the angels are
intricately bound up in this order from the very beginning of
creation.

This order is first seen in the ranks of the angels themselves,
who were created on the first day of creation. The two highest
ranks are the Angels of the Presence and the Angels of Sanctification, and these are followed in order by angels in charge of fire,
the winds, and other natural phenomena. In all, there are at least
twenty-one classes of angel: they may number twenty-two, if we
are to count the angels who are over the abysses (plural) as two
classes.[10] The importance of the number twenty-two will be made
plain later. The complete list of their ranks is found in *Jub*. 2.2.
Of the greatest significance is the fact that the two highest orders,

the Angels of the Presence and the Angels of Sanctification, observe the Sabbath Day in heaven from the very beginning of time; and the Sabbath is the very goal of creation itself, the crown and glory of God's order of things, just as it is in Scripture (Gen. 2.2–3). Thus the Angel of the Presence tells Moses:

> And He completed all of his work on the sixth day, everything which is in the heavens and the earth and the seas and the depths and in the light and in the darkness and in every place. And he gave us (the angels) a great sign, the sabbath day, so that we might work six days and observe a sabbath from all work on the seventh day. And he told us – all the Angels of the Presence and all the Angels of Sanctification, these two great kinds, that we might keep the Sabbath with Him in heaven and on earth. (*Jub.* 2.16–18)

Quite why these angels must keep the Sabbath on earth as well as in heaven is soon made plain: the descendants of Jacob, named here at the very beginning of the book, are to be set apart for God from all other peoples on earth to keep Sabbath. These people God will sanctify and bless just as he has sanctified and blessed the Sabbath (*Jub.* 2.19), because God has foreseen Jacob, marked him down as eldest son, and sanctified him for himself for ever (*Jub.* 2.20). The angel sums up the matter in the following verse, saying that God created the Sabbath so that Jacob's descendants should be like him, so that

> they might keep the Sabbath with us on the seventh day, to eat and drink and bless the one who created all things just as He blessed and sanctified for Himself a people who appeared from all the nations so that they might keep the Sabbath together with us. And he caused their desires to go up as pleasing fragrance, which is acceptable before him always. (*Jub.* 2.21–2)

As Israel keep Sabbath on earth, the angels would appear to be present with them. To say that *Jubilees* labours the matter of the Sabbath would be an understatement. Lest we should be in any doubt, the blessedness and holiness of Sabbath is again set in association with the blessedness and holiness of Jacob in 2.24; the Sabbath is holier than all other days (2.26), and whoever observes it is holy and blessed for all time, like the Angels of the Presence and Sanctification (2.28). And only Israel on earth, and the two highest classes of angels in heaven and on earth, keep this sacred day with God (2.30–1). The author returns to the Sabbath at the very close of his book, setting out the halakhah appropriate for the day, and asserting most significantly that the Sabbath shall be 'a day of the holy kingdom' for all Israel among all their days for ever.[11]

Almost equal in importance to the Sabbath is the Feast of Pentecost, which *Jubilees* understands as the Feast of the Covenant-oath. This matter has been much discussed:[12] we need note here only that this feast, like Sabbath, was kept in heaven (*Jub.* 6.17–18) and is likewise to be observed by Israel for all time (*Jub.* 6.20–2). Indeed, the same may be said about all the festival days: they are observed in heaven, and Israel is bound to observe them on earth, at the correct time. Hence the importance of the calendar: if Israel make errors in its calculation, then they will observe New Moons, Sabbaths, and Festivals which are out of kilter with those in heaven, and God's intended order of things is disrupted (6.33–7).

In keeping Sabbath and the other festivals, then, Israel is to be perfectly at one with only the two highest classes of angels. The expression 'Angels of the Presence' presumably represents an original Hebrew *mal 'ᵃkê happanîm*, literally, 'the Angels of the Face', that is, those angels who have access to the very presence of God himself. Why Israel should be on an equal footing with such exalted beings is no doubt explained by an incident in the life of their ancestor Jacob, whose name was changed to Israel after he had wrestled with a heavenly being at a place he named Peniel,[13] 'Face of God', saying: 'For I have seen God face to face, and yet my life is preserved' (Gen. 32.30). More must be said of this incident presently; for the moment, we should note that the Bible seems to suggest that Jacob-Israel was one who had seen God, and that the author of *Jubilees* developed this biblical datum in such a way that a bond is forged between Israel on earth and those beings in heaven who see God, the 'angels of the Presence'.

The phrase 'the Angels of Sanctification' probably represents Hebrew *mal 'ᵃkê haqqôdeš*, which means either 'the Angels of the Sanctuary' or 'the Angels of Holiness'. These are the celestial ministers of the heavenly Temple who minister before God continually: when Levi is chosen to exercise the priestly office, it is said that his sons will minister before the Lord just as the angels do (*Jub.* 30.18). And when Isaac blesses Levi, he prays that God bless his sons by drawing them near to serve him in his sanctuary like the Angels of the Presence and the *Holy Ones* (*Jub.* 31.14).[14] These angels are, in all likelihood, the ones who sing the *qᵉduššâh*, the Trisagion or Sanctus which Isaiah the prophet had heard when he saw the Lord enthroned as King in the Temple (Isa. 6.1–3).

One further bond links these angels and the people of Israel:

both share the mark of God's covenant, the mark of circumcision. The angels are created with this mark, and all male Israelites are bound to be circumcised. Commenting on this, *Jubilees* remarks:

> Because the nature of all the angels of the Presence and all the angels of Sanctification was thus from the day of their creation. And in the presence of the angels of the Presence and the angels of Sanctification he sanctified Israel so that they might be with Him and with His holy angels. (*Jub.* 15.27)

So close is Israel's assimilation to these highest angels that God alone has authority over this people: no angel or spirit has any power over Israel, for God alone is their ruler (*Jub.* 15.32).

Thus through keeping Sabbath, New Moon, and the Festivals, and through observing the rite of circumcision, Israel on earth replicate exactly a heavenly reality confined to the two highest classes of angels. In this way, heavenly realities are made present on earth. God's kingship itself, properly and without limitation exercised in heaven, is thus operative on earth, where just and faithful Israelites observe the commandments of the Torah as set out by *Jubilees*: for then God alone is King over them, and the Sabbath is the day of the holy kingdom. But if heaven is made present on earth by a just and faithful Israel, it is equally God's intention that Israel should be lifted to heaven: Israel is circumcised so that they may be with God and his holy angels (15.27). What *Jubilees* envisages as God's intention is nothing less than perfect union, oneness, between heaven and earth as represented by the highest angels and Israel, a union not only of 'place' but also of time in a perfect calendar encompassing the natural and the super-natural.[15]

The key representative role of Jacob

Yet to say this is not to exhaust the teaching of *Jubilees* on the bonds which unite the earthly and the heavenly worlds. The mystery of the Sabbath, and its status as blessed and sanctified which corresponds exactly to the status of Jacob and of the angels, is further expounded in a remarkable passage early in the work. There it is noted that before the first Sabbath, God had created twenty-two kinds of works, and that from Adam until Jacob there were twenty-two patriarchal figures (*Jub.* 2.23). The twenty-second and last creation of God is, of course, Adam the protoplast and origin of the whole of humanity: *Jubilees* presents Jacob, the twenty-second patriarch, as somehow analogous to the protoplast. But whereas the former was cast out of the garden of Eden, which *Jubilees* regards as one of four places sacred to God on earth (*Jub.* 4.26), Jacob is blest and holy, like the Sabbath (2.23), is father of the Israelites who share privileges with the highest angels, and institutes the priesthood of Levi (32.3) which will serve on Mount Zion, the fourth of those earthly places listed as sacred to God in *Jub.* 4.26.

Not only this, but Jacob recapitulates in himself the blessings of earlier patriarchs, as a result of which the stability and continuity of the created order is guaranteed. So when Abraham blesses Jacob, he declares:

> And all of the blessings with which the Lord blessed me and my seed will be for Jacob and his seed always. And in his seed my name will be blessed and the names of my fathers Shem and Noah, and Enoch and Mahalalel, and Enos, and Seth, and Adam. And they will serve to establish heaven and to strengthen the earth and to renew all of the lights which are above the firmament. (*Jub.* 19.23–5)

This link between Jacob and the stability and order of creation is also implied by another piece of information which *Jubilees* presents only obliquely. There are twenty-two letters in the Hebrew alphabet: our current text of *Jubilees* says nothing of this, but does state clearly that Hebrew is the original language, 'the tongue of creation' (12.26) which, before Adam's transgression, had been the universal language spoken also by the animals (3.26).[16] Jacob, the twenty-second patriarch, is ancestor of the people Israel, whose native tongue is Hebrew, the language by which the universe was brought into being: it is also the language of the angels, who are responsible for re-introducing it into the world by teaching it to Abraham (12.25).[17] And yet another link between heaven and earth through the angels and Jacob may be established if the author of *Jubilees* was of the same opinion as Josephus (*Contra Apionem* I.38) that there were twenty-two books in the Hebrew Bible.[18] Whether or not this last point has substance, it is undeniably the case that *Jubilees* records how, on the twenty-second day of the seventh month, an angel presented to Jacob seven tablets recording the whole history of his descendants (31.21).

The centrality of Jacob in this discussion of Israel and the angels compels us to enquire closely who this Jacob might be, and what his character might represent. Among the Jewish people, there is nothing so indicative of a person's essence or character as the name which he or she bears. It is a matter of common knowledge that Jacob's name was changed to Israel, a fact twice recorded in Genesis (32.24–30; 35.9–12). The way in which

Jubilees re-writes these two narratives is highly revealing, and has important ramifications.

The first narrative records a famous incident when Jacob, left alone at the ford of Jabbok in the night before he is due to meet his potentially hostile brother Esau, wrestles with a mysterious adversary who wounds his thigh. The latter is described as a man by Gen. 32.24; but in verse 28 it becomes clear that this is no ordinary mortal, since he says to Jacob: 'Your name shall no more be called Jacob, but Israel; for you have striven (*śārîtā*) with God and with men, and have prevailed.' Such is the RSV's rendering of this verse, which we shall follow for the moment. The story next makes Jacob ask the wrestler what his name is; no answer is given, but the stranger blesses Jacob, and goes away. It is then that Jacob calls the place Peniel, because he has seen God face to face, and his life is preserved (v. 30).[19]

Jubilees 29.5–6, which covers the narrative of Gen. 32.24–30, altogether omits the encounter with the 'man', the wrestling, the struggle, and the wounding of Jacob's thigh. The incident is radically reduced: Jacob is presented as setting out for Gilead and meeting Laban his father-in-law: 'But the Lord did not permit him (i.e. Laban) to deal cruelly with Jacob, because He appeared to him in a dream at night' (*Jub.* 29.6). Thus at a stroke the mysterious stranger of the Bible becomes the well known Laban, and God appears to Jacob simply, it would seem, to give him reassurance that all is well. Certainly the re-naming of Jacob as Israel is entirely left out.[20]

The second narrative, Gen. 35.9–12, records how God appeared to Jacob on his second visit to Bethel, announced that his name would no longer be Jacob, but Israel, and promised that a nation and a congregation of peoples, together with kings, would arise from him. In stark contrast with the treatment accorded to the first narrative, *Jubilees* massively expands this biblical account, and sets it within a lengthy description of Jacob consecrating Levi, who has been designated for the priestly office. Jacob proceeds with this once he knows that Rachel is pregnant with Benjamin, and that his sons, leaving aside Levi, will therefore number twelve (32.3); this number is important for Jacob, since Rebecca had earlier said that the number of Jacob's sons should correspond to the number of months in the year (25.16). They next celebrate the Feast of Sukkoth (Tabernacles or Booths); pay appropriate tithes; and Jacob plans to build a sanctuary at Bethel (*Jub.* 32.1–16). Then, on the twenty-second day, 'the Lord appeared to him in the night and blessed him and said to him, "Your name will not be called Jacob, but you will be named

Israel"' (*Jub.* 32.17). There follows a re-writing of God's promise
to Jacob-Israel: *Jubilees* states that kings will issue from him who
shall rule the whole world; and his descendants are promised a
universal rule of the earth, which they shall inherit (32.18–19).

The upshot of all this is that God, not a mysterious stranger,
imposes the name Israel on Jacob during the Feast of Sukkoth on
the twenty-second day of the seventh month. Jacob suffers neither
struggle nor injury, and receives his new name at the moment
when the predestined priesthood of Levi, which will serve God
on earth in the manner of the angels in heaven (30.18; 31.14), is
consecrated for service. The number of the sons of Israel is also
complete, corresponding to the divinely ordered months of the
year: all is in readiness for Israel's function to begin.

It is, perhaps, not surprising that *Jubilees* so fundamentally
alters these two biblical narratives. Since the book has so heavily
emphasized that Israel is on an equal footing with the highest
angels, it might appear perverse to record a struggle between
Jacob and some heavenly being. Yet what compelled *Jubilees* to re-
structure the biblical data, it may be argued, is a difficulty within
the biblical text itself. It will be recalled that the mysterious being
who encountered Jacob is said in Gen. 32.28 to have re-named
him Israel, 'because you have striven (*śârîtâ*) with God and with
men'. Such was the RSV's translation, which understands the
Hebrew word reproduced here as if it derived from root *śrh*, 'to
struggle, exert oneself'.[21] It is possible that Josephus (*Ant.* I.333)
was of a similar mind, when he explained the name Israel as
meaning an opponent of an angel, *ton antistatên angellôi*.[22] For the
most part, however, ancient translators and commentators did
not follow this line of interpretation, but preferred one of two
widely represented renderings.

Thus the Septuagint, the Syriac, Theodotion, the Old Latin,
and the Vulgate translated the word as 'you have been strong', as
from the Hebrew root *śrr*, 'be firm, hard'.[23] But Palestinian Jews
clearly preferred another translation, represented by Aquila,
Targum Onqelos, the Targums Pseudo-Jonathan and Neofiti, the
Targum fragments from the Cairo Geniza, and one recension of
the Samaritan Targum. All these took the Hebrew to mean 'you
have been a prince, you have been a ruler', understanding *śârîtâ*
as if it derived from the root *śrr*, 'to be a prince, to rule'. It is this
interpretation of the name Israel which Jerome sets forth in his
Hebrew Questions on Genesis, even though in his Vulgate he
adheres to the Septuagint translation of *śârîtâ*.[24] On this view of
things, the name *Israel* signifies that Jacob is now a *ruler* or a
prince, Hebrew *śar*, with God; and the title *śar* is the very word

used in the biblical book of Daniel (e.g. 10.13, 20, 21) to designate the angelic rulers of the nations and no less a figure than the
Archangel Michael himself.

Jacob as the angel-prince imitating heaven's worship

Exegesis of the name Israel as 'a prince-angel with God' almost
certainly accounts for much of what *Jubilees* has to say about the
intimate correspondences which exist between Israel and the
angels, and which serve to bring into 'one-ness' the world below
and the world above. Even the form of the name Isra-el is similar
to the names Micha-el, Gabri-el, and Rapha-el, the angels who
have most intimate contact with God as 'Angels of the Presence'.
But what of Israel's association with the Angels of Sanctification?
Is this explained solely by the fact that the Israelite priesthood
descended from Levi, as it ministers to God in carrying out the
rituals of the earthly Temple, corresponds to the ministry of the
Angels of Sanctification (Angels of the Sanctuary, Angels of
Holiness) in the heavenly realms? Certainly such correspondence
is unambiguously admitted by *Jubilees*, as we have seen; but the
book may also have taken for granted, without explicit acknowledgement, an ancient interpretation of Israel as the one who
sings God's praises.

It is not difficult to bring the name Israel into association with
the praise of God, given the techniques of the ancient exegetes.
We need only remind ourselves that Hebrew, in addition to the
roots *srh*, *srr*, and *srr* has a verbal root *syr*, 'to sing', and a corresponding noun *syr*, 'song', which may also be used to designate a
particular form of Psalm, as, for example, in the titles of Psalms
65–8, 75, 76, 88 and others. There was always the possibility,
then, that exegetes might interpret the name Israel with reference
to this root.[25] The scriptural Psalms themselves are formal compositions of great complexity, many of which were sung by the
Levites in the course of the Temple service on earth; and apart
from the Scriptures, the production of Psalm-like hymns was very
much a part of the piety and spirituality of Second Temple
Judaism. We need only recall the *Hodayot*, or Thanksgiving hymns
found at Qumran. These were composed by an individual or
group keenly aware of communion between the angels and the
lower world.[26]

But most instructive in this regard is the first-century AD work
entitled *Liber Antiquitatum Biblicarum*, falsely ascribed to Philo.[27]
Here, Israel's leaders often hymn God for his great deeds (see, for
example, 21.15; 32.1–17). And it is this work which identifies

Jacob's adversary at the Jabbok, referring to the incident 'when he wrestled in the dust with the angel who had responsibility over the hymns' (*LAB* 18.6). But Targum Neofiti of Gen. 32.25 goes further, and actually names the angel as Sariel: here we have Hebrew *śar*, 'angel-prince', and the possibility of a pun on the two names *śry'l* and *yśr'l*.[28] And according to this same Targum of Gen. 32.27, Sariel addresses Jacob: 'Let me go away, for the rising of the column of the dawn has come; because the time has arrived for the angels of the height to utter praise; and I am the chief of those who utter praise.'[29] For this Targum, as also for Targum Pseudo-Jonathan, the angel who gives to Jacob the name Israel, understood as 'because you have been a prince with God', is none other than the chief of the angelic chorus which ever praises God in heaven. It remains uncertain whether the haggadah of *Liber Antiquitatum Biblicarum* and the Targums set out here was known to *Jubilees*; but all these texts in their different ways insist that Israel is the one who praises God on earth, and that this praise is mysteriously coupled with that offered by the angels in heaven.

Jubilees has insisted, in its re-writing of the Bible, that Jacob received his new name Israel at Bethel, not at the ford of Jabbok. It was at Bethel, on his first visit to that place, that he had dreamed of a ladder set up linking heaven and earth, with the angels going up and down upon it, and the Lord himself standing at the top of it (Gen. 28.12–13). *Jub.* 27.21–2 more or less faithfully reproduces the biblical account of Jacob's ladder; but in view of what this book has told us about Jacob and the angels elsewhere, it may be worthwhile to note comments made about this episode by two other post-biblical texts. Foremost among these is Wisd. 10.10–12, which tells how Wisdom herself directed Jacob as he fled from Esau, so that he comes to Bethel: 'She showed to him the kingdom of God, and gave to him knowledge of the holy ones (or: holy things).'[30] This book has interpreted Jacob's dream at Bethel, with the angels, the ladder, and the Lord standing at the head of it, as a revelation of God's kingship: it is to Jacob, the ancestor of Israel, that this is revealed, as is knowledge of the holy ones, that is, the angels, or of holy things, possibly the rites of the Temple. The Targums are much more explicit, for they put a speech into the mouth of the angels who stand by the ladder, which is described as fixed, q*by'*, on the earth: 'Come, see the pious man (*ḥsyd'*) whose image (*eikôn*) is fixed (q*by'*) on the Throne of Glory.' Here the notion that Jacob himself is the locus of God's kingdom on earth is graphically expressed: his very likeness is as surely fixed on God's kingly throne as is the ladder on which the angels go up and down, thereby uniting the realms of heaven and earth in the presence of Jacob who is Israel.[31]

Earthing the heavenly 'sacramentum'

Already in the third century BC, the book of Tobit testifies to a belief that the angels are truly present with just and faithful Jews who not only keep the commandments of the Torah, but who imitate God's own actions and deeds. Tobias had imitated God in burying the dead: he also regarded the Festivals laid down in the Torah as an *everlasting decree*, regularly observing them; as a result, the archangel Raphael assists him. The book of *Jubilees* offers an extended theological reflection on these principles enunciated by the author of *Tobit*.

The angels properly belong in heaven, where God sits on the Throne of Glory as King; and it is in the nature of kings that they have 'secrets' or 'secret counsel' – Aramaic *râz*, Greek *mustêrion*, Latin *sacramentum*. As members of the heavenly court, angels may have access to the King's *sacramentum*, and it is such secrets that the Angel of the Presence reveals to Moses in *Jubilees*. Central to the mysteries revealed to Moses is the belief that when Israel acts in accordance with the Torah, then she makes present on earth the actions and attitudes of the two highest classes of angels in heaven, the Angels of the Presence and the Angels of Sanctification.

This mystery, *sacramentum*, is a fundamental truth on which, ultimately, the whole universe depends. For *Jubilees* makes it clear that Israel's place in God's order of things is 'written in' to the very process of creation itself; and Israel's proper function is to provide that place of unity, that 'one-ness' between the upper and lower worlds in both time and space where God's Kingship may properly be exercised in earth, as it is in heaven. In short, the people Israel are to be in complete harmony with the angels just as their father Jacob was, when at Bethel he saw the heavenly beings ascend and descend the ladder linking heaven and earth, mortal men and the Lord God of Israel.

For many ancient Jewish exegetes, the very name Israel signified 'angel-prince of God', encapsulating the character and essence of the Patriarch and his descendants. *Jubilees* most probably took this exegesis for granted, setting out more and more clearly its implications. Thus Israel's spiritual life is to be determined by her own character and status as equal to the angels: meticulous observance of the Torah as interpreted by *Jubilees* is the privilege which she shares with the angels in heaven. In this essay, we have not been concerned to detail the consequences of Israel's failure to live up to her name, in accordance with her character; it will be clear, however, that such a failure would constitute the profanation of God's mystery, his *sacramentum*, with the possibility that the stability of the universe itself might be put at risk.

Notes

General note:

The translations of *Jubilees* quoted here are taken from that of O. S. Wintermute, 'Jubilees', in *The Old Testament Pseudepigrapha*, vol. 2, ed. J. H. Charlesworth (London: Darton, Longman & Todd, 1985), pp. 35–142. For the text of the Aramaic Targums, we have used A. Sperber, *The Bible in Aramaic*, vol. 1, *The Pentateuch According to Targum Onkelos* (Leiden: E. J. Brill, 1959); E. G. Clarke, with collaboration by W. E. Aufrecht, J. C. Hurd, and F. Spitzer, *Targum Pseudo-Jonathan of the Pentateuch* (New Jersey: Ktav, 1984); A. Díez Macho, *Ms. Neophyti 1*. Tomo I Génesis (Madrid-Barcelona: Consejo Superior de Investigaciones Cientáfic, 1968); M. L. Klein, *Genizah Manuscripts of Palestinian Targum to the Pentateuch*, vol. 1 (Cincinnati: Hebrew Union College Press, 1986); translations are ours.

1. See, for example, Gen. 16.7–11; 22.11–15; Num. 22.22–35; 2 Kings 1.3–15; Zech. 1.9, 12, 14; 1 Chron. 21.15–20. For a study of angels in the Hebrew Bible, see E. T. Mullen, *The Assembly of the Gods: The Divine Council in Canaanite and Early Hebrew Literature*, Harvard Semitic Monographs 24 (Atlanta: Scholars Press, 1980); and for an excellent brief survey of biblical and postbiblical material, see Carol A. Newsom, article 'Angels', *The Anchor Bible Dictionary*, vol. 1 (New York: Doubleday, 1992), pp. 248–53.

2. For the date and provenance of *Tobit*, see discussion of the full range of opinions in E. Schürer, *The History of the Jewish People in the Age of Jesus Christ*, vol. III.1, rev. and ed. by G. Vermes, F. Millar, and M. Goodman (Edinburgh: T. & T. Clark, 1986), pp. 222–31.

3. See Targum Pseudo-Jonathan (PJ) of Deut. 34.6, which notes that the Archangels Michael and Gabriel helped God to bury Moses, with the assistance of Metatron, Yophiel, Uriel, and Yephiphyah. Cf. also *b. Sotah* 13b–14a; *Deut. Rabb.* 31:14; *Mekhilta de R. Ishmael Beshallah* 1:118 ff.; A. Shinan, *The Aggadah in the Aramaic Targums to the Pentateuch*, 2 vols. (Jerusalem: Makov, 1979), vol. 1, pp. 155–60, [in Hebrew]; C. T. R. Hayward, 'Jacob's Second Visit to Bethel in Targum Pseudo-Jonathan', in *A Tribute to Geza Vermes*, ed. P. R. Davies and R. T. White (Sheffield: JSOT Press, 1990), pp. 182–3.

4. See Wisd. 2.22; 6.24 (= Septuagint 6.22); cf. 12.5 (rendering *mustas*); Dan. 2.18, 30, 47; he also reproduces as Latin *mysterium* the Greek *mustêrion* in Judith 2.2; Dan. 2.19, 27, 28, 29, 47. For *sacramentum* rendering *mustêrion* in the New Testament, see Eph. 1.9; 3.3, 9; 5.32; Col. 1.27; 1 Tim. 3.16; Rev. 1.20; 17.7.

5. See Dan. 2.18, 19, 27, 28, 29, 30, 47 (twice); 4.6.

6. For full discussion, see C. Rowland, *The Open Heaven. A Study of Apocalyptic in Judaism and Early Christianity* (London: SPCK, 1982), pp. 75–189.

7. For the most recent discussion of the date and provenance of *Jubilees*, see J. C. VanderKam, article 'Jubilees', *The Anchor Bible Dictionary*, vol. 3, pp. 1030–1; cf. also Schürer, *History of the Jewish People*, Vol. III.I, pp. 308–18; and K. Berger, *Das Buch der Jubiläen: Jüdische Schriften aus hellenistisch-römischer Zeit* Band II Lieferung 3 (Guütersloh: Gerd Mohn, 1981), pp. 295–301. Fragments of the original Hebrew text of *Jubilees* have been found at Qumran, for a discussion of which see J. C. VanderKam, *The Book of Jubilees*, Scriptores Aethiopici 88, Corpus Scriptorum Christianorum Orientalium 511 (Louvain: Peeters, 1989), pp. vi–ix. Direct reference is made to *Jubilees* in CD XVI.2–4, and there is a clear, but debated relationship between this work and *11QTemple*: see J. C. VanderKam, 'The Temple Scroll and the Book of Jubilees', in *Temple Scroll Studies*, ed. G. J. Brooke (Sheffield: JSOT Press, 1989), pp. 211–36. For the influence of *Jubilees* on New Testament writings, see R. H. Charles, *The Book of Jubilees* (London: A. & C. Black, 1902), pp. lxxxiii–lxxxv.

8. For discussion of the calendar in *Jubilees*, see A. Jaubert, 'Le Calendrier des Jubilées et de la Secte de Qumrân. Ses Origines bibliques' (*Vetus Testamentum* 3, 1953), pp. 250–64; and 'Le Calendrier des Jubilées et les jours liturgiques de la Semaine' (*Vetus Testamentum* 7, 1957), pp. 35–61; J. M. Baumgarten, 'Some Problems of the Jubilees Calendar in Current Research' (*Vetus Testamentum* 32, 1982), pp. 485–9.

9. The heavenly tablets contain the secrets of the calendar (1.29; 6.17, 29, 31, 35; 16.28; 18.19; 49.8; 50.13); specific ritual laws (3.10, 31; 15.25; 32.10, 15); rules for ethical conduct (4.5, 32; 28.6; 33.10; 39.6); and criminal law (30.9). See H. Bietenhard, *Die himmlische Welt im Urchristentum und Spätjudentum* (Tübingen: J. C. B. Mohr, 1951), pp. 242–4.

10. The angels control all natural phenomena; and it should be noted particularly that the created order itself is, for *Jubilees*, both a physical and a spiritual reality; so M. Testuz, *Les idées religieuses du livre des Jubilées* (Paris: Minard, 1960), pp. 46–7. If they number twenty-two classes, then they and Israel share yet another characteristic. But they probably number twenty-one, and may thus be counted as, ultimately, slightly inferior to Israel. The difficulty of counting their exact numbers is further complicated by textual problems: see Wintermute, 'Jubilees', p. 55.

11. See *Jub.* 50.9, 'And a day of the holy kingdom for all Israel is this day among their days always'. When the Temple in Jerusalem has been built for ever, then God will appear in the sight of all: 'And everyone will know that I am the God of Israel and the father of all the children of Jacob and king upon Mount Zion forever and ever. And Zion and Jerusalem will be holy' (*Jub.* 1.28).

12. See, for example, Testuz, *Les Idées religieuses*, pp. 146–9; Wintermute, 'Jubilees', p. 67; VanderKam, 'The Temple Scroll and the Book of Jubilees', especially pp. 219–20.

13. See *Gesenius' Hebrew Grammar*, ed. E. Kautzsch and rev. A. E. Cowley (Oxford: Clarendon Press, 1910), p. 252; J. Skinner, *A Critical and Exegetical Commentary on Genesis* (Edinburgh: T. & T. Clark, 1912), p. 410; and G. von Rad, *Genesis*, tr. J. H. Marks, 2nd edn (London: SCM, 1963), pp. 318–19.

14. They are the same as the Angels of Sanctification: see Charles, *Jubilees*, p. 186, and 'The Book of Jubilees', in *Apocrypha and Pseudepigrapha of the Old Testament* (= *APOT*), vol. 2 (Oxford: Clarendon Press, 1913), p. 60.

15. Such ideas were taken up and developed by writers of various documents discovered at Qumran. See *1QM* 12 for a very clear example of how intimate was the communion between God, the angels, and the members of the group represented in this Scroll. For the unity of earthly and heavenly worship at Qumran, see especially *4QShirot 'Olam Ha-Shabbat* and the commentary of Carol Newsom, *Songs of the Sabbath Sacrifice: A Critical Edition* (Atlanta: Scholars Press, 1985), pp. 65–72.

16. Charles, *Jubilees*, pp. 17–18, and *APOT* vol. 2, p. 15, suggested that 2.23 originally read: 'as there were twenty-two letters and twenty-two sacred books and twenty-two heads of mankind from Adam to Jacob, so there were made twenty-two kinds of work', which is the text of the verse transmitted by Epiphanius of Salamis, *De Mensuris et Ponderibus* 22. Charles, in the work cited first above, p. 18, notes the appearance of this tradition in other Christian authors, and in the late Jewish work *Midrash Tadshe* 6.

17. For Hebrew as the language of creation, see also PJ and Targum Neofiti (TN) of Gen. 11.1; *Gen. Rab.* 18.4. For the opinion that the angels do not understand Aramaic, see *b.Shabbat* 12b. According to *Jub.* 12.25, Hebrew had not been spoken since the collapse of the tower of Babel.

18. See above, note 15. The tradition that God looked into the Torah in order to create the universe is certainly as old as Philo, *De Opificio Mundi* 3, 16; cf. *Gen. Rab.* 3.5. It may be presupposed by ben Sira 24, which equates the Torah with Wisdom, the eternal principle which sustains and undergirds the created order, and which was present when God made the universe.

19. Josephus, *Ant.* I.334, understood Peniel in Gen. 32.31 as 'the face of God'; see also Aquila, 'the face of the Mighty One', and Septuagint, 'the form of God'. As is well known, Philo regularly

understood the name Israel as if it were *'īš rô'eh 'ēl*, 'a man seeing God'; see, for example, *Leg. Alleg.* II.34; III.15.

20. For discussion of the treatment accorded by *Jubilees* to both these scriptural passages, see J. C. Endres, *Biblical Interpretation in the Book of Jubilees* (Washington: Catholic Biblical Association of America, 1987), pp. 110–14; 165–8. See also pp. 228–31 for the priority accorded to Jacob over Abraham by *Jubilees* in the matter of God's election of the Fathers.

21. This is the most common translation of the word in modern versions: see Hos. 12.4–5, where Jacob is evidently engaged in combat with an angel, but note also the comments of M. Gertner, 'The Masorah and the Levites. An Essay in the History of a Concept' (*Vetus Testamentum* 10, 1960), pp. 272–84.

22. Josephus is quite clear that Jacob actually overcame an angel of God in this struggle.

23. Septuagint and Theodotion have *enischusas*; Old Latin *invaluisti*; Vulgate *fortis fuisti*; and the Syriac *'štrrt*.

24. Aquila has *êrxas*; TN, the Samaritan Targum A, and the Geniza Manuscripts of Targum have *'trbrbt*; PJ has *'ytrbrbt*; and Targum Onkelos has *rb 't*. See also Jerome, *Hebraicae Quaestiones in Genesim*, Corpus Christianorum Series Latina LXXII (Turnhout: Brepols, 1959), pp. 40–1. Symmachus reads *êrxô*, 'you began', as if deriving the word from the Aramaic root *šry*, 'to begin'. Although this reading seems strange, it may make good sense when it is remembered that the Aorist Indicative Middle of *archein* often has the sense 'begin a religious ritual, sacrifice'. Symmachus was, perhaps, aware of traditions in *Jubilees* and PJ of Gen. 35.11 that Jacob's name was changed to Israel during a celebration of the Feast of Sukkoth at Bethel, when also the future Levitical priesthood was established. For evidence that Symmachus was a Jew not unaware of Rabbinic and pre-Rabbinic tradition, see A. Salvesen, *Symmachus in the Pentateuch* (Manchester: University of Manchester Press, 1991), pp. 283–97.

25. See further Gertner, 'The Masorah and the Levites', pp. 241–72.

26. See B. P. Kittel, *The Hymns of Qumran: Translation and Commentary* (Chico: Scholars Press, 1981).

27. For discussion of this work and its date, see Schürer, *History of the Jewish People*, vol. III.1, pp. 325–31; and G. W. E. Nickelsburg, 'The Bible Rewritten and Expanded', in *Jewish Writings of the Second Temple Period*, ed. M. E. Stone (Assen: van Gorcum, 1984), pp. 107–10. For the quotation given below, we have used the Latin text of *LAB* edited by G. Kisch, *Pseudo-Philo's Liber Antiquitatum Biblicarum* (Notre Dame: University of Notre Dame, 1949): the translation is ours.

28. See G. Vermes, 'The Archangel Sariel. A Targumic Parallel to the Dead Sea Scrolls', in *Christianity, Judaism, and Other Greco-Roman Cults*, Studies for Morton Smith at Sixty, Part 3, ed. J. Neusner (Leiden: E. J. Brill, 1975), pp. 159–66, esp. pp. 164–5.

29. For other occurrences of the name Sariel in postbiblical literature, see Vermes, 'The Archangel Sariel', pp. 159–63.

30. *edeixen autôi basileian theou kai edôkenautôi gnôsin hagiôn.* See also J. Vilchez, *Sabiduria* (Estella: Lizarra, 1990), pp. 303–5; and C. Larcher, *Le Livre de Sagesse ou La Sagesse de Salomon*, vol. 2 (Paris: J. Gabalda, 1983).

31. See also *Gen. Rab.* 78.3. There is some evidence that Jacob was later regarded in certain circles as the incarnation of an angel called Israel: this is apparent from the *Prayer of Joseph*, of which only small fragments survive. See J. Z. Smith, 'The Prayer of Joseph', in *The Old Testament Pseudepigrapha*, vol. 2, ed. J. H. Charlesworth (London: Darton, Longman & Todd, 1985), pp. 699–712.

PART TWO
OUR BODIES TAKEN INTO HIS: INCARNATION EXTENDED

'I am the bread which came down from heaven . . . if any one eats of this bread, he will live for ever; and the bread which I shall give for the life of the world is my flesh' (John 6.41, 51 RSV). Just as the first chapter of John's Gospel can be seen as laying the foundations for all Christian sacramentalism in the notion of the incarnation as sacrament, so chapter six may be viewed as legitimating the extension of that principle to what are more conventionally known as sacraments, through that incarnational body now working its effects mysteriously upon our own. But what of the difficulty, already raised by John Macquarrie in his opening contribution: that the acts traditionally labelled sacramental lack the personal character of the incarnation, and might therefore seem a degeneration from it? Each of the contributors to this section seeks to answer that objection. In the course of doing so they stress the transformative character of the relationship, that it is never just a case of receiving 'things' but also of being drawn by Christ into a new personal identity as part of his extended body, the Church.

For Wolfhart Pannenberg baptism, properly understood, should provide a fresh focus for personal spirituality. Instead of the usual Protestant obsession with guilt, we ought to see ourselves as given a new identity by the rite, one which we are then called to foster and deepen throughout our lives. Rowan Williams shares that emphasis on a new identity given in baptism. But, whereas for Wolfhart Pannenberg it is personal incorporation into the life of the godhead that is central, with Rowan Williams there is much greater stress on a horizontal dimension, in the generation of a new society.

Though the next three pieces all address traditional areas of fierce controversy in the history of Christianity, they do so in a way in which continues to illustrate concern not only to avoid any diminution of the personal character of the sacraments but a wish to enhance the sense in which they can be said, like Christ in his earthly life, to aim at our transformation. Nicholas Wolterstorff and Gerard Loughlin are both primarily concerned with the eucharist, and both make considerable use of modern philosophy to elucidate their ideas. There any obvious similarity ends. Wolterstorff uses a philosopher in the English analytic tradition, J. L. Austin (d. 1960), to defend Calvin's stress on the primacy of divine action, while Loughlin uses two more recent writers in the continental tradition, Derrida and Marion, to defend Aquinas' doctrine of transubstantiation. Nonetheless, they share far more than may initially appear. Most obviously, what worries Wolterstorff about transubstantiation is what he sees as its lack of a personal relationship, while this is the very thing which Loughlin seeks to demonstrate in his presentation of transubstantiation as a pure gift of divine love.

The section then ends with a helpful reminder of the danger of too facile a categorization of the various denominational positions. Hostility to what was seen as the automatic, non-personal character of sacramental absolution was one major factor in the Reformation. But long after Aquinas had written, part of the medieval tradition was still advocating a view (as in the English mystic, Walter Hilton) to which the Reformation could not possibly have taken exception. On this account, the re-formation or transformation of the individual under the personal influence of divine grace is, like the incarnate Christ's demand for conversion, what the sacrament is all about.

4

Baptism as Remembered 'Ecstatic' Identity

WOLFHART PANNENBERG

Traditionally Protestant spirituality has had a strong penitential focus, but the work of Freud has made problematic the deliberate cultivation of guilt feelings. Wolfhart Pannenberg urges an alternative focus in a lively sense of God's providential care. The revival of eucharistic worship has made Christians more conscious of belonging to each other, but this needs to be set in its context of an identity given through Christ in baptism. For Luther justification was not a momentary act, but the continuous remembrance of us being placed ecstatically 'outside ourselves' in the relation of Christ as Son to the Father. The baptismal imagery of death used by both Jesus and Paul is not merely metaphorical, but points to our final destiny at physical death as full participation in the life of the Trinity, the ultimate goal towards which God's providential care can direct us.

The crisis in Protestant spirituality

Traditional Protestant piety was more or less non-sacramental. This was certainly true of continental Protestantism in Germany, in France, Scandinavia and elsewhere. The Protestant churches could be described as churches of the Word by contrast to the Roman Catholic Church as church of the sacrament. The Word was understood in terms of law and gospel – the law in the Lutheran tradition mainly in the function of accusing and demonstrating human sinfulness, the gospel as God's promise of salvation that came true in Jesus Christ. In the Calvinist tradition the law was also taken as God's guidance for the believer's life, but in both these main forms of Protestantism the word of God in law and gospel was related to the process of human conversion, of repentance and regeneration. Since these issues were in the focus of traditional Protestant spirituality, its typical form can be characterized as penitential piety. The roots of this piety can be re-traced to the late Middle Ages. Though the Reformation opposed the mentality of workrighteousness that went so easily along with medieval emphasis on penance, it still retained that emphasis in its doctrine on justification. Workrighteousness was overcome by the emphasis on faith alone, faith in God's promise of salvation in Jesus Christ. But still the issue of penance and conversion remained in the centre of Christian spirituality. There was a variety of developments of this issue. Penance and conversion could be considered as happening again and again in the course of a Christian life, especially under the impact of listening to the preaching of the Word on Sundays. It could also be considered as a unique experience producing a lasting moral change in the life of the individual. The latter became characteristic of much of the pietistic movement, and it could easily lead to hypocrisy regarding the moral condition of the reborn Christian. The emphasis on the need for continuously repeated conversion, on the other hand, could issue in a neurotic mentality where confessing oneself as sinner came to be considered as the decisive and only condition for obtaining justification. Nourishing one's own consciousness of sinfulness could thereby take the place of medieval workright-eousness. This was, of course, a perversion of the doctrine of the Reformation on justification through faith alone, but it seems to have been remarkably widespread until the cultivation of guilt feelings without a basis in concrete moral or criminal offences came under the attack of Freudian psychoanalysis and was exposed as neurotic.

In the present situation, the traditional Protestant emphasis on the spiritual experience of conversion seems to be available to less and less people. It has survived to some extent in the field of poli-tical rhetoric, where the confession of sins on behalf of one's nation or society (instead of one's own private sins) does not only provide the speaker with a feeling of his or her personal righteous-ness, but sometimes also gains social recognition as a prophetical voice. Otherwise, however, in the life of individuals, the traditional penitential attitude by and large disappeared so completely, together with the social recognition of traditional moral norms, that it is natural to long for a restoration of the values of tra-ditional morality. Such restoration, however, will hardly be achieved on a broad scale by revivalist preaching, because the experiential core of penitential piety is so utterly discredited. A recovery of Christian spirituality needs different clues to the depth of Christian experience. In the first place, answers must be given to the question of how human persons in the climate of a secularized culture can become aware of the divine reality that not only transcends, but embraces and penetrates our life and all finite reality. The disintegration of traditional Christian spirituality and beliefs produced a situation where many secularized Christians were driven to turn to the Eastern religions and to their practice of meditation in order to recapture some awareness of the transcendent, the feeling of divine presence. There are resources in our own Christian heritage, however, that can be reappropriated to achieve that purpose. Fortunately, for all its dominant impact penitential piety was never the only form of Christian spirituality, not even in the Protestant churches. The most important other factor, perhaps, was the awareness of God's providence and the trust in God's providential care and design, expressed in so many hymns. It goes along with our self-awareness as creatures who are always dependent upon the mysterious and incomprehensible reality that surrounds and transcends us and that we call God. Confidence in God's providence, of course, requires some knowledge of the personal character of that mysterious reality and of the purposes of God's providential activity. In the earlier Protestant churches, such knowledge was provided by faith in the biblical revelation of God. Since the Enlightenment it has to some extent been replaced by natural theology.

Faith in God's providential working was a basic issue as early as in the proclamation of Jesus himself: 'Look at the birds of the air: they neither sow nor reap nor gather into barns, and yet your heavenly Father feeds them . . . Consider the lilies of the field, how they grow; they neither toil nor spin; yet I tell you, even Solomon in all his glory was not arrayed like one of these' (Matt. 6.26ff. RSV). In the same way and with even greater care the Creator provides for his human beings. Such confidence in God's providence will always remain basic in Christian spirituality. In the present situation, in competition with the spiritual attractions of other religions, Christians should strengthen their hold of this basic attitude of faith in God. But it needs to be complemented and deepened by other, more specific forms of Christian spirituality, and it is at this point that a new appropriation of the spiritual resources preserved in the sacraments of the Church can be helpful.

The eucharistic experience of belonging

The twentieth century has witnessed a revival of eucharistic participation in many Christian churches. While formerly the eucharist used to be a special concern of high church tendencies within the Protestant churches, now eucharistic communion has become a lively focus again in the ordinary liturgical life of local congregations. That in itself is a highly important event in the spiritual history of Christianity. The rediscovery of the communion among the participants as a central element of the eucharistic celebration was a fresh experience not only in the Protestant churches. Roman Catholic spirituality was always focused on the celebration of the eucharist, but in its centre there was not so much the meal, as the offering of the consecrated elements to God by the priest. The distribution of the consecrated bread to the faithful could be treated as if it were a separate rite. Thus the rediscovery of the central place of the meal in the celebration of the eucharist was something new in Roman Catholic liturgy and spirituality too. All the churches had to learn in a new way that the neglect of the body of Christ in the act of eucharistic communion, the failure of discerning the body of Christ from ordinary food, which Paul warned against in 1 Cor. 11.29, concerns the communion among the participants as members of one body, the body of Christ whom they received in eating the eucharistic bread. The apostle warns against the privatization of the act of communion with Christ that abstracts from the ecclesial consequences of that communion. The ecumenical movement among the Christian churches was profoundly strengthened by the rediscovery of the communal character of the eucharistic meal, because now it became apparent that the churches, when they celebrate the eucharistic meal in seclusion from one another by not admitting other Christians to their communion, use the sacrament in opposition to the intention of Jesus Christ in the words of institution. After all, it is not any particular group of people that celebrates their sense of communion among themselves, when the eucharist is celebrated in a Christian worship. Rather, it is the communion of all those who are members of Christ, and therefore no one who is to be considered a Christian must be excluded. In earlier centuries, when heretics were considered no longer Christians, it was certainly easier to celebrate the eucharist in good conscience while preventing those persons from participation. In our ecumenical age, however, wherever we acknowledge each other as Christians across denominational barriers, it has become a violation of the eucharist as instituted by our Lord, if those other Christians are excluded from communion. Awareness of this painful situation has become a major incentive to ecumenical commitment, aiming at such a degree of convergence and mutual acceptance among the churches that eucharistic communion can be resumed.

The problem I pointed to does not only concern the ecumenical relations between church bodies and occasional eucharistic hospitality for Christians from other denominations. It also concerns the self-understanding of each local congregation in celebrating the eucharist. The ecclesial communion represented by the communion of the participants of the eucharistic meal is not confined to that particular congregation, but is identical with the entire Christian Church, the communion of all those who share in the one Christ. This catholic communion becomes manifest in the local congregation when celebrating the eucharist. Thus again, the local congregation would be mistaken, if its members took the eucharist as a celebration of their own fellowship. Rather, in the first place it is a communion with Jesus Christ that is offered in the eucharistic bread to each individual member of the congregation, and second it is the derivative communion among all those who share in the one body of Christ. In the local congregation this worldwide communion becomes manifest, and therefore the local congregation cannot mistake itself for a self-sufficient entity, but is always under the obligation of keeping in communion with all other individual Christians and their local congregations or church bodies. Ecumenicity is of the very essence of the eucharistic experience, and it is not by accident that in recent decades an ecclesiology of communion based on the eucharist has become the emerging model of restoring the ecclesial unity among all Christians.

What has been said so far on eucharistic communion is not just theoretical reflection. It can be part of the experience of participation in the eucharistic service in as much as experience and interpretation are inseparable. Interpretation is not something secondary that may come after the experience. Quite generally, in experiencing something as something particular, interpretation is already involved. It is a matter of education that we are aware of what we see or hear, and it is not in principle beyond the capacity of any congregation or its individual members to know to some extent what actually they are doing in church. As soon as the pastor lives up to his duty to tell them what they are doing in the liturgy, there will no longer be any complaints that the liturgy is full of obsolete ancient formulae that no ordinary person presently can understand. As soon as those words are made understood, however, the liturgy becomes a different kind of experience. It becomes an experience of the unity of all Christians united in Christ who is present in the eucharist.

The eucharistic presence of Christ, of course, is not something directly accessible to experience. It is a matter of faith. This faith constitutes the eucharistic experience, an experience of devotion and adoration, but also of reassurance – a reassurance of belonging to Christ as a member of his body.

Eucharistic roots in infant baptism

This consciousness of belonging, which is so central in the Christian experience, is rooted in baptism. Therefore, there is a relationship between the eucharistic experience and baptism. Its importance is such that the spiritual meaning of eucharistic participation in Jesus Christ can be fully appreciated only in connection with baptism, because it is through baptism that each of us becomes a member of Christ's body, which we are confirmed to be in the eucharistic communion.

Unfortunately, in most forms of Christian spirituality, baptism is too little appreciated. Our own baptism, of course, is not a matter of individual experience, since most of us were baptized as little children. I do not object to this practice of paedobaptism, contrary to the judgements of many modern theologians. Children's baptism means that God has claimed our life before we even become aware of ourselves. Its effect is being remembered and reappropriated afterwards. The continuous remembrance and appropriation of our baptism to our consciousness of ourselves is the medium of its importance in our Christian spirituality. Such continuous remembrance and appropriation of our baptism formed the focus of Luther's theology of baptism, which unfortunately was subsequently largely neglected within the Lutheran Church. It has been said with good reason that Luther's theology of baptism was the concrete form of his doctrine on justification by faith.[1] This suggests the measure of the loss that occurred in the Lutheran Church, when Luther's theology of baptism was forgotten. Justification by faith alone became a momentary experience under the impact of the proclamation of law and gospel, while in Luther's thought it was the continuous remembrance of what happened to us once for all in our baptism. According to Luther, the preaching of the Word helps us along in this task of daily commemoration of our baptism, but it was not conceived of as merely a momentary event. That there is continuity in our lives as Christians is entirely due to our baptism as it is continuously commemorated, and the proclamation of the Word is to be referred to that continuous task of a Christian life experience.

The fact that Luther was an advocate of paedobaptism can strike one as paradoxical in view of his emphasis on justification by faith. Should not faith be a prerequisite of baptism so that a person should receive baptism only on the condition of a personal confession of faith? Luther explicitly rejected this view by insisting that there must be something prior to faith that we can hold on to. Faith is not constitutive of baptism, but belongs to the process of receiving and appropriating one's baptism. Even where adults are baptized, they can never guarantee their own abiding faith and its continuing strength. It is God's action in claiming our life that our faith is related to. Personally, I myself was baptized as a child, like so many are, without much Christian education, and my family came to be alienated from the Christian faith to the point of even leaving the Church. But when I came to become a Christian in my years of adolescence, it became increasingly important to me that God had been there in my life all along claiming it for his service in the event of my baptism. In many individual cases the personal appropriation of one's baptism by faith occurs only later in life. And, of course, it is only in the process of that appropriation through faith that the act of baptism is effective in one's personal life. The sacramental rite, taken by itself, is merely a sign. It is an effective sign in the process of remembrance and appropriation in faith, which is the life-long process of Christian experience.

The anticipatory allusions within the baptismal rite highlight the way in which the appropriation of one's baptism is a life-long process. According to Paul, we are baptized into the death of Christ (Rom. 6.3) in order to share also in the hope of his resurrection. This is not meant to be a metaphor, but the future death of the baptized one is anticipated in the act of baptism. The baptismal rites of the ancient Church exhibited this meaning much more concretely than later forms of administering the sacrament, because the baptized person was actually submerged in the water. The future death of the person and therefore his or her entire life history is anticipated in the rite of baptism in order to be implanted into the person of Jesus Christ, into his cross and his resurrection. Consequently, the subsequent life history of the baptized person until the actual occurrence of his or her death is to carry out what was anticipated in the event of one's baptism. Day after day the life of the Christian is to mortify the old Adam and to turn once more to the new life that is promised us in Christ's resurrection.

This is what happens in the commemoration of baptism. Therefore, in Luther's thought penance was nothing else but the continuous commemoration and re-enactment of what happened to us once and for all in the act of our baptism. As the act of our baptism anticipates our future death and therefore the entire life history of the baptized person yet to be spent, it is in the appropriation of our baptism by faith that we carry out its meaning in shaping our lives such as to transform it into the life of a Christian.

The Pauline idea that in the act of baptism the baptized person is implanted into the death of Christ, was hardly invented by the apostle. There are indications that Jesus himself saw his baptism by John the Baptist to be connected not only with his ministry of proclaiming the kingdom of God, but also with his personal fate of death at the hands of his opponents. Thus in Mark 10.38 Jesus is reported to have asked his disciples: 'Are you able to drink the cup that I drink, or to be baptized with the baptism with which I am baptized?' (RSV). The image of drinking the cup was an old prophetic image of undergoing a disastrous fate, of perishing in an act of divine judgement. Divine judgement, the final one, had also been the issue of the baptism administered by John. The text suggests that Jesus perceived a connection between the foreseeable catastrophe of his own mission and the baptism he had received by John. So the interrelatedness of ritual anticipation and execution in life that is characteristic of Christian baptism, may be rooted already in Jesus' own understanding of his baptism by John. The use of the word 'baptism' as referring to the fate he was going to face is also expressed in another word in the Jesus tradition, Luke 12.50: 'I have a baptism to be baptized with; and how I am constrained until it is accomplished' (RSV). Here again, the word 'baptism' clearly refers to the passion that lay ahead, and yet it is inconceivable in the language of Jesus without the connotation of the baptism he earlier received from John.

So being baptized into the death of Jesus, as it occurs in Paul, is full of rich connotations. It carries on the notion of discipleship, of sharing in the fate of Jesus. It most specifically implies the idea of carrying one's cross like Jesus did (Matt. 10.38), that is, taking the consequences of discipleship in the same way Jesus accepted the consequences of his own particular mission. All this is involved in our daily commemoration of our baptism, and not least so the question of our own particular vocation and the consequences that entails, corresponding to Jesus' cross that he had to take upon himself.

Mystical elevation to a new identity in the Spirit

The most profound connection, however, between our Christian
baptism and that of Jesus himself is in the gift of the Spirit.
According to early Christian tradition the gift of the Spirit set
Christian baptism apart from that of John the Baptist and of his
disciples (Acts 19.2f.). John's baptism was not thought to confer
the divine Spirit; rather, it symbolically anticipated the final
judgement and therefore was considered a baptism of repentance
(19.4). It was a unique event, rather than a common one, when
in the case of Jesus' baptism by John, as the gospels report it, the
Spirit was received. Since there is other evidence that Jesus
indeed was a charismatic, it is not implausible that he traced the
presence of the Spirit in himself back to the experience of his
baptism by John. Jesus' own baptism, then, became the origin of
the connection of the gift of the Spirit with the baptismal rite in
the Christian Church. But the gift of the Spirit indicates the
saving presence of the eschatological reality of the kingdom of
God. The charismatic presence of the divine Spirit in Jesus'
ministry is bound up with the characteristic difference of Jesus'
message from the Baptist in announcing the imminent future of
the kingdom. The point of that difference is that in Jesus' proclamation that future becomes present already as a saving event.
That anticipatory presence of the kingdom coincides with the
presence of the Spirit, and as it happened in Jesus it also happens
in Christian baptism. By being buried into the death of Christ, as
Paul says, the baptized Christian receives a share in the Spirit of
Christ, the creator Spirit of God whose presence in us warrants
our future resurrection to a new life which will be the work of the
same Spirit, since he already is the creative source of our present
life.

Thus the gift of God's Spirit in baptized Christians enshrines
the promise of their future participation in the life of the risen
Christ. Therefore, the joyous anticipation of the final victory of
life over death is inseparable from the commemoration of our
baptism and should pervade our Christian existence. There is,
however, one element in the appropriation of baptism that even
surpasses that joy of life in the midst of this earthly and death-
bound pilgrimage. The innermost mystery of the baptismal identity of the Christian is addressed by Paul in Romans 8. It is
contained in the fact that by receiving the Spirit Jesus was shown
to be the Son of God, the eternal correlate of the Father. In the
case of Jesus, to be sure, the possession of the Spirit in receiving
him from the Father belongs to his personal identity as being the

eternal Son. Christians, on the other hand, in the act of their baptism, only receive a share in Christ, and the gift of the Spirit is closely connected with sharing in the life of the Son. We only become adopted children of God, and this happens by being lifted above ourselves, when we are implanted into Jesus Christ in the act of baptism. But in commemorating and appropriating our baptism by faith we share in the sonship of Jesus Christ, in the eternal relationship of the Son to the Father as it was revealed on earth in the history of Jesus. Do we realize what that implies? It means participating in the innermost life of the Trinity, in the eternal communion of love between the Son and the Father, and it is because of this participation in the Son's relationship to the Father that we are entitled to address the unspeakable mystery of God in the way Jesus did in the words of the Lord's Prayer. How easily are the words of that unique prayer trivialized. We rarely realize what we are doing when we say the Lord's Prayer. It is not the way we might address in terms of our own imagination as sinful human beings the tremendous and often terrible mystery that wields the world. It is only by participating in Jesus' relationship to God that we may call him our father, and in doing so we are surrounded by and taken up into the life of the Trinity, because it is only in the place of the Son that we can address God in the words of his prayer. In using this prayer, we do not have God opposite to ourselves, because it is within the trinitarian communion of the Son with the Father that this prayer takes place.

Authentic Christian spirituality, then, is characterized by some sort of mystical elevation, an elevation that raises us beyond ourselves and is always accompanied by the humble awareness of the spiritual poverty of our existence outside that state of elevation, which puts us outside of ourselves in the place of the Son and thus in communion with the Father. Such elevation happens to us in the event of our baptism, but also in each commemoration of our baptism in the act of faith. According to Luther faith is trust in God that places us outside ourselves. It is the specifically Christian form of mystical experience, and it pervades all aspects of a Christian life. As it occurs in the commemoration of our baptism, so the same elevation occurs in the commemoration of the death of Christ in celebrating his eucharist. Therefore, the eucharistic liturgy begins with the exhortation: 'Lift up your hearts', and the congregation responds: 'We lift them up to the Lord'. It is only in such a state of exaltation that we properly celebrate the eucharistic memorial of the Lord's Supper, united with the liturgical minister, when he or she speaks 'in the person of Christ' the words of institution. And it is in the state of such exaltation beyond ourselves that we receive in the eucharistic bread and wine Jesus himself and the presence of the kingdom that he made manifest in celebrating the meal.

All the different aspects of Christian spirituality belong together, and perhaps the best way of approaching its treasure is through meditation on the meaning of baptism. It is baptism that opens up to our Christian experience that intimate relationship to God as Father that comes to expression in the Christian confidence in God's providence that belongs to the best heritage of our Protestant tradition. In the view of an outside observer who abstracts from the foundations of such confidence in Jesus' relationship to the Father and in the baptized Christian's participation therein, the Christian confidence in God's providential care can easily appear to be naive and unrealistic, virtually unaware of the terrors of human existence in this world. This impression disappears as soon as one realizes the framework of such faith in God's providence, as it is constituted through partaking in Jesus' relationship to the Father. As this is rooted in baptism, so on the other hand baptism provides the precondition for celebrating the eucharist, because it implants us into Christ so that we can lift up our hearts to commemorate the death of Christ in celebrating his eucharist. While baptism confers membership in the Church to the individual by incorporating that individual person into the communion of the body of Christ, the eucharistic communion expresses the communal character of such participation in Christ in anticipation of the kingdom to come, which happens in the celebration of the meal that Jesus himself celebrated in the days of his earthly ministry. Thus it all belongs together: without the eucharist, baptismal piety could degenerate into some individualistic mysticism, but the connection of the eucharistic remembrance with the commemoration of our baptism clarifies that it is only in Christ that we can properly celebrate the eucharist, as it is only in Christ – outside ourselves – that the members of the congregation are united through the eucharistic communion, together with all other Christians of all generations in the one body of Christ. That reality of communion in Christ should pervade and transform the earthly relationships of people within each local congregation as well as in the ecumenical relations between such congregations. But the manifestation of the communion within the one body of Christ in the historical reality of the Christian churches is, as we well know, sadly broken, sometimes beyond recognition. It is the more important to realize that the scars and fractures occur on the level of the efficacy of the Church's spiritual reality in our provisional experience, while the source of our faith takes priority over such phenomena and will finally overcome their limitations as it will transform our lives in all respects.

In a secularized culture like ours and in a situation where we are deeply challenged by the invitations of other religions promising new and supposedly more effective approaches to spiritual experience, the Christian churches and their members might seek recourse again to the spiritual resources that are preserved in the sacraments of the Church. Christians need not feel ashamed or empty when looking at the splendours of eastern mysticism. We only have to recover the forgotten spiritual treasures of our own tradition. Where is the religious mysticism that surpasses the participation in the inner life of the Trinity that is made accessible to each baptized Christian and is actually realized in the experience of Christian prayer? We only have to become aware once more of the spiritual treasures we have been granted, especially in the sacraments of the Church. We have to overcome the superficial way of administering and attending the liturgy and the sacraments as if they were merely ancient forms of ritual. If they are not understood, their celebration quickly turns boring. But they carry divine life within themselves. It just waits to be rediscovered.[2]

Notes

1. P. Althaus, *The Theology of Martin Luther* (Philadelphia: Fortress Press, 1966), pp. 352–74.
2. My most recent detailed discussion of the sacraments of baptism and eucharist (unfortunately, not yet translated into English) is to be found in my *Systematische Theologie* (Göttingen: Vandenhoeck & Ruprecht, 1993), vol. 3, pp. 265–369.

5

Sacraments of the New Society

ROWAN WILLIAMS

*Rowan Williams finds himself deeply dissatisfied with any notion
of sacramentality which suggests its natural emergence from the
created order. Using the Prayer Book liturgy by way of illustration,
he suggests that baptism is essentially about dislocation: about
giving the child a new identity which, because it is based on no
existing social relations, is a gift of pure equality within the
Church as the new society. Likewise, because at the Last Supper
Christ mediated himself through the betrayal of friends and the
vulnerability of things, the eucharist should be seen as the gift of
the new society in which a costly interdependence is accepted as
the norm.*

Sacraments as rites of dislocation

The Christian sacraments are not just epiphanies of the sacred;
or rather, the *way* in which they are epiphanies of the sacred is by
their reordering of the words and images used to think or experience social life. Without at this stage introducing any specifically
theological language, we can say that a Christian community
involved in activities it calls 'sacramental' is a community *describing* itself in a way that is importantly at odds with other sorts of
description (secular or functional ones).

More precisely, the sacramental action itself traces a transition
from one sort of reality to another: first it describes a pre-sacramental state, a secular or profane condition now imagined, for
ritual purposes, in the light of and in the terms of the transformation that is to be enacted; it tells us that where we habitually
are is not, after all, a neutral place but a place of loss or need. It
then requires us to set aside this damaged or needy condition,

89

this flawed identity, so that in dispossessing ourselves of it we are able to become possessed of a different identity, given in the rite, not constructed by negotiation and co-operation like other kinds of social identity. The rite requires us *not* to belong any more to the categories we thought we belonged in, so that a distinctive kind of new belonging can be realized. When this transition takes place, the presence and the power of the sacred is believed to be at work. I shall not try to discuss how far you can usefully employ the term 'sacrament' outside the Christian framework; but diverse religious traditions certainly recognize corporate actions designed to reconstruct or radicalize a common identity, above all in sacrifice and festival.

Christianity is distinct in the non-seasonal frequency of its ritual celebrations, and in the way in which its two commonest sacramental actions recapitulate aspects of a single story, the paschal narrative of Jesus' death and resurrection; and that may suggest that the themes of transition and transformation are more insistently present in Christian language than in some other traditions. While theologians have sometimes rather loosely talked about the sacramental 'principle' in Christianity as an affirmation of some inherent capacity in material things to bear divine meanings, the actual shape and rhetoric of sacramental *actions* says more about how such meanings emerge from a process of estrangement, surrender and re-creation than we might expect if we begin only from the rather bland appeal to the natural sacredness of things that occasionally underpins sacramental theology.

Baptismal identity is given, not chosen

That, I know, is an alarmingly abstract beginning. What I hope to do in what follows is to trace how these ideas operate concretely in baptism and the eucharist, so as to see more clearly what the society is that is imagined and, according to the believer, realized in these actions. Details of ceremony and formula, of course, vary greatly, but clearly comparable patterns are present across confessional frontiers, if only because the central *actions* with water, bread and wine are invariable. To begin with baptism: the 1662 Book of Common Prayer begins its baptismal liturgy with particular sharpness, telling us that all are born in sin, and that the gift looked for in baptism is something 'which by nature [the child to be baptized] cannot have'; and it proceeds to rehearse stories of transition and rescue – Noah and his family, 'the children of Israel thy people'. The apparently neutral condition of the infant is thus redescribed as one of danger or unfreedom, liability to divine 'wrath'; what is necessary is incorporation into the society that is within the ark, where it becomes possible to be 'rooted in charity'. Prayers are said for the 'death' of the child's existing human identity and the distorted affects that go with it, and God is petitioned to number the child among his chosen. After the immersion or affusion, the child is said to be 'grafted into the body of Christ's Church', and prayer is further made that the child may share Christ's resurrection as it has already, symbolically, shared his death. In conclusion, the duties of the baptized are spelled out, reiterating the theme of death and resurrection: what is symbolically done here, the putting to death of 'corrupt affections', is to be renewed daily in concrete behaviour.

What ought to strike us is how both the kinds of belonging evoked here – the condition of sin, belonging with Adam, and the new life of belonging in or with Christ – are not *elective* matters, not things over which the subject has any control. First there is the unsought and unwelcome solidarity of being in danger, then the 'grafting' into a new reality. The danger is associated with misdirected 'affections', which we could almost render as malfunctioning instinct and desire – we want, are drawn by, are moved by, what will kill us; so that, by contrast, the new life is implicitly associated with new attractions, a new sensibility. We are first drawn by objects that fill gaps in our self-construction, so that what we desire is repletion, which is immobilization, a kind of death. We must receive the grace to want the endlessness of God. But unlike the developments of sensibility or desire in our ordinary conscious life, this has nothing to do with being *educated* into new perception: there is a gift bestowed (though its exact nature is not spelled out) which orients us in a certain way, and what must follow is a discipline to ensure we do not lose sight of it.

What the gift might be is a notable site of contention in theology, as it happens, but it is (at least) evoked, if not comprehensively defined, by the use of words like 'regeneration' and 'adoption'. The only thing in the language of the rite that looks like an elective move, a matter of choice of policy, is the decision to bring the child to baptism in the first place. This is described as a 'charitable work' which God 'favourably alloweth', but it is itself only a response to the scriptural promise of Christ to receive and bless children; and the reference to charity here points us back to the *givenness* of the bonds between those grafted into Christ and 'rooted in charity'. In short, we look in vain, in the course of this liturgy, for an autonomous subject choosing its companions. The subject coming to baptism is not only a subject incapable of choice, an infant, it is also enmeshed in unchosen relations and subject to irresistible and destructive compulsions; in the course of the rite, it is symbolically stripped of all this and given a new context and new associates, new goals and (implicitly at least) new desires. Everything about the rite seems to push *choice* to the margin.

Equality in the new, communal identity

Now I know and you know that the 1662 Book of Common Prayer is a document very heavily charged with polemic, and with many apparently innocent phrases that in fact are carefully designed to say or not say certain things. The Baptismal Order has to balance a whole set of not easily compatible theological constraints, and what it takes for granted is controversial to most modern ears. We do not like constructing the 'danger' of the unbaptized in terms of divine wrath, and we are a bit more uneasy than our forebears were about the obliteration or displacement of personal commitment in a rite whose New Testament roots seem to be a good deal more interested in moments of choice. I shall not try to solve any of these tangles, or to pronounce on the (typical) tightrope walking between Calvinism and Catholicism evidenced in this particular text; I want only to draw out a little further the picture of ourselves that the rite suggests, and to note how that picture might affect our social imagination. For beyond the particular character and contour of this one rite, heavily conditioned by its historical setting, there are features of the rite itself, in its universal outlines and imagery, that press the same questions on us. If *this* is the nature of the transition between secular identity and sociality and Christian identity and sociality, what do we have to think, as Christians, about social identities?

The first point I would like to make is that the rite leaves no space for an identity constructed by the will starting from scratch. Whether or not we are comfortable with the way the Book of Common Prayer dismantles the illusory neutrality of 'just' being born as a member of the human race, the baptismal event necessarily reminds us that we are born into a context we did not choose, and our options are already limited for us. We cannot choose our company – obviously not, as infants, but as adults too – since the solidarity of the secular world continues to distort our perceptions and taste even when we *think* we are choosing.

The second point is that what constitutes our belonging

together, morally and spiritually, is our corporate relation to God. That is to say that what unites us with other human beings is not common culture or negotiated terms of co-operation or common aims, but something *external* to human community itself, the regard of God upon us. In the Book of Common Prayer's terms (which are actually the terms of the majority of Christians, historically speaking), we are either bound together by being 'seen' by God as distant, as strangers, or bound together in a common assurance that we are received, affirmed, adopted. The status of other subjects, morally and spiritually, is wholly beyond our determination – though, in Christian tradition, not wholly beyond our knowledge: a very ambiguous element in all this, since a quick reading of the difference between baptized and unbaptized would lead to a very sharp exclusivism. What softens and 'unsettles' such exclusiveness is the constant possibility of transition and the essential independence of this transition from any human corporate policy. We may find it odd that sixteenth-century Spanish theologians had to argue about whether the native peoples of the Americas were human (and so able to be converted to the Catholic faith), but, as they and their compatriots well knew, there was an immediate political linkage between being capable of receiving baptism and the capacity to be a 'citizen'.[1] To be even potentially the object of affirming regard and adoption makes certain policies such as systematic enslavement of one group by another a good deal more problematic. Subsequent history shows how easily even grave theological tensions can be lived with, if the price is right; but we need to remember that the appropriateness of baptizing slaves was still being questioned in British colonies in the eighteenth century: some at least dimly saw the dangerous connections here.

The baptismal perspective, in insisting that we are caught up in solidarities we have not chosen, is an admittedly uncomfortable partner for the post-Enlightenment social thinker. It gives disappointingly little ground for developing a discourse of human rights or claims, since it sidesteps the whole milieu of the tribunal in which I can enforce what is owing to me: in the baptismal perspective, we confront something we cannot 'plead' with. The decisions have already been taken. Yet *if* – and it is an enormous if – we are quite serious about the radical difference of God or the radical liberty of God, the consequent picture of human status is perhaps still more challenging than the conventional construction of 'rights'. Not only is a fundamental equality established by the indiscriminate regard of God, but, still more significantly, a fundamental compatibility and interdependence in human goals when rightly perceived. In that God's affirming regard is given to the subject specifically as a member of a community, the implication is that, within that community, what is good or desirable for each is consistent with what is good and desirable for all others.

The new desires that replace the 'corrupt affections' of pre-baptismal humanity must therefore be desires free from competitive patterns or rivalry; as Augustine put it in his treatise on the Trinity, our wanting of the good and our loving of the just is, in the communion of faith, a desire for the same good to be in all.[2] It is a love of love itself, desiring that all should realize the same self-forgetful longing for the good of the other. This may not be a discourse of 'rights' in the modern sense, but it offers something that such a discourse often fails to deliver, a sense of the interlocking of different kinds of good or welfare. There cannot be a human good for one person or group that necessarily excludes the good of another person or group. The passage from talking of rights to talk of a common good in which I recognize the unity of my desire with the desire of all is enabled by what baptism, sacramentally understood, speaks of: a divine reality with which claim and negotiation are impossible. In this light, critical questions become possible about our actual desires and how far they remain in essence competitive or exclusive – how far, that is, the symbolic death and dispossession is consciously realized, how far the givenness of new desires is appropriated or understood.

Hegel, writing about baptism, captures the tensions here:[3] the new identity of the baptized self is 'implicit spirit, which must become explicit'; this process may entail, subjectively, a 'real, infinite anguish', but the fact of the Church's existence declares that, at the level of the community, at the level of speech and understanding, the battle has been won. The reality of the common life in which spirit recognizes itself in the life and welfare of the other has already been established in the foundational events of the Church, and does not *depend* on any group or individual in later history successfully realizing it at any particular time. Or, in more conventionally theological language, baptism, most fundamentally, announces the givenness, once and for all, of the new humanity in Christ.

The Last Supper as itself an act of renunciation

It is this same pivotal conviction of the givenness of the new world that constitutes the sacrament of the Lord's Supper as socially disturbing in a comparable way. Here again, sometimes more obviously, sometimes more subtly, we are dealing with narratives or dramas of transition. The eucharist recollects an event already complex, already 'doubled' – the Last Supper interpreted as a sign of Jesus' death and its effects, or, from the other end, the death of Jesus metaphorized as a breaking and sharing of bread. The central transition here, as in baptism, is a death, a death here presented as a passage (once again) into new solidarities: the wine poured out as a sign of the shedding of blood is the mark of a *covenant* being made, on the analogy of God's covenant with Israel. The movement, then, is towards a declared commitment on God's part, sealed or assured by Jesus' death.

If we follow here the same interpretative lines we used earlier, the conclusion is that the 'pre-sacramental' state is one in which God's commitment is not assured, or not perceptible to us as certain. The profane or secular condition from which we start is one of uncertainty: we are shown ourselves initially as those who are unable to trust the faithfulness of God. Put this alongside the fact that all eucharistic liturgies in the mainstream of Western Christian tradition begin with some sort of penitential acknowledgement, and the further conclusion suggests itself that our sins have something to do with the fundamental condition of untrustfulness. Some rites – notably the much maligned Communion Order of 1662, but also, in a very different idiom, the Byzantine liturgy – heighten the tension by returning at significant moments to the rhetoric of penitence and unworthiness, up to the very moment of communion. It seems that until we have actually received the tokens of the covenant we remain locked in sin, in the hostility to God and each other that flows from lack of assurance in God. When we physically receive the pledge of that assurance, we become 'covenanted' ourselves to God and each other (the Book of Common Prayer speaks of our being thus made 'living members' of a 'holy fellowship'). The divine initiative of promise creates a *bonded* community, a 'faithful people' (to quote 1662 again).

But this transition depends on a transition at another level. The material elements of bread and wine are to be made holy by the prayer that associates them with the flesh and blood of Jesus. Whatever the particular theology of eucharistic presence in a tradition, there is invariably a setting-aside of the elements and a narrative recalling Jesus' self-identification with the bread and wine as 'representative' bits of the created order, a convention whose origins go back to some of the earliest eucharistic texts and eucharistic theologies we have: Irenaeus, in the second Christian century, can refer to them as 'first fruits', as if they were a sort of harvest thanksgiving offering,[4] and the resonance of this with the imagery of Christ as 'first fruits' from the dead (1 Cor. 15.20) is obvious. The harvest of the natural order becomes the harvest of God's action: Christ as the first visible sign of God's new order is shown under the form of the first signs of fruition or fulfilment in the inanimate creation. The identification itself establishes a continuity (a fidelity) in what God does in the natural order and in history. The transition, the symbolic transformation of the bread and wine, uncovers a deeper unity between radically different orders.

Not simply a natural or obvious unity, however: it is effected or uncovered by a particular act, a particular word in the history of revelation. Jesus 'passes over' into the symbolic forms by his own word and gesture, a transition into the vulnerable and inactive forms of the inanimate world. By resigning himself into the signs of food and drink, putting himself into the hands of other agents, he signifies his forthcoming helplessness and death. He announces his death by 'signing' himself as a thing, to be handled and consumed. This *further* level of transition is the most basic and the most disturbing here: the passage into the community of those who trust God's faithfulness is effected by God in Christ passing from action into passion; the act of new creation is an act of utter withdrawal. Death is the beginning of the new order, and this divine dispossession points back to questions about the very nature of the creative act itself, as more like renunciation than dominance.

Jesus giving himself over into the hands of the disciples anticipates his own *being given over*, his betrayal. The classical liturgies follow Paul in 1 Cor. 11 in explicitly locating the action 'in the same night that he was betrayed'; and in thus bringing the betrayal within the symbolic scope of the action of taking and breaking bread, the text finally brings into focus the way in which the rite overall embodies the making of a covenant. God's act in Jesus forestalls the betrayal, provides in advance for it: Jesus binds himself to vulnerability before he is bound (literally) by human violence. Thus, those who are at table with him, who include those who will betray, desert and repudiate him, are, if you like, frustrated as betrayers, their job is done for them by their victim. By his surrender 'into' the passive forms of food and drink he makes void and powerless the impending betrayal, and, more, makes the betrayers his guests and debtors, making with them the promise of divine fidelity, the covenant, that cannot be negated by their unfaithfulness. The relinquishing of power in the face of the impending violence of desertion and denial paradoxically allows the Jesus of this narrative to shape and structure the situation, to determine the identity (as guests, as recipients of an unfailing divine hospitality) of the other agents in the story. And so the sequence of transitions finally effects the transformation of the recipients of the bread and wine from betrayers to guests, whose future betrayals are already encompassed in the covenanted welcome enacted by Jesus. The eucharistic ritual narrative thus condenses into itself the longer and more diffuse historical sequence of passion and resurrection – the betrayal followed by divine vindication and the return of Jesus as host at the table (as in Luke 24 and John 21). What is thus laid out as a sequence, the discovery of the dependability of God's acceptance on the far side of the most decisive human rejection, is, in the action of the Last Supper, anticipated in a single gesture, the gesture in which Jesus identifies himself with the 'passive' stuff of the material creation.

So the overall movement from untrustfulness to covenant faith is sustained and explicated in a whole series of interlocking transitions, of which, as I said earlier, some are dramatically obvious (the consecration of the elements, and their actual consumption), some less so, but equally insistent and important. As with baptism, the symbolic end-point is the community created and bound together by an external assurance, something not evolved or negotiated, something that precedes and outlives particular fractures and failures (betrayal, denial). The most intimate may be a traitor; the most rebellious is already invited as a guest. There is no need to labour the point that the eucharist is at least the climax of Jesus' extending of and accepting of hospitality in relation to the marginal or disreputable in the course of his ministry: the offer of the assurance of God's favour is there inseparable from the acceptance of a specific welcome, the agreement to sit down at table with Jesus. The covenant is, in practice, the guarantee of hospitality. The other becomes the object of love and trust because 'invited' by God, and so, in some sense, trusted by God. God's promise to be faithful, even in advance of betrayal, points towards a community whose bonds are capable of surviving betrayal, and which thus can have no place for reprisal, for violent response to betrayal and breakage, or for pre-emptive action to secure against betrayal. There is no promise that people will not be unfaithful and untrustful towards each other, but there is an assurance that the new humanity does not depend on constant goodwill and successful effort to survive: its roots are deeper. If it is, properly, defenceless, that is because it does not need defending and *cannot* be defended by means that deny its basic assurances (again a theme familiar in Augustine, as in the final book of the *City of God*).[5]

Renunciation in nature's difference

Into this pattern too comes an insight about materiality, about our physical environment. The material creation itself can appear as the sign of a divine renunciation: the processes of the world have their integrity, their difference from God, and God's purpose is effected in this difference, not in unilateral divine control, just as the saving work of Christ comes to completion in a renunciation, a surrender of control. This puts at least some questions against an instrumentalist view of material objects. Simone Weil's remarkable imagery about the world of 'dead' matter as the active incarnation of God because it represents the supreme integrity of divine self-effacement as the only way in which divine love can be received by us without idolatry and distortion, is pertinent here: 'He emptied himself of his divinity by becoming man, then of his humanity by becoming a corpse (bread and wine), matter'.[6]

The objects of the world, seen in the perspective of the eucharist, cannot be proper material for the defence of one ego or group-ego against another, cannot properly be tools of power, because they are signs of a creativity working by the renunciation of control, and signs of the possibility of communion, covenanted trust and the recognition of shared need and shared hope.

There is, then, in sacramental practice, something that does indeed reflect on how we see matter in general; but it is not, I think, a 'sacramental principle' enabling us to recognize divine *presence* in all things. It is more that the divine presence is apprehended by seeing in all things their difference, their particularity, their 'not-God-ness', since we have learned what the divine action is in the renunciation of Christ, his giving himself into inanimate form. And so we can rightly learn to be theologically and morally wary of an anthropocentrism that denies difference or integrity to the material environment, that sees matter always as 'raw' material, the building-blocks of something we are to determine. Matter serves human meanings, and we cannot be so 'deeply Green' as to say that the world must be left untouched by human meanings and human practices; but it is not there simply *to* serve human meanings. The eucharist hints at the paradox that material things carry their fullest meaning for human minds and bodies – the meaning of God's grace and of the common life thus formed – when they are the medium of *gift*, not instruments of control or object for accumulation. If I may quote words written some years ago: 'in spite of a proper caution about speaking too loosely of the elements as "offered" to God in the Eucharist, we still need to say that the moment of *relinquishing what is ours* is crucial in the eucharistic process.'[7]

Solidarities we do not choose

What the eucharist thus intimates about matter is that it is itself transfigured into significance in the most comprehensive way when it is dealt with in such a way as to show not dominance but attention or respect, the withdrawal of the controlling ego; and this has some obvious implications for a religious aesthetic as well as a religious economics. But it also pinpoints what is generally difficult and challenging in a sacramental theology of the kind sketched here. Sacramental practice seems to speak most clearly of loss, dependence and interdependence, solidarities we do not choose: none of them themes that are particularly welcome or audible in the social world we currently inhabit as secular subjects. We are told, in effect, that the failure to see ourselves and find ourselves in one or another kind of corporateness is a failure in truthfulness that is profoundly risky. Our liberty to choose and define our goals as individuals or as limited groups with common interest is set alongside the vision of a society in which almost the only thing we can know about the good we are to seek is that it is no one's possession, the triumph of no party's interests. The search for my or our good becomes the search for a good that does not violently dispossess any other – and this not on the basis of rights whose balance must be adjudicated, but because of a conviction that the creative regard calling and sustaining myself is precisely what sustains all. And what makes this something different when an imposed collectivism is the fact that it is appropriated by no force but by trust, by the recognition of the hidden unities of human interest: our own transition, our own 'passover', into the need of the other, wherever and whoever the other may be.

Jean Vanier, in one of his meditations on the experience of the L'Arche communities, observes that being alongside the 'handicapped' frightens the supposedly 'normal' or 'able' person because it obliges them to recognize, sooner or later, the poverty and vulnerability they have in common with those regarded as subnormal; so much more than mere objects of the compassion or benevolence of the competent, the decision-makers.[8] Beyond such fright or disorientation lies the difficult knowledge that I *need* the good, the healing, of the 'handicapped' for my good, as they do my good, my wholeness; and the dignity of being free to give to another is part of what a working Christian community can uncover in those who are marginal, useless or embarrassing to the secular imagination. And a French philosopher associated with L'Arche has added that the common life in such a context obliges us to redefine the whole idea of autonomy: it is not the self's ability to select and freely execute its goals, but the skill of knowing whose aid and companionship you need and the freedom to depend on that.

This is unmistakeably an outworking of the sacramental vision. The recognition of a shared poverty may sound an evasion of some harsh social questions, but what it essentially points to is the challenge of how there might be a social order in which the disadvantaged and even the criminal could *trust* that the common resources of a society would work for their good, and in which those who, at any given moment, enjoyed advantage or power would be obliged to examine how their position could be aligned with the given fact of common and mutual need, how they would act so as to release others to become 'givers' to them. Now this is not a social *programme* and the sacramental life of the Church does not exist to inspire political attempts to improve society. But the sacraments faithfully performed hold up a mirror to other forms of sociality and say that these are at risk and under judgement. The Church declares, symbolically if all too seldom in its own social concreteness, that there is a form of common human life that 'means' or communicates the meanings of God, and it is a form of life in which unchosen solidarities are more significant than 'elective affinities',[9] and the status of an invited or desired guest is accessible to all. Because of the assured trustworthiness of God, the possibility of a society characterized by fidelity can be imagined, a society in which mutual commitment consistently judges and limits sectional acquisitiveness.

It is this capacity to imagine a 'faithful people' that seems to me the most significant irritant offered by sacramental practice to the contemporary social scene. One of the most ill-diagnosed features of the present crisis in capitalist society (fast being exported to aspiring capitalist societies elsewhere) is the decline of *trust*. Privation today brings cynicism in its wake: there is little reason for anyone to believe that others are dependable, that resources work for the common good. If this is a fundamental perception or experience of the social order, it becomes practically impossible to 'socialize' people who see their world like this – the young or the old, marginal or suspect communities of any kind, those in prison, the disabled. This invites an adversarial relation to those institutions felt to have *betrayed* the disadvantaged, directly or indirectly (why are schools in impoverished areas regular targets for arson?). We can easily misunderstand the much-discussed problem of a so-called 'culture of dependency' among the disadvantaged. It is not, surely, that the ideal of collective welfare as such is disabling: welfarism *becomes* disabling when society is such that recipients or clients of social and health services are frozen in the attitude of suppliants, never becoming fellow-agents with those administering aid. They need but are not needed. It is not surprising, in such circumstances, that a discourse of rights *and* claims becomes more and more strident and – often – uncritical, unexamined.

As will be clear, I do not think myself that this addresses the underlying problem, which is the sense, in the United Kingdom as elsewhere in the North Atlantic world, that there are no social bonds that cannot be renegotiated in the interest of those already advantaged, and thus that there is no ground or precious little possibility of any investment in construction and collaborative action, inside or outside classical political and social institutions. It has been said of our educational flounderings in recent years that the problem arises from the fact that we have no notion of what it is we want to 'induct' young people into in terms of a form of common life; and at present the very possibility of common life in this sense, a practice oriented towards a non-sectional, interdependent set of goods, seems remote and theoretical.

I have tried in this essay to outline some aspects of the logic of Christian sacramental action in baptism and eucharist so as to bring out what they assume about social identities. In so far as they raise for us questions about unities of interest beyond our choosing and our control and about the foundations of social trust or fidelity, they should disturb us a good deal. There is little enough symbolic therapy (if I may coin a term) in our societies to reinforce a sense of common need or dependence, and a contingency and vulnerability we share as finite agents. All the more important, then, to resist anything that trivializes or shrinks the symbolic range of our sacramental practice – baptism as essentially a mark of individual confession, the eucharist as a celebration of achieved local human fellowship. They are too important as reminders, to believers and non-believers, of the need to put to death corrupt attachments to a false anthropology. Let them still speak of nakedness, death, danger, materiality and stubborn promise.

Notes

1. See 'On the American Indians', in F. de Vitoria, *Political Writings* (Cambridge: Cambridge University Press, 1991), pp. 231–92; A. Pagden, *Spanish Imperialism and the Political Imagination* (New Haven: Yale University Press, 1990); A. Pagden, *European Encounters with the New World* (New Haven: Yale University Press, 1993).
2. Augustine, *Works* VII, Nicene and Post-Nicene Fathers (Edinburgh: T. & T. Clark, 1873), Book VIII chs vi–vii, pp. 211–17.
3. G. F. Hegel, *Lectures on the Philosophy of Religion, One volume edition; The Lectures of 1827* ed. P. C. Hodgson (Berkeley: University of California Press, 1988), p. 477, no. 231.
4. Irenaeus, *The Writings* V:I, Ante-Nicene Christian Library (Edinburgh: T. & T. Clark, 1868), *Adversus Haereses* IV, 17–18, p. 430.
5. Augustine, *City of God* ed. D. Knowles, tr. H. Bettenson (Harmondsworth: Penguin, 1972), p. 1088.
6. S. Weil, *The Notebooks* tr. A. Willis (London: Routledge & Kegan Paul, 1956), p. 283.
7. R. Williams, *Resurrection* (London: Darton, Longman & Todd, 1982), p. 111.
8. See, for example, *The Broken Body* (London: Darton, Longman & Todd, 1988); and also *Community and Growth* (London: Darton, Longman & Todd, 1989).
9. To borrow a famous phrase from Goethe, as in his celebrated novel of 1809 about romantic love. See J. W. von Goethe, *Elective Affinities* (Harmondsworth: Penguin, 1971).

6

Sacrament as Action, not Presence

NICHOLAS WOLTERSTORFF

Nicholas Wolterstorff suggests that Calvin's understanding of the eucharist may be helpfully elucidated through the use of modern philosophy. Unlike Aquinas' symbolic system according to which consecration adds a presence, in the new causal powers that now inhere in the water or the bread and wine, for Calvin it is all about an enacted promise. The drama of the liturgy assures us that the promise of redemption is still in effect; or, using the terminology of the philosopher J. L. Austin, it has 'perlocutionary force'. Wolterstorff suggests that this gives the sacraments a highly personal character, especially when combined with Calvin's stress on the role of the Spirit preparing the mind for such an enacted confirmation.

Sign-agency in Aquinas and God-agency in Calvin

Consider a standard medieval explanation of what constitutes a sacrament – for example, that of Thomas Aquinas. A sacrament, says Aquinas, is a *sign of a sacred reality*. He adds, by way of elaborating a few of the assumptions behind that formula, that 'the term "sacrament" is properly applied to that which is a sign of some sacred reality pertaining to men; or – to define the special sense in which the term "sacrament" is being used in our present discussion of the sacraments – it is applied to that which is a sign of a sacred reality inasmuch as it has the property of sanctifying men.'[1] Now compare that to the definition of sacrament which John Calvin gives at the opening of his discussion of sacraments in the *Institutes*: a sacrament, says Calvin, 'is an outward sign by which the Lord seals on our consciences the promises of his good will toward us in order to sustain the weakness of our faith; and we in turn attest our piety toward him in the presence of the Lord and of his angels and before men.'[2]

Though the differences between these two definitions are striking, some of those differences do not really make any difference. Sacraments are for the purpose of sustaining the weakness of our faith, says Calvin. Aquinas would have no disagreement with that – not, at least, if he understood Calvin's understanding of *faith*; he just happens not to build it into his definition of 'sacrament'. Then there is Calvin's claim that the sacraments are, secondarily, attestations of piety. Though I do not think Aquinas would quite want to endorse that, he would have no objection to saying something similar.

Where my interest lies in this essay is a desire to call attention to, and reflect on, a difference between the two accounts which does not strike us at first, because it belongs to the underlying conceptuality of the definitions rather than to the details I have emphasized in the previous paragraph. Let me rephrase the definitions just a bit so as to highlight the difference I have in mind. A sacrament, says Aquinas, is a sign which both signifies a sacred reality and effects sanctification in human beings, or to adapt an Augustinian formula which was a favourite of the tradition: a sacrament is a sign which effects in human beings that sacred reality which it signifies. Now, by contrast, Calvin: a sacrament is a sign whereby God seals God's promises to us so as thereby to sustain our weakness. Or as he would also be willing to put it: a sacrament is a sign whereby God effects in us the promise which God seals to us with that sign. Speaking specifically of the eucharist, Calvin says that in 'the sacred mystery of the Supper', God 'inwardly fulfills what he outwardly designates'.[3]

You see the difference: in Aquinas it is the sign which is the agent: the sign inwardly effects what the sign outwardly signifies. In Calvin, it is God who is the agent: God inwardly fulfills by way of the sign what God outwardly designates with the sign.

Now I do not by any means wish to contend that Calvin never used the language of sign-agency in his discussion of sacraments, that he always and only used the language of God-agency. Though the God-agency language is clearly dominant, he does, not at all surprisingly, every now and then speak of the signs as doing things. Furthermore, immediately after he has given the definition I cited, along with another, briefer one which seems to me very unsatisfactory for his purposes, he says:

Whichever of these definitions you may choose, it does not differ in meaning from that of Augustine, who teaches that a sacrament is 'a visible sign of a sacred thing,' or 'a visible form of an invisible grace,' but it better and more clearly explains the thing itself. For since there is something obscure in his brevity, in which many of the less educated are deceived, I have decided to give a fuller statement, using more words to dispel all doubt.[4]

Calvin strikes me as somewhat disingenuous here, probably out of respect for Augustine. He represents himself as merely clarifying points left obscure in Augustine's definition. He was indeed clarifying points left obscure. I suggest, however, that he was at the same time altering the fundamental conceptuality of thinking about the sacraments from a sign-agency conceptuality to a God-agency conceptuality.

This use of the God-agency conceptuality, as I am calling it, became standard fare in the Reformed confessions. Let me give you a sampling. You will have to put up with some sixteenth-century verbosity! The Reformed Gallican Confession of 1559, apparently written by Calvin himself, begins its account of the sacraments [§34] ambiguously, but then resolves the ambiguity in the God-agency direction. The account runs like this:

the sacraments are added to the Word for more ample confirmation, that they may be to us pledges and seals of the grace of God, and by this means aid and comfort our faith, because of the infirmity which is in us, and that they are outward signs through which God operates by his Spirit, so that he may not signify any thing to us in vain.[5]

The Scots Confession of 1560, going rather aggressively out of its way to repudiate the accusation of Zwinglianism, says that the sacraments

were instituted by God . . . to exercise the faith of his children, and, by participation of the same sacraments, to seal in their hearts the assurance of his promise, and of that most blessed conjunction, union and society, which the elect have with their Head, Jesus Christ. And thus we utterly damn the vanity of they that affirm sacraments to be nothing else but naked and bare signs. No, we assuredly believe . . . that in the Supper rightly used, Christ Jesus is so joined with us, that he becomes very nourishment and food of our souls.[6]

The Second Helvetic Confession of 1566, at the beginning of the chapter dealing with the sacraments says:

Sacraments are mystical symbols, or holy rites, or sacred actions, ordained by God himself, consisting of his Word, of outward signs, and of things signified: whereby he keeps in continual memory, and recalls to mind, in his Church, his great benefits bestowed upon man; and whereby he seals up his promises, and outwardly represents, and, as it were, offers unto our sight those things which inwardly he performs unto us, and therewithal strengthens and increases our faith through the working of God's Spirit in our hearts; lastly, whereby he does separate us from all other people and religions, and consecrates and binds us wholly unto himself and gives us to understand what he requires of us.[7]

And the Belgic Confession of 1561:

our gracious God, on account of our weakness and infirmities, hath ordained the sacraments for us, thereby to seal unto us his promises, and to be pledges of the good will and grace of God towards us, and also to nourish and strengthen our faith, which he hath joined to the word of the gospel, the better to present to our senses, both that which he signifies to us by his Word, and that which he works inwardly in our hearts, thereby assuring and confirming in us the salvation which he imparts to us. For they are visible signs and seals of an inward and invisible thing, by means whereof God worketh in us by the power of the Holy Ghost.[8]

Later, in its article on the Holy Supper this same Confession gives the most crisp expression of the God-agency conceptuality that I know of when it says that God 'works in us all that he represents to us by these holy signs'.[9] Lastly, in the Heidelberg Catechism, though the Catechism was a compromise document, and is non-committal on the question of whether God effects by sacraments what God promises thereby, the God-agency conceptuality is there as in all the others: 'The sacraments are visible, holy signs and seals, appointed of God for this end, that by the use thereof he may the more fully declare and seal to us the promise of the Gospel.'[10]

The linguistic pattern is clear. The question is what, if any, significance is to be attached to the fact that Calvin, and those influenced by him in the sixteenth century, were so strongly inclined to use the language of God-agency rather than the language of sign-agency in their discussions of the sacraments.

Not a difference over causal principles

The thought which comes first to mind is that Calvin and the Calvinists were *occasionalists* in their thought – occasionalism being the doctrine that only persons, divine and human, have causal powers. On the occasionalist view, fire does not cause wood to be consumed by burning; fire has neither that causal power nor any other. Rather, God causes wood to be consumed by burning, and does so *on the occasion of* the wood being brought into contact with fire. But I think it is very clear that Calvin was not an occasionalist. In fact, Calvin both formulated a very occasionalist-sounding objection to his account and proceeded to answer the objection. He states the objection thus: 'the glory of God passes down to the creatures, and so much power is attributed to them, and [God's glory] is thus to this extent diminished'. He answered the objection as follows:

> we place no power in creatures. I say only this: God uses means and instruments which he himself sees to be expedient, that all things may serve his glory, since he is Lord and Judge of all. He feeds our bodies through bread and other foods, he illuminates the world through the sun, and he warms it through heat; yet neither bread, nor sun, nor fire, is anything save insofar as he distributes his blessings to us by these instruments. In like manner, he nourishes faith spiritually through the sacraments, whose one function is to set his promises before our eyes to be looked upon, indeed, to be guarantees of them to us.[11]

'We place no power in creatures', says Calvin. But in saying this he is obviously not expressing occasionalism but a thoroughgoing form of theistic instrumentalism. Bread, sun, fire – all are instruments of God's beneficent actions toward us. That presupposes that bread has the causal power of nourishing us; otherwise God could not make it available to us for the beneficent purpose of nourishing us. And so forth.[12]

But now the contrast between Aquinas and Calvin which I claimed to see, and which I expressed as the contrast between the use of a sign-agency conceptuality in thinking about the sacraments and a God-agency conceptuality, seems to be slipping away from us. For Aquinas affirms exactly what I have just quoted Calvin as saying. It appears that we have only a verbal contrast – a *purely verbal* contrast. Aquinas also addresses an occasionalist-sounding objection, which he phrases thus: 'Some, however, assert that the sacraments are not the cause of grace in the sense of actually producing any effect, but rather that when the sacraments are applied God produces grace in the soul.' Aquinas replies that 'we have it on the authority of many of the saints that the sacraments of the New Law not merely signify but actually cause grace. Therefore we must adopt a different approach based on the fact that there are two kinds of efficient causes, principal and instrumental.' It is the latter of these, the concept of *instrumental cause*, that is relevant here:

> An instrumental cause . . . acts not in virtue of its own form, but solely in virtue of the impetus imparted to it by the principal agent. Hence the effect has a likeness not to the instrument, but rather to that principal agent, as a bed does not resemble the axe which carves it but rather the design in the mind of the carpenter. And this is the way in which the sacraments of the New Law cause grace. For it is by divine institution that they are conferred upon man for the precise purpose of causing grace in and through them . . . now the term 'instrument' in its true sense is applied to that through which someone produces an effect. This is why we are told in Titus, *He saved us by the washing of regeneration.*[13]

If there really is, on the point I have been emphasizing, a difference of conceptuality between Aquinas and Calvin, and not merely a difference of language, that difference cannot consist in Calvin embracing occasionalism and Aquinas resisting it. Both reject occasionalism.

A symbol system or discourse system

I am not at ease, however, with letting the unsatisfactoriness of this first thought be the end of the matter. The difference of linguistic pattern is so dominant and so striking as to make me reluctant to conclude that there is nothing more to it than a fortuitous difference of linguistic emphasis. So let me pursue another way of construing how Calvin was thinking, in the hope that this will illuminate why he speaks as he does. Perhaps it will also explain why Calvin thinks he has answers to two objections which have repetitively been lodged against him ever since he first published his thoughts on the sacraments.[14]

I have in mind the charge that, on his account, nothing new happens in the sacrament, and the charge that, on his view, the sacraments cannot possibly effect what they signify. The 'nothing new' charge arises from the fact that the promise which God supposedly seals by way of the sacrament is something which

God has already made and which the recipient of the sacrament, as a hearer of the preached word and a person of faith, is already acquainted with and has already accepted. The matter, that is, the content, of the preached word is Jesus Christ; but Jesus Christ is also the matter of the sacrament. The 'no effect' charge arises from the fact that the bread and wine not only remain bread and wine in substance, but do not acquire any new causal powers. Perhaps God *on the occasion of* the sacrament works the effect in the recipient of uniting him or her more closely with Christ; but how could God possibly work that effect *by way of* the sacrament? Though Calvin may profess instrumentalism, doesn't his resistance to acknowledging any substantial or causal change in the bread and wine force him into that quite other doctrine of occasionalism?

We are all by now familiar with Ferdinand Saussure's distinction between language and discourse – between *langue* and *parole*. A language as such is just a code: words and grammar. To understand the role of language in human society we have to add to the code the use of that code in discourse. For all the familiarity of Saussure's distinction, however, it is clear that a wide and deep stream in contemporary philosophy of language would not accept it – or more precisely, would not accept it as marking a *fundamental* distinction. Everybody would agree that there is more than just the code; not everybody would agree that, at the deepest level, what must be added to the code is discourse. One party would agree that it is discourse which must be added. But the other party would say that what must be added is what might be called, following Nelson Goodman, *symbol systems*, in which the signs belonging to the system are assigned denotations which those signs then designate.[15] Those combinations of the signs which are well-formed sentences are then true or false depending on how the denotations of the terms are related in reality.

Of course the discourse party is willing to speak of signs as having designations, and of sentences as being true or false; but it regards those attributions as parasitic on the phenomena of persons referring to entities with signs and of persons using sentences to say things which are true or false. Correspondingly, the symbol-system party is willing to speak of persons as referring to things with terms and of persons saying true and false things with sentences; but it regards such speech as grounded ultimately on the phenomena of terms designating in symbol systems and of sentences being true or false. It should be added that a given thinker's use of one of these conceptualities rather than the other is not always grounded on the conviction that it truly is more fundamental; even less often is it grounded on the *argued* conviction that it is more fundamental. And in fact I know of no discussion which thoroughly and systematically compares the powers of the two conceptualities.

My initial suggestion is that a good many of the differences between Aquinas' account of the sacraments and Calvin's stem from the fact that Aquinas was thinking in terms of symbol systems whereas Calvin was thinking in terms of discourse. More must be said about discourse, however, if we are fully to understand Calvin's thought.

A discourse of assured promise

On the contemporary scene there are, broadly speaking, three ways of thinking about discourse. One is the Romantic expressivist way: discourse consists, at bottom, of the speaker using signs to express his or her inner life. Another is the quasi-behaviourist way: discourse consists at bottom of using signs to produce effects in auditors or readers. On the quasi-behaviourist way of thinking, communication rather than expression is viewed as the essence of language. The third way of thinking about discourse prominent on the contemporary scene is the speech-action way, pioneered by J. L. Austin.[16]

At the heart of the speech-action way of thinking is the distinction, to use Austin's terminology, between *locutionary* actions, *illocutionary* actions, and *perlocutionary* actions. Let me explain. Suppose I relieve your anxiety by promising that I will buy new tyres for the car, and that I do so by leaving a note for you on which I have inscribed the words, 'I'll buy new tyres for the car this afternoon.' In that case, my locutionary act is the act of inscribing the words, 'I'll buy new tyres for the car this afternoon.' My illocutionary act is the act of promising you that I will buy new tyres for the car this afternoon; my act of inscribing those words *counts* as my act of making that promise. And my perlocutionary act is my act of relieving your anxiety by making that promise to you. Of course, my performing that perlocutionary act presupposes that I have also performed another perlocutionary act, the act, namely, of communicating to you *what and that* I have promised.

It would be comically anachronistic to suggest that Calvin was thinking about the sacraments in terms of speech-action theory. Such prescience was not his! So let me instead state the suggestion I want to pursue like this: the best model for understanding how Calvin was thinking about the sacraments is the model of speaking proposed by speech-action theory. Let us try out this suggestion by thinking in accord with the model for a while. Naturally there are many facets of Calvin's thought about the sacraments which I will not be able to say anything about. In particular, I will confine my discussion to the sacrament of the eucharist.

The prying apart of illocutionary actions from locutionary actions is a crucial part of the model. Once we have that distinction in hand, then immediately we notice that the same sorts of actions which are illocutionary actions – and in many cases not just the *same sorts* of actions but *the very same* actions – can be performed not only by uttering or inscribing words, and not only by doing such other things with words as pointing to them or signing them, but can be done without using words at all, using instead pictures, semaphore signals, gestures, and so forth. Of course, in these latter cases they would not, strictly speaking, be *illocutionary* actions, since they would not be performed by way of locutionary actions; nonetheless they would belong to the same ontological category. Thus we can make sense at once of Calvin's insistence that, in spite of the difference in medium between sacrament and preaching, it should 'be regarded as a settled principle that the sacraments have the same office as the Word of God: to offer and set forth Christ to us, and in him the treasures of heavenly grace'.[17]

We should understand Calvin as saying, in that passage, that the *content* of the sacraments is the same as the *content* of the preached word; both of them present to us the promise of our redemption in Jesus Christ. What Calvin emphatically wants to say, however, is that the illocutionary act – the illocutionary *stance*, as Austin sometimes called it – is different. Calvin himself over and over uses the metaphor of a seal: by way of the sacrament God presents to us the promise made in Jesus Christ and seals, confirms, or ratifies, that promise: 'the seals which are attached to government documents and other public acts are nothing taken by themselves, for they would be attached in vain if the parchment had nothing written on it. Yet, when added to the writing, they do not on that account fail to confirm and seal what is written.'[18]

The metaphor obviously appealed strongly to Calvin's followers; it is used in all the Reformed confessions. But if I at all understand what Calvin is getting at here, and how a seal on a document functioned, the metaphor is not a wholly felicitous one. A document does not count as the discourse of the official until the seal – or nowadays, the signature – of the official has been attached. *Then and there*, when the seal is attached, the official says whatever the document makes him say. But that is not at all analogous to Calvin's thought. God's promise of redemption was already made in Jesus Christ, and is proclaimed by Scripture and preaching. It is not made episodically when and where the sacrament is celebrated. Calvin's thought – if I may make so bold as to offer an improvement on what he says – Calvin's thought is rather this: by way of offering the sacrament, God *here and now* assures the assembled that God's promise to redeem them remains in effect. In the sermon God tells us, by way of the words of the preacher, of the promises already made in Jesus Christ. In the sacrament God does not so much *tell* us of those promises made in Christ as *here and now assure us* that they remain in effect. He here and now assures us that the promise remains in effect, rather than merely telling us about a promise once made.

This especially is a point which symbol-system theory leaves obscure, but which discourse theory of the speech-action sort can clarify. The promise is not made *here and now*. Nor is it just the case that it is *here and now said* that the promise *was* made; that is the fundamental function of the proclamation. What in the sacrament is done *here and now* is the *issuing of the assurance* that the promise once made remains in effect. That is what is new, or part of what is new: the assurance of which, as Calvin sees it, we frail human beings are so very much in need. Sacraments, he says, 'are like seals of the good will that [God] feels toward us, which by attesting that good will to us, sustain, nourish, confirm, and increase our faith'.[19]

Promise clearer in the sacrament than in preaching

What is also true for Calvin is that the *medium* of the sacraments is of indispensable importance. Though the promise presented in Scripture and preaching, and presented in the sacraments and confirmed as remaining in effect, is the same promise, it is not at all true that the sacramental medium is dispensable. Calvin is convinced, for one thing, that assurance by way of the sacramental medium is more reassuring in its effects than is the presentation of the promise by Scripture and preaching. 'The sacraments, therefore, are exercises which make us more certain of the trustworthiness of God's Word.' They make us more certain because God 'attests his good will and love toward us more expressly than by word'.[20]

It is not a point most of us would have expected Calvin to

make! Yet there it is: The sacraments present the promises of God
to us in Jesus Christ more clearly than does 'the word, because
they represent them for us as painted in a picture from life'.[21] So
'the Lord here not only recalls to our memory . . . the abundance
of his bounty, but, so to speak, gives it into our hand and arouses
us to recognize it'.[22] By way of the sacrament, God graphically
presents to us the promise made in Jesus Christ, and in so doing
assures us that the promise remains valid. God dramatically
represents closer union with the body and blood of Christ and in
so doing assures us that the promise to secure such union for us
remains valid.

Let us allow Calvin to develop the point in his own words:

> . . . from the physical things set forth in the Sacrament we are
> led by a sort of analogy to spiritual things. Thus, when bread
> is given as a symbol of Christ's body, we must at once grasp
> this comparison: as bread nourishes, sustains, and keeps the
> life of our body, so Christ's body is the only food to invigorate
> and enliven our soul. When we see wine set forth as a symbol
> of blood, we must reflect on the benefits which wine imparts
> to the body, and so realize that the same are spiritually
> imparted to us by Christ's blood. These benefits are to nourish,
> refresh, strengthen, and gladden. For if we sufficiently consider
> what value we have received from the giving of that most holy
> body and the shedding of that blood, we shall clearly perceive
> that those qualities of bread and wine are, according to such an
> analogy, excellently adapted to express those things when they
> are communicated to us.[23]

The gestural metaphor of being offered bread and wine is open-
ended in meaning, however; so much so that after following out
the meaning for a while we come to a point where we can no
longer say what the metaphor means. It points beyond our grasp,
to mystery. Yet we *experience* what it means, experience it without
understanding it. Or so, at least, Calvin described his own case:

> Now, if anyone should ask me how this takes place, I shall not
> be ashamed to confess that it is a secret too lofty for either my
> mind to comprehend or my words to declare. And, to speak
> more plainly, I rather experience than understand it. There-
> fore, I here embrace without controversy the truth of God in
> which I may safely rest. He declares his flesh the food of my
> soul, his blood its drink. I offer my soul to him to be fed with
> such food. In his Sacred Supper he bids me take, eat, and drink

his body and blood under the symbols of bread and wine. I do not doubt that he himself truly presents them, and that I receive them.[24]

Earlier I remarked that the prying apart of illocutionary acts from locutionary acts characteristic of speech-action theory enables us to illuminate several aspects of Calvin's thought on the sacraments. Let me point to one more such aspect. When we are introduced to the distinction between locutionary and illocutionary acts, it is natural to have in mind the situation in which a *given person* performs an illocutionary act by performing a locutionary act – asserts something by speaking, makes a promise by writing something on a sheet of paper, and so forth. But in fact the agent of the two acts need not be the same. The President may come down with an attack of laryngitis just before he is slated to give his State of the Union address. Someone else may then read his speech for him; if so, then by that person's uttering the words, the President makes his proposals. That is how we must think of the sacramental case before us. By the appointed minister of the Church uttering the words and performing the actions of the sacrament, God presents the promise made in Jesus Christ and assures us that the promise remains in effect. The minister does not do it; God does it. God is the agent. With hammering insistence the Reformed confessions assert that *God* is the one who signifies and seals the promises.

For Aquinas acquires an additional causal power

The main thing remaining is to consider how our model illuminates some of what Calvin says about the perlocutionary effect of God's discourse in the sacrament. Here I think it will help to have, as a foil, some of what Aquinas says on the matter of sacramental effect, for he remarks that 'the sacraments of the New Law are designed to produce two effects, namely to act as a remedy against sins, and to bring the soul to its fulness in things pertaining to the worship of God in terms of the Christian life as a ritual expression of this'.[25] The first effect Aquinas calls 'grace'; the sacraments are an instrumental cause of grace. The second he calls 'sacramental character'; the sacraments are an instrumental cause of sacramental character. The question is how these instrumental effects come about. Given the causal powers of bread, wine, water, and oil, how can God bring about those effects? Hammers and saws do not build houses; we human beings have to build houses by using hammers and saws as instruments. But our doing so presupposes a definite set of causal powers on the part of hammers and saws. The causal powers of an egg, for example, are quite irrelevant to cutting boards or sinking nails. Aquinas states the application of the general point to the sacramental case thus: 'once we assert that a sacrament is an instrumental cause of grace it is straightway necessary to assert also that there is a certain kind of instrumental power in the sacrament designed to produce the sacramental effect'.[26]

In order to help us think about the instrumental causation which takes place in the sacraments, Aquinas offers some analogies. Here is one:

> ... cutting is proper to an axe in virtue of the sharpness intrinsic to it, whereas the function of making a bed belongs to it only inasmuch as it is an instrument used in a craft. So too it is with the sacraments. They touch the body and so produce upon it the sort of effects which are connatural to them as physical entities. But in the very act of doing so they also operate as instruments, producing effects upon the soul in the power of God. For instance the water of baptism, by the very fact of washing the body of its own connatural power, washes the soul too in virtue of being an instrument of the divine power.[27]

The analogy, though it may in a general way enhance our understanding of instrumental causation, does not help us understand what goes on in the sacrament. It is the natural sharpness of an axe that makes it useful to us in making a bed; but how is God enabled, by using water with its physical cleansing properties, to infuse grace (and sacramental character) into the soul of the one dipped in the water of baptism?

So Aquinas offers another analogy:

> ... there is nothing to prevent a spiritual power being in a body provided it is instrumental – in other words in virtue of the fact that a body can be impelled by some spiritual substance to produce some spiritual effect. Thus too in the human voice itself as perceptible to the senses a certain spiritual power resides to arouse the mind of the hearer in virtue of the fact that it proceeds from a mental concept, and in this way there is a spiritual power in the sacraments inasmuch as they are ordained by God to produce a spiritual effect.[28]

Here Aquinas goes beyond the axe and bed analogy. Sounds made by the human voice have 'a certain spiritual power' to arouse the mind of the hearer which they do have as such; they acquire that causal power, under certain circumstances. Nothing like that happens in the case of the axe; the axe does not acquire any additional causal powers. So this second analogy comes closer to Aquinas' thought about the sacraments than does the first. But it, too, will not quite do; Aquinas does not think that bread and wine acquire the causal power to infuse grace in the way in which the sounds of the human voice acquire the causal power to arouse the mind of someone. The analogy remains distant.

So let us try again, moving on from Aquinas' general discussion of sacraments to his particular discussion of the eucharist. He observes:

> It is not because of the natural power of the water that any spiritual effect is caused in Baptism, but because of the power of the Spirit which is in the water . . . But what the power of the Spirit is to the water of Baptism, that the very body of Christ is to the appearances of bread and wine. They are operative only because of the very body of Christ that they contain.
>
> A sacrament is so called because it contains something sacred. A thing can be sacred in two ways; in itself absolutely, and in relation to something else. The difference between the Eucharist and other sacraments having a material element is this: whereas the Eucharist contains something that is sacred in itself absolutely, namely, Christ, the water of Baptism contains something that is sacred in relation to something else, that is, it contains the power of sanctifying us.[29]

Now the point is becoming clear: the water used in baptism has acquired special causal powers, spiritual powers, in addition to its ordinary physical powers. Likewise in the eucharist special causal powers come to be associated with the bread and wine. The dynamics are somewhat different between the two sacraments, however. The bread and wine do not themselves acquire additional causal powers. Rather, the bread is transubstantiated into the body of Christ and the wine into the blood of Christ; and those inherently have spiritual powers. The accidents of the bread and wine, which remain after the alteration of substance, retain the ordinary causal powers of bread and wine. By contrast, the water of baptism really does have new spiritual powers.

When and how does this drastic alteration of substance, and this acquisition of new causal spiritual powers, take place? In and by the consecration of the elements:

. . . in the other sacraments [than eucharist] the consecration
of the matter consists merely in a certain blessing, as a result
of which the consecrated matter receives an instrumental spiritual power; this derives from the minister who is a living
instrument able to reach to inanimate instruments. But in this
sacrament the consecration of the matter consists in a miracu-
lous change of the substance, which only God can bring about.
So it is that the minister has no other act in effecting this sacrament than to pronounce the words.[30]

Calvin's judgement on this whole theory of transubstantiation
and acquisition of additional causal powers is clear: he wants
nothing to do with it. God has not attached to the sacramental
elements 'some sort of secret powers . . .'[31] It is an error to 'think
that a hidden power is joined and fastened to the sacraments by
which they of themselves confer the graces of the Holy Spirit
upon us as wine is given in a cup'.[32]

Calvin's very different account: the promise appropriated

But how then do the sacraments gain their effect, of strengthening
us in faith – which for Calvin is the same as uniting us more
closely with the divine-human person, Jesus Christ? For that they
do have this effect, Calvin repetitively insists. There are two parts
to Calvin's answer.

In the first place, if we are to be united more closely with
Christ by God's sacramental presentation of the promise and
assurance that that promise remains in force, then we must *understand* that God is presenting that, and is assuring us of that, by
this sacrament. The fundamental function of the sacramental
words is to bring about such understanding. Calvin expresses his
agreement with his opponents that a sacrament, strictly speaking,
'consists of the word and the outward sign' together. But then he
immediately adds: 'we ought to understand the word not as one
whispered without meaning and without faith, a mere noise, like
a magic incantation, which has the force to consecrate the element.
Rather, it should, when preached, make us understand what the
visible sign means.'[33] So he says: 'Accordingly, when we hear the
sacramental word mentioned let us understand the promise, proclaimed in a clear voice by the minister, to lead the people by the
hand wherever the sign tends and directs us.'[34]

In short, the perlocutionary effect of the sacrament, if we may

call it that, is not produced simply by the uttering of the sacramental words and the performance of the sacramental actions –
any more than the perlocutionary effect in speech is produced
simply by the sound or the look of the words. It occurs only when
the recipients discern the illocutionary acts performed – only
when they discern that God is assuring them that the promise
made in Jesus Christ remains in effect for them. If your anxiety is
calmed by the note I leave on the kitchen table, that is because
you do not merely see the words but discern what I was saying
with those words.

On the other hand, we saw earlier that the perlocutionary
effect of the sacrament is also not produced simply by discerning
the assurance; the *signs* whereby the assurance is made are also of
fundamental importance. It is God's assuring us that the promise
remains in effect *by offering us this meal* that unites us more closely
to Christ. To use the jargon of our model: it is this illocutionary
act produced by this locutionary act that produces this perlocutionary act.

But more is needed than meditation on the dramatic representation, and understanding of what God is saying thereby, if the
sacraments are to work their intended effect. Receptivity on the
part of the recipient is also necessary. And that comes about by
the work of the Holy Spirit within us; we do not just do it on our
own. God 'illuminates our minds by the light of his Holy Spirit
and opens our hearts for the Word and sacraments to enter in,
which would otherwise only strike our ears and appear before our
eyes, but not at all affect us within'.[35]

> ... the sacraments properly fulfill their office only when the
> Spirit, that inward teacher, comes to them, by whose power
> alone hearts are penetrated and affections moved and our
> souls opened for the sacraments to enter in. If the Spirit be
> lacking, the sacraments can accomplish nothing more in our
> minds than the splendor of the sun shining upon blind eyes, or
> a voice sounding in deaf ears.[36]

What immediately follows this passage in the text of the *Institutes* is a great flowering of metaphors for the work of the Spirit
in the recipient of the sacrament. What I find fascinating is that
all of them are metaphors for the Spirit's making us receptive in
heart and mind. Here are some of the metaphors:

> ... just as the eyes see by the brightness of the sun, or the ears
> hear by the sound of a voice, so the eyes would not be affected
> by any light unless they were endowed with a sharpness of

vision capable of being illumined of themselves; and the ears would never be struck by any noise, unless they were created and fitted for hearing. But suppose it is true . . . that what sight does in our eyes for seeing light, and what hearing does in our ears for perceiving a voice, are analogous to the work of the Holy Spirit in our hearts, which is to conceive, sustain, nourish, and establish faith. Then both of these things follow: the sacraments profit not a whit without the power of the Holy Spirit, and nothing prevents them from strengthening and enlarging faith in hearts already taught by that Schoolmaster.[37]

In summary: 'what increases and confirms faith is precisely the preparation of our minds by [the Spirit's] inward illumination to receive the confirmation extended by the sacraments'.[38] When that happens, then 'the believer, when he sees the sacraments with his own eyes, does not halt at the physical sight of them, but by those steps (which I have indicated by analogy) rises up in devout contemplation to those lofty mysteries which lie hidden in the sacraments',[39] thus becoming united with Jesus Christ, the God-man.

Personal action: the awesome impact of ordinary bread and wine

There you have it: a philosopher's attempt to use the model provided by speech-action theory to illuminate Calvin's doctrine of the sacraments! There are many aspects of Calvin's doctrine about which I have said nothing. Perhaps some of those could also be illuminated by thinking about them in accord with the speech-action model. I hope, though, to have said enough to help us decide whether thinking of Calvin's account along these lines proves illuminating – and in particular, whether it makes his account less elusive than it has proved to most readers ever since it was first published.

Let me close by mentioning two overall impressions that I am left with. What strikes me, in the first place, is something about the understanding of the liturgy that emerges from Calvin's account. To enter the liturgy, as Calvin understands it, is to enter the sphere not just of divine presence but of divine action. God, in Calvin's way of thinking, is less a presence to be apprehended in the liturgy than an agent to be engaged.

What strikes me, in the second place, is the extraordinary significance that Calvin assigns to God's offering us these material elements of bread and wine and our eating and drinking them. I

know, of course, that Calvinism is often thought to be a highly
rationalistic form of Christianity; no doubt it has often been that.
But just ordinary bread and ordinary wine – no special causal
powers: Calvin believes that by way of these, dramatically presented and understandingly and receptively received, God
strengthens our faith by uniting us more closely to the humanity
as well as the divinity of Jesus Christ. Never, to my knowledge,
has ordinary material stuff been freighted with such momentous
significance.

Kilian McDonnell, imbued with the Thomistic conviction that
the sacramental elements are infused by God with special spiritual powers, is struck by the freedom from material means which
God enjoys on Calvin's view, as he understands that. In his book,
John Calvin, the Church and the Eucharist, he says that on Calvin's
view,

> God uses bread to nourish us because he chose to do so, but
> he does not in any sense remain bound to objects even after
> having chosen them. Nor does he give to them a power which
> is proper to himself. To feed man unto salvation is a work of
> God and the sacraments never possess this as an immanent
> power. The Eucharist is never an object, but a personal instru-
> ment. The Eucharist does not have, either from nature or from
> God, a power of nourishing spirituality which it possesses in a
> definitive sense. There is no power given to the eucharistic
> bread so that the bread possesses that power now and need not
> again, and ever again, receive the power to nourish spiritually.[40]

McDonnell considerably overstates and even distorts the
Thomistic view which he professes to embrace. Let us take the
case of baptism, since, as we have seen, its structure is somewhat
less complex, on Aquinas' analysis, than that of the eucharist. It
was Aquinas' view that the water used in baptism is in fact 'ever
and again' infused with special spiritual powers, by consecration;
water does not possess 'in a definitive sense' the power of cleansing
us spiritually. Further, Aquinas was as eager as was Calvin to say
that the eucharist is not 'an object, but a personal instrument'.
And on the Thomistic view as well as on the Calvinistic – indeed,
on every Christian view – God is not 'bound to' objects after
choosing them.

All that pertains, however, to the view which McDonnell uses
to contrast with Calvin's; it is, I contend, a very distorted version
of Thomism. As to Calvin's view itself: it wears to my eye a very
different appearance from that which it wears to the eye of
McDonnell: God took the risk of trusting ordinary bread and

ordinary wine, when devoutly and meditatively received under the power of the Spirit in the sacrament, to unite us more closely with Jesus Christ. It is true that that does not imply that God is bound by bread and wine. But it certainly does imply that God places on these humble, eminently material, stuffs, an awesome load of significance. Or perhaps the more accurate thing to say is that the *drama* of God offering us bread and wine as a sign and assurance of Christ offering us his body and blood, and our then eating that bread and wine – it is on that simple dramatic representation performed with ordinary bread and ordinary wine that God places an awesome load of significance. Never has dramatic representation been freighted with such awesome import.

Notes

1. Thomas Aquinas, *Summa Theologiae*, tr. David Bourke (London: Eyre & Spottiswoode, 1975), 3a, 60, 2.
2. J. Calvin, *Institutes of the Christian Religion*, Library of Christian Classics 2 (Philadelphia: Westminster, 1960), 4, 14, 1, p. 1277.
3. Calvin, *Institutes*, 4, 17, 5, p. 1364.
4. Calvin, *Institutes*, 4, 14, 1, p. 1277.
5. P. Schaff, *The Creeds of the Evangelical Protestant Churches* 3 (London: Hodder & Stoughton, 1877), pp. 378–9.
6. Schaff, *Creeds* 3, pp. 467–8.
7. Schaff, *Creeds* 3, p. 285 (my translation).
8. Schaff, *Creeds* 3, p. 474.
9. Schaff, *Creeds* 3, p. 429.
10. Schaff, *Creeds* 3, p. 328.
11. Calvin, *Institutes*, 4, 14, 12, p. 1287.
12. Thus I strongly disagree with Kilian McDonnell's comment, in his *John Calvin, the Church and the Eucharist* (Princeton: Princeton University Press, 1967), p. 37 that 'the Scotistic and Occamist philosophies, together with the mystical movement and the *devotio moderna* piety, are important for the general background to Calvin's eucharistic doctrine . . . They manifest themselves in a flight from secondary causality, and . . . in a reassertion of the sovereignty of God as the only cause.'
13. Aquinas, *Summa Theologiae*, 3a, 62, 1.
14. See the discussion in the recent book by B. A. Gerrish, *Grace and Gratitude: the Eucharistic Theology of John Calvin* (Minneapolis: Fortress Press, 1993).
15. N. Goodman, *Languages of Art: An Approach to a Theory of Symbols* (London: Oxford University Press, 1969).
16. J. L. Austin, chapter 10, 'Performative Utterances' in *Philosophical*

Papers (Oxford: Clarendon Press, 1961), pp. 133–252, a subject developed in *How to do Things with Words* (Oxford: Clarendon Press, 1962).

17. Calvin, *Institutes*, 4, 14, 17, p. 1292.
18. Calvin, *Institutes*, 4, 14, 5, p. 1280.
19. Calvin, *Institutes*, 4, 14, 7, p. 1282.
20. Calvin, *Institutes*, 4, 14, 6, p. 1281.
21. Calvin, *Institutes*, 4, 14, 5, p. 1280.
22. Calvin, *Institutes*, 4, 17, 37, p. 1414.
23. Calvin, *Institutes*, 4, 17, 3, p. 1363. Given this probing by Calvin of the import of the dramatic representation, I find it very strange that McDonnell would say that, on Calvin's view, God 'uses bread as a means because he chooses to use bread, and though the bread is an apt symbol of nourishment, the significance of the means is not so much that it is bread, as that it is chosen. There is something almost accidental in the choice of this particular means' (*Calvin, the Church and the Eucharist*, p. 166). Of course Calvin believes that God could have worked by other means: all theologians in the Christian tradition have believed the same. But Calvin was very far indeed from thinking that the choice of sacramental elements was accidental; to be united with the body of Christ, we must meditate on the import of these very elements.
24. Calvin, *Institutes*, 4, 17, 32, pp. 1403–4.
25. Aquinas, *Summa Theologiae*, 3a, 63, 1.
26. Aquinas, *Summa Theologiae*, 3a, 62, 4.
27. Aquinas, *Summa Theologiae*, 3a, 62, 1.
28. Aquinas, *Summa Theologiae*, 3a, 62, 4.
29. Aquinas, *Summa Theologiae*, 3a, 73, 2.
30. Aquinas, *Summa Theologiae*, 3a, 78, 1.
31. Calvin, *Institutes*, 4, 14, 14, p. 1289.
32. Calvin, *Institutes*, 4, 14, 17, p. 1292.
33. Calvin, *Institutes*, 4, 14, 4, p. 1279.
34. Calvin, *Institutes*, 4, 14, 4, pp. 1279–80.
35. Calvin, *Institutes*, 4, 14, 8, p. 1284.
36. Calvin, *Institutes*, 4, 14, 9, p. 1284.
37. Calvin, *Institutes*, 4, 14, 9, pp. 1284–5.
38. Calvin, *Institutes*, 4, 14, 10, p. 1285.
39. Calvin, *Institutes*, 4, 14, 5, p. 1280.
40. McDonnell, *Calvin, the Church and the Eucharist*, p. 167.

7

Transubstantiation: Eucharist as Pure Gift

GERARD LOUGHLIN

The philosopher Jacques Derrida has maintained that the notion of gift is an impossible ideal: by definition it must receive no return, but even to acknowledge a gift as such is already to make some kind of return. Though conceding this point, Gerard Lough-lin uses the writings of another French philosopher, Jean-Luc Marion, to argue that it is precisely when the eucharist is con-ceptualized in terms of transubstantiation that it most nearly approaches this ideal. In this respect Marion's approach, he sug-gests, should be contrasted favourably with much contemporary Roman Catholic thinking. Notions like 'transfiguration' put too much emphasis on a return from our own self-consciousness. This can be illustrated from two very different understandings of time which each approach generates. On the modern view our present situation determines our understanding of eucharistic presence, whereas what is required is a view of presence which through its notion of memorial and eschatological anticipation uses past and future to shape our present: as the pure gift of divine love.

The narrative ritual

A group of friends gather for a meal, each bringing something to the table. They bring bread and wine. Their host brings himself. He has called them together, to share food and drink with one another. He tells them that in sharing the bread and drinking the cup they are sharing in him. He has given himself to them. He has given them his life.

On a thorsday a soper y made
With frendis and foys to make hem glad

123

Of brede and wyne the sacrament
Euyr to be oure testament . . .[1]   *you are*

The eucharist is a narrative that enfolds the participants within the biblical story, not simply in each performance but in the cycle of performances throughout the Church's liturgical year. The biblical story is present not only in the readings of the lectionary, but in the very language of the liturgy which, through penitence and acclamation, comes to focus on the life, death and resurrection of Jesus Christ. The participants' absorption into the story is made possible through their absorption of the story in and through its ritual enactment.[2] They are not simply witnesses of the story, but characters within it. They do not simply recall the forgiveness of sins but ask and receive forgiveness; they do not repeat the praise of others but give praise themselves; they do not merely remember the night on which Jesus was betrayed but, mindful of their own daily betrayal, gather with the apostles at that night's table, themselves called by the one who in that darkness called his disciples to eat with him. Above all, they do not merely remember the giving of the bread and the passing of the cup, but, receiving the bread and passing the cup amongst themselves, they too share in that night's food.[3]

Toward the end of his book on *The Promise of Narrative Theology*, George Stroup discusses the eucharist. He notes how it brings Church and Christ together in the performance of the scriptural story:

> It is the Christian narrative which mediates between the bread, the body of Christ, and Jesus Christ's spiritual presence. To 'remember' him is not simply to bring Jesus of Nazareth to mind but to 'actualise' those narratives in which he has his identity, to engage in that form of confession which fuses the narrative identity of the self to the narrative history of Jesus Christ.[4]

The Word of God is present in the word of Scripture and in the bread and wine of the eucharistic sacrament whenever a person is incorporated into the Christian narrative: 'the Word is present when the Spirit enables personal and communal identity to be fused to the narrative history of God's grace'.[5] As the bread is broken and dispersed among the people so they are brought together, united by the One who is dispersed among them.[6] In this essay I want to reflect on Christ's gift of himself in the narrative ritual of the eucharistic meal.

Eating narratives

What is given in the eucharist? Without question, and perhaps almost without notice, the eucharist gives first and quite simply, the story of a meal. At a certain time and in a certain place – 'On the night he was betrayed' – a group of friends gather for a meal. Not once upon a time, but at a certain time. Not anywhere or somewhere, but there in Jerusalem. The eucharist narrates a story of particular events in the past. But it is this story of past events that commands the present narration: 'Do this in memory of me'. The eucharist is not a pious memorial that merely recalls the past, for even before it begins to remember it is called into the present by the past. Its becoming is not of itself. It becomes what it is, always already, from the past.

The eucharist is story and meal, narrative and food. When the meal is over, the one who has gathered his friends together shows the depth of his love for them by taking bread, breaking it and giving it to them. He gives them wine, and he tells them the story that is about to unfold and is unfolding even as the eucharist is being performed, it itself called into being by the story it narrates. He gives the story that the eucharist first and quite simply now gives. It is given by him for all.

The eucharist – story and meal, praise and performance – is the gift of Christ, and Christ – the Body of Christ, which is Christ-and-the-people-of-Christ-incorporated, inscribed in Christ's own story – is the gift of the eucharist. In the eucharistic meal Christ gathers his friends together. For this is the nature of charity: to be with one another so as to love one another; to nourish and build up the one body of Christ.

The impossible gift

The eucharist is the pure gift of God. It is the good gift, the gift beyond measure, the gift of the trinitarian charity. But Jacques Derrida teaches that the gift is impossible. First, a gift must be given without return. Second, all giving receives a restitution. Therefore the gift is impossible.

Jacques Derrida identifies the gift in relation to the law (*nomos*) of exchange, the economy or circle of giving and return. The gift is that which interrupts economy, because it is that which is not returned. It does not and must not circulate.[7]

> For there to be a gift, there must be no reciprocity, return, exchange, countergift, or debt. If the other *gives* me back or

owes me or has to give me *back* what I *give* him or her, there will not have been a gift, whether this restitution is immediate or whether it is programmed by a complex calculation of a long-term deferral or différance.

Derrida asserts that this is the 'semantic precomprehension of the word "gift" in our language or in a few familiar languages'.[8]

The gift is *aneconomic* and thus impossible, and not simply impossible but *the* impossible. It is, Derrida writes, the very figure of the impossible. 'It announces itself, gives itself to be thought as the impossible.'[9] Why is the gift impossible? Derrida argues that the conditions for the possibility of the gift are at the same time the conditions of its impossibility: 'these conditions of possibility define or produce the annulment, the annihilation, the destruction of the gift'.[10] The conditions of the gift are stated in the following axiom: 'In order for there to be gift, gift event, some "one" has to give some "thing" to someone other, without which "giving" would be meaningless.'[11] But the gift – the giving of some thing to someone – is impossible because there is no giving without return.

If there is to be a gift the donee must not make a return nor be indebted, and the donor must not expect a return or restitution. But this means that the donee must not recognize the gift as a gift. 'If he recognizes it as gift, if the gift *appears to him as such*, if the present is present to him *as present*, this simple recognition suffices to annul the gift.'[12] This is because the recognition is already to give back a 'symbolic equivalent'. The donor, likewise, must not recognize the gift as a gift: 'otherwise he begins, at the threshold, as soon as he intends to give, to pay himself with a symbolic recognition, to praise himself, to approve of himself, to gratify himself, to congratulate himself, to give back to himself symbolically the value of what he thinks he has given or what he is preparing to give'.[13] This is the impossibility or double-bind of the gift. 'For there to be gift, it is necessary that the gift not even appear, that it not be perceived or received as gift.'[14]

It would seem that if there is to be a gift it must be forgotten. But it cannot be forgotten by the conscious mind alone. It must also be forgotten by the unconscious, it must not remain there or elsewhere as repressed. For that would be to keep the gift by exchanging places, by displacing. The gift is recognized in the unconscious and thus annulled. If there is to be a gift there has to be an absolute forgetting; nothing must be left behind. Derrida says that this absolute forgetting, this forgetting of forgetting, which is at the same time not nothing, cannot be understood in philosophical, psychological or psychoanalytic categories. Rather, it is on the basis 'of what takes shape in the name *gift*' that we can hope to think about absolute forgetting.[15] Thus the gift becomes the condition of forgetting, as its establishment – the forgetting condition. Gift and forgetting are 'each in the condition of the other', forgetting in the condition of the gift and the gift in the condition of forgetting.[16]

Derrida, taking his way by Heidegger, likens the logic of the gift to that of Being and Time. Being is not but there is Being; Time is not but there is Time:

> Heidegger recalls that in itself time is nothing temporal, since it is nothing, since it is not a thing (*kein Ding*). The temporality of time is not temporal, no more than proximity is proximate or treeness is woody. He also recalls that Being is not being (being-present/present-being), since it is not something (*kein Ding*), and that therefore one cannot say either 'time is' or 'being is'.[17]

In being-present and in present-time, Being and Time withdraw; there is a forgetting of Being and Time. The gift, if there is a gift, also withdraws, forgotten in the very moment of giving.

The logic of the impossible gift comes into play as soon as there is a subject, as soon as there is a donor and a donee, a giver and a recipient. So one must conclude that 'if there is gift, it cannot take place between two subjects exchanging objects, things or symbols'.[18] The question of the gift, therefore, has to be placed before that of the subject, just as the question of Being is placed before it is determined as substantial being.

Is it then possible that in the eucharist Christ is given to us as unconditional charity, as gift? Is it possible that Christ escapes the law of exchange, the circle of return? Instead of a gift, are we not rather given an obligation, a contract and a covenant? Or is the eucharist the proper name of the gift, of the impossible? So that all gifts, if there be any, are types of this gift?[19]

I now propose to approach these questions by way of the question of how we may best articulate – at the level of doctrinal grammar – the giving of the eucharistic gift. This is the question of transubstantiation. It is a question because transubstantiation is the name, not of an explanation, but of a rigorous recollection of the eucharistic mystery. St Thomas begins his account of the change of bread and wine into the body and blood of Christ by reminding us that 'we could never know by our senses that the real body of Christ and his blood are in this sacrament, but only by our faith which is based on the authority of God'.[20] The doctrine of transubstantiation adds nothing to, but only articulates, the eucharistic mystery of faith. The argument to be considered is that transubstantiation is the best articulation we have.

Transubstantiation and its transcriptions

St Thomas Aquinas teaches that in the eucharist we are fed spiritual food under the species of bread and wine, the proper matter of the sacrament.[21] It is a spiritual food because it contains Christ crucified, bodily himself. Christ comes to us in this sacrament out of friendship, for as Aristotle teaches, friends want to live together. The eucharist is the sign of supreme charity or love.[22]

Christ is in the sacrament because the substance of the bread is changed into that of the body, and the substance of the wine into that of the blood. The change is supernatural and effected by God alone. It is 'not a formal change, but a substantial one. It does not belong to the natural kinds of change, and it can be called by a name proper to itself – "transubstantiation".'[23]

What are we to make of such a doctrine as transubstantiation, with its ancient ideas of 'matter' and 'form', 'substance' and 'accident'? Must we not, with Richard Dawkins, find it 'daft'?[24] Perhaps it is, in the sense that what Aquinas does with the concepts he borrows from Aristotle makes little sense within Aristotelian ontology.[25] But perhaps this is not a problem, for may we not argue that transubstantiation has its own distinctive logic?

A more serious charge against transubstantiation is that it 'fixes and freezes' the person of Christ in an 'available, permanent, handy, and delimited thing'. Transubstantiation – as Jean-Luc Marion notes – is then 'the imposture of an idolatry that imagines itself to honour "God" when it heaps praises on his pathetic "canned" substitute (the reservation of the eucharist), exhibited as an attraction (display of the Holy Sacrament), brandished like a banner (processions), and so on'.[26] God becomes a very real presence, but the presence of a mute thing, placed at the disposal of the community.

In view of such criticism, it is not surprising to find transubstantiation rendered in other than Aristotelian idiom. Thus we are offered transignification and transfinalization, and told that in such transcriptions, 'substance, being, essence, meaning, significance and end' can be 'completely identical'.[27] They remain transubstantial because they seek to articulate Catholic faith in the eucharistic presence of Christ. They seek – as Herbert McCabe puts it – to avoid, on the one hand, a merely metaphorical or symbolic understanding of the eucharist, and, on the other hand, a physicalist understanding of the eucharist which supposes some disguised chemical change in the bread and wine.

An accessible re-writing of transubstantiation is offered by Gareth Moore in his short essay, 'Transubstantiation for beginners' (1986). He suggests that, for the believer, the consecrated bread and wine are understood no longer according to their appearance but according to their context. It is context which constitutes the eucharistic change. He gives the example of a five pound note. Apart from the institution of money it is just a piece of brightly coloured paper. But given the institution of money and the forms of life in which a five pound note functions, it is no longer just a piece of paper. There is also a difference, a substantial difference, between a genuine and a forged five pound note. One is issued by authority, the other not. Institution and use makes the five pound note what it is.

In the same way, a piece of bread becomes something other than just a piece of bread by being taken up and used in a certain way in the life of the Church. A consecrated host differs from a perhaps identical piece of bread by being embedded within a certain institution and its way of life. To understand it we must look not only at it, but around it.[28] To believe in paper money is to live in a money economy; to believe in transubstantiation is to live as part of the Church, 'to live the life of the Church centred around the Eucharist'.[29]

However attractive – because comprehensible – Moore's re-writing of transubstantiation as transignification, it is not immune from criticism. Jean-Luc Marion offers a powerful critique of such re-writing in his essay 'The present and the gift'.[30] He does so in favour, not of wimpish symbolism, but of real, red-blooded transubstantialism.

Christ not at our disposal

Jean-Luc Marion teaches that what matters with regard to particular accounts of the eucharistic mystery is whether or not they put the eucharistic presence at the disposal of the community or the community at the disposal of Christ:

> [If] it is still Christ, the priest in *persona Christi*, who gives to the community the new meanings and goals of the bread and wine, precisely because the community does not produce them,

does not have them at its disposal, or perform them; then this gift will be welcomed as such by a community that, receiving it, will find itself nourished and brought together by it.[31]

But if it is the community that gives the 'new meanings and goals of the bread and wine', then the bread and wine will be less the mediation of God's presence in the community, as the community's awareness of itself in its search for God's presence. For then, even as it receives the bread and wine, it will still be seeking and finding only its own collective consciousness.[32] It would seem that Moore's account – as far as it goes – is in danger of doing this: making God's presence dependent on the institution and performance of the community.

Marion suggests that in such renderings of the eucharistic mystery, it is not so much that the presence of Christ is relocated from the bread and wine to the community, as that Christ's presence ceases to be distinct from the collective consciousness. Christ's presence endures for as long as the community is present. Presence becomes dependent on present consciousness. Once that consciousness has disappeared, the community dispersed, there is nothing left to constitute and maintain presence. The consecrated bread can be thrown out or burnt. With the community gone, divine presence is relegated to the past.[33]

As Marion develops this theme, eucharistic presence is 'measured by what the attention of the human community presently accords to it'.[34] He describes it as a perfect inversion of perpetual adoration. Rather than the eucharistic presence ceaselessly provoking our attention, it is our attention that provokes and governs the eucharistic presence.[35] And because our attention is intermittent, presence is interim.

It is thus that Marion turns the tables on those who would find in transubstantiation a reification of eucharistic presence, a form of idolatry putting God at the disposal of the community. Eucharistic theologies that seek to understand the divine presence in terms of the community's will, attention or consciousness, are places where idolatry 'knows its triumph'.[36]

This is where Marion thinks the theology of transubstantiation can help. First, in order to appreciate that the eucharistic presence is not determined by ourselves, we must so distinguish it from ourselves that we can admit its distance from us. It is Christ who determines our union with him, his presence with us. Marion argues that 'the theology of transubstantiation alone offers the possibility of distance, since it strictly separates my consciousness from Him who summons it. In the distance thus arranged, the

Other summons, by his absolutely concrete sacramental body, my attention and my prayer.'[37]

Transubstantiation has the virtue of keeping the distance that marks out the Other from ourselves. 'In becoming conscious of the thing where eucharistic presence is embodied, the believing community does not become conscious of itself, but of another, of the Other par excellence.'[38] Even if transubstantiation risks a material idolatry, it avoids the supreme spiritual idolatry of supposing Christ's presence our self-consciousness. The very thing for which Hegel chided Catholicism – that 'the spirit of all truth is in actuality set in rigid opposition to the self-conscious spirit'[39] – marks out an escape from this most subtle of idolatries:

> What the consecrated host imposes, or rather permits, is the irreducible exteriority of the present that Christ makes us of himself in this thing that to him becomes sacramental body. That this exteriority, far from forbidding intimacy, renders it possible in sparing it from foundering in idolatry, can be misunderstood only by those who do not want to open themselves to distance.[40]

It is a matter of choosing between the idol and distance, between ourselves and the transcendent God.

A transubstantiation of language?

Herbert McCabe also turns to language for his re-written transubstantialism, but avoids Marion's criticism by insisting that the change of language – with which he replaces the change of substance – is given not by, but to the community. The eucharistic gift is thus understood as the gift of a new language, a new society and a new body: the body of Christ.

For McCabe, the risen body of Christ is present in the eucharist in the mode of language, in the signs we use. 'Our language has become his body.'[41] Or, we might say, his language has become our body. McCabe understands language as an extension of the human body. Language allows us to do far more in the world than we could if we only had our bodily parts and senses, our sight and hearing, our teeth and hands. Language allows us to realize a social, communicated world as our habitat:

> The human body extends itself into language, into social structures, into all the various and complex means of living together, communicating together what men have created, but all of

them are rooted in the body; there is no human communication which is not fundamentally bodily communication.[42]

Language changes, usually slowly and without notice, but sometimes suddenly and dangerously, and when it does, the bodies whose extensions it is, change also. McCabe is interested in radical change, social revolution. The world after revolution cannot be described in pre-revolutionary language, for revolution is a complete change of language and world. At best, the revolutionary can picture the world that comes after in parables.[43] New worlds come only through revolution, through death and resurrection. A new world is thus a new language, a new communication; and it is this – a new world, language and communication – that are given in the eucharist. Christ comes to us as a new medium of communication.[44] He gives us nothing other than himself and his language: body and word. He offers us his friendship.[45]

In the first century of our era, the gift of Christ's body and word were returned with death. But as the gift of God it was not destroyed. Once given it is not taken back. On the other side of death, on the other side of the revolution, the body of Christ is more alive, more bodily, than before. He is 'available in his bodiliness more than he was, he is now able to be present to all men and not just to a few in Palestine'.[46] The body of the risen Christ, that comes to us in the eucharist, comes to us from our promised future; it is post-revolutionary, more bodily.

Thus re-written, the doctrine of transubstantiation teaches that the bread and wine undergo a revolutionary change, changing not into something else, but more radically into food and drink; for 'Christ has a better right to appear as food and drink than bread and wine have.'[47] This is because food and drink signify the sharing of a common world, of bodily communication. McCabe holds that apart from sexual union, there is no more primitive and fundamental form of bodily communication than the sharing of food. The common meal is a symbol of unity because it is rooted in the life of the body. Food is a language in which we communicate and come together. Thus Christ is the true bread because in him we come truly together; he is more truly food than food itself.

When people gather for the eucharist, they gather for a meal that is at the same time the language of their bodily communication; and this language-meal is not their own, but comes to them from beyond the site of their gathering, from beyond and after the revolution. It is a language they can barely speak; but it is the language in which they can most truly communicate; be most bodily, most alive. McCabe thus articulates the eucharistic change as a change of language. In the eucharist, 'the language itself is transformed and becomes the medium of the future, the language itself becomes the presence, the bodily presence of Christ'.[48] This account is transubstantial because, while the 'accidents' of pre-revolutionary language remain, its 'substance' is post-revolutionary. The signs are the same, but their signifieds have changed; they are barely comprehensible.

Gifted time: present shaped by past and future

It is time to start a return to the question of the impossible gift; but I shall do so by way of Marion's own transcription of transubstantiation. In it he seeks to refuse metaphysics, and above all, the metaphysics of time as this has been constituted from Aristotle to Hegel. This is in keeping with his larger project to think God other than by way of Being, as prior to Being, as pre-ontological: God without Being.[49]

As we have seen, Derrida suggests that the gift as such can be thought only prior to the subject, prior to the relation of giver and given that annuls the gift in the very moment it is given. But for Marion the gift comes first, prior to being, subject and relation. Thus it is, and remains, pure gift. It is not given between some; rather, all are given. Nor are they given some thing; they are simply given. Love's gift of being is more commonly known by way of the doctrine of creation. Thus creation is another name for gift; another name for eucharist. Jean-Luc Marion argues that the idolatry of eucharistic consciousness is dependent upon a certain conception of time. It views time as the present moment which determines past and future. If there is presence it is now, valid only 'as long as the present of consciousness measures it and imparts the present to it starting from the consciousness of the present'.[50]

This is the ordinary conception of time, and it constitutes the 'function, stake, and characteristic' of metaphysics as a whole, from Aristotle to Hegel.[51] The present moment, the here and now, assures consciousness of that which is, in the present moment. The here and now constitutes the past as that which ends when the present begins, and the future as that which begins when the present ends. Past and future are negatively determined; both nonpresent and nontime. Therefore they do not and cannot give an assurance of being to consciousness; that assurance is only conferred by the present. It is only in the here and now that there can be eucharistic presence. Thus a theology that would reduce eucharistic presence to the present moment of collective consciousness in the here and now, turns out to be more metaphysical than the transubstantiation it would criticize. 'Idolatry finds its metaphysical completion in the very enterprise that claimed to criticize an apparently metaphysical eucharistic theology.'[52]

Marion seeks to think eucharistic presence without yielding to the three forms of idolatry he identifies: the material idolatry of the transubstantial thing, the spiritual idolatry of collective consciousness, and the temporal idolatry of the ordinary conception of time:

> Can the Eucharistic presence of Christ as consecrated bread and wine determine, starting from itself and itself alone, the conditions of its reality, the dimensions of its temporality and the dispositions of its approach? Does Eucharistic presence suffice for its own comprehension?[53]

The eucharistic gift is not determined by the ordinary conception of time; it is not determined as the presence of the present moment, of the here and now. Rather the present is determined, is given, by the eucharistic gift. It is the present of the gift. 'Eucharistic presence must be understood starting most certainly from the present, but the present must be understood first as a gift that is given.'[54] Time must be understood according to the order of the gift; it must be understood as that which is given, rather than as that which gives. Time must be understood as gift: as creation.

Presence is to be understood starting from the gift. It is the gift which constitutes presence in the present. The eucharistic gift includes the fundamental terms of the temporality of the gift.[55] According to the order of the gift, the eucharistic present is temporalized not from the here and now, but from the past, the future and finally the present. From the past it is temporalized as memorial; from the future as eschatological announcement, and from the present as 'dailyness and viaticum'.[56] This is not the metaphysical concept of time, which understands the whole from the present; rather it is a gifted concept of time, which understands the present from the whole. It follows, according to Marion, that eucharistic presence is to be understood 'less in the way of an available permanence than as a new sort of advent'.[57]

The eucharistic present is temporalized from the past as memorial, but not in the sense of remembering what is no longer, of calling to mind a nonpresence. That would be to think the past from the here and now. 'It is a question of making an appeal, in the name of a past event, to God, in order that he recall an engagement (a covenant) that determines the instant presently given to the believing community.'[58] Thus the past event is understood as the pledge of the present moment: the advent of the Messiah. In the eucharist the people do not recall to mind the death, resurrection and ascension of Christ, as if they might have forgotten this, but rather remember before God that this event has not ceased to determine their day and future. 'The past determines the reality of the present – better, the present is understood as a today to which alone the memorial, as an actual pledge, gives meaning and reality.'[59]

Once we understand the temporalization of the present from the past we also understand its temporalization from the future. For the memorial is the pledge of an advent completed from the future. It is not simply a waiting, but an asking and a hastening of Christ's return. Already the future determines the present moment as its anticipation. 'The eucharist anticipates what we will be, will see, will love . . . In this way, "sometimes the future lives in us without our knowing it".'[60] Marion's quotation from Proust will remind us of McCabe's unknown language, and of the gift that is the forgetting condition.

Past and future are not the nonpresence of the ordinary conception of time, but the very determinants of the eucharistic present. What then of this present that they make possible? 'Each instant of the present must befall us as a gift: the day, the hour, the instant, are imparted by charity.'[61] The present day is never our possession. Marion invokes the figure of manna. Each day is given and gathered as was the manna in the wilderness. The Christian day, like Christian bread, is given daily and daily requested of the Father.

The eucharistic present is given by Christ: a present that is always anterior to itself because always already given in the memorial; and always in anticipation of itself because always already called to announce its completion from the future.[62] And in this gift of the present is the presence of the one from whom it comes. What we may call eucharistic time – the eucharistic present as moment and gift, temporalized from the past and the future, from the memorial and the anticipated glory – is the paradigm of every present moment, of every time as gift. 'The temporal present during which the eucharistic present endures resembles it: as a glory haloes an iconic apparition, time is made a present gift to let us receive in it the eucharistically given present.'[63]

The present of the eucharistic presence comes to us, confused by us, under the form of the here and now. This is because our charity does not have enough lucidity to see the present moment as a present gift.[64] We are incorrigibly, spontaneously idolatrous; we want to take possession of the day.

Jean-Luc Marion seeks to save transubstantiation from metaphysics for what may be loosely called a postmodern theology, by transcribing it from the idiom of ontology into that of temporality; not the temporality of metaphysics itself – the order of the here and now – but a properly Christian temporality that becomes the paradigm of every present moment.[65] It is the temporality of the Christian story.

In and through the present moment of the here and now there is given to us the good grace; a moment that is given, always already, from the past in which it is pledged and from the future it anticipates and in which it is completed. The narrative of our present is shaped equally by our past and by our expectations for the future. And in this given moment we receive the presence of Christ in the bread and wine he hands to us.

The gift of Christ himself enabling a return

Aquinas discusses gift as the personal and proper name of the Holy Spirit. It would seem that gift is not the personal name of the Spirit because it is the name of God's essence in relation to creation.[66] To this, Aquinas answers that a gift is given from someone to another, handed over and thus possessed, first by the donor – who has the gift to give – and then by the recipient – who is given the gift to have.

The gift of God is possessed either as essence, when the gift is identical with the giver; or as created thing, when the gift is different from the divine donor; or, thirdly, when the gift is related by origin to the giver. The Son belongs to the Father by origin, as does the Spirit to Father and Son. 'As one who belongs to the giver through origin, then, the Gift of God [Spirit] is distinct personally from the giver [Father and Son] and is a personal name.'[67]

> The gift is the very 'being-given', or givenness of God: God as 'donation'. . . . God's giving never leaves God's hands, in which are held all things as 'being-given' . . . God's 'gift', like God's 'utterance', names an eternal relationship of origin.[68]

Aquinas also teaches that gift is the proper name of the Spirit, as denoting the relationship of origin to Father and Son. However, outside of Aquinas' theology of the trinitarian relations – within a more mobile trinitarianism – we may surely name the Son as gift also. As Aquinas notes: 'There is Isaiah, "A Son is given to us." To be gift, then, fits the Son as much as it does the Holy Spirit.'[69] Christ is also given; and here as well, giver and gift are one.

In this giving of Christ we are given to one another also, in so far as we are incorporated into the body of Christ, written into his story, called on to the stage to perform his drama. Gift and given, Christ and the donees who receive him, are one. To receive the gift of God is to be incorporated into the Triune life, into the eternity of donation, of giving and receiving back again. Indeed, the unity of the body of Christ is the unity of giver, gift and given – of teller, story and listener; of playwright, play and player; of host, meal and guest – and the unity of the Body is the presence given in the present of the eucharist.[70]

In this way, perhaps, we can begin to say how the impossible logic of the gift is overcome in the gift that is simply the giving of God. For this giving exceeds the ontological conditions and limits of the 'impossible gift'. All the terms of the gift – donor, donation and donee – are collapsed into the one event that is finally the Body of Christ. God gives only himself. When God gives, nothing passes from God to someone else; rather God draws near. Nor is God given to someone else, for the 'someone else' is the being of the gift. 'It is a gift to no-one, but rather establishes creatures as themselves gifts.'[71] This is not to conceive God's giving as a 'pure gesture', giving only giving, without content.[72] For always what is given must be understood from Christ, and thus from the Body of Christ. The 'Body' is the being of the gift.

Here it seems that we must allow for an element of exchange or return in the divine donation. Yes – as John Milbank after Marion notes – it is right to say that no return can be made to God, 'since there is nothing extra to God that *could* return to him. God gives "to" no-one, but creates all *ex nihilo*, causes all by his grace, exemplary purity of gift, whose absolute gratuity and spontaneity removes it from all taint of exchange'.[73] Here, however, Milbank points us to the seeming paradox of 'absolute gratuity with absolute exchange'.[74] For what is given absolutely is an absolute return, for return to God is the being and beat of the human heart. We are made for God. And this is our possibility as free creatures – who are always already forgetting our giftedness – because of Jesus Christ, who is the perfect return of God's gift.

In him, 'infinite return is realised as perfect return, God's return of himself to himself, and it is disclosed to us that the divine created gift, which realises an inexorable return, is itself grounded in an intra-divine love which is relation and exchange as much as it is gift'.[75]

Thus we must recognize what Millbank calls the 'exchangist character of the divine gift'.[76] But in also recognizing the inexorability of God's gift – its character as grace such that its reception and return are inevitable and are themselves given by God – it becomes difficult to maintain the distinction between exchange and gift necessary to Derrida's problematic (the spatial passage of donation from donor to donee). For what is given is the return or exchange, if 'exchange' has meaning here.

The gift of return is given in the death of Christ on the cross – 'a man making an infinite and complete return to God' – which as sinners we refuse, but as members of the Body, accept.[77] It is this gift we receive in the eucharist; for which there can be no return other than to return to the God by whom and for whom we are given absolutely.[78]

Notes

1. A fifteenth-century poem quoted in Miri Rubin, *Corpus Christi: The Eucharist in Late Medieval Culture* (Cambridge: Cambridge University Press, 1991), pp. 307–8. It pictures Christ as the charter of our redemption. 'The Eucharist is God, and his offering, the charter [testament or gospel], is at once evidence of a sacrifice, and the sacrificed body itself' (p. 308).

2. On the importance of ritual for narrativist theology see Ronald L. Grimes, 'Narrative and ritual criticism', in *Ritual Criticism: Case Studies in Its Practice, Essays on Its Theory* (Columbia, South Carolina: University of South Carolina Press, 1990), pp. 158–73. I am grateful to Samuel Wells for drawing my attention to this work.

3. See further Catherine Pickstock, 'The sacred as polis: language as synactic event', *Literature and Theology*, 8 (1994), pp. 367–83, p. 376.

4. George Stroup, *The Promise of Narrative Theology* (London: SCM [1981] 1984), p. 254.

5. Stroup, *Promise of Narrative Theology*, p. 258.

6. See Pickstock on the rite of the synaxis in Pseudo-Dionysius's *Ecclesiastical Hierarchy* ('Sacred polis', p. 374). 'This, then, is what the hierarch reveals in the sacred rites, when he uncovers the veiled gifts, when he makes a multiplicity of what had originally been one, when the distributed sacrament and those receiving it are made perfectly one, when a perfect communion of all the participants is

achieved.' Pseudo-Dionysius, *The Complete Works*, tr. Colm Luibheid (New York: Paulist Press, 1987), p. 222 (444c). See further Paul Rorem, *Pseudo-Dionysius: A Commentary on the Texts and an Introduction to Their Influence* (New York: Oxford University Press, 1993), pp. 99–104.

7. Jacques Derrida, *Given Time: I Counterfeit Money*, tr. Peggy Kamuf (Chicago and London: University of Chicago Press, 1992), p. 7. Derrida's discourse is poised against Marcel Mauss's famous work of 1923–4, *The Gift: The Form and Reason for Exchange in Archaic Societies*, tr. W. D. Halls (London:Routledge, 1990) – for it 'speaks of everything but the gift' (Derrida, *Given Time*, p. 24).

8. Derrida, *Given Time*, p. 12. As Aquinas notes, 'a gift, according to Aristotle, is literally a giving that can have no return, i.e. it is not given with repayment in mind and as such denotes a giving out of good will'. St Thomas Aquinas, *Summa Theologiae*, vol. 7, tr. T. C. O'Brien (London: Eyre & Spottiswoode, 1976), 1a, 38, 2, *responsio*.

9. Derrida, *Given Time*, p. 7.
10. Derrida, *Given Time*, p. 12.
11. Derrida, *Given Time*, p. 11.
12. Derrida, *Given Time*, p. 13.
13. Derrida, *Given Time*, p. 14.
14. Derrida, *Given Time*, p. 16.
15. Derrida, *Given Time*, p. 17.
16. Derrida, *Given Time*, p. 18.
17. Derrida, *Given Time*, p. 20.
18. Derrida, *Given Time*, p. 24.
19. John Milbank, in a profound article published too late for proper digestion here, also takes up Derrida's problematizing of the gift and seeks a theological response in the idea of Christian *agapé* as 'purified gift-exchange', as 'delay and non-identical repetition', purged of all 'archaic agonistic components'. See John Milbank, 'Can a gift be given? Prolegomena to a future trinitarian metaphysic', *Modern Theology*, 11 (1995), pp. 119–61, p. 131.
20. St Thomas Aquinas, *Summa Theologiae*, tr. William Barden (London: Eyre & Spottiswoode, 1965), 3a, 75, 1.
21. Aquinas, *Summa Theologiae*, 3a, 74.
22. Aquinas, *Summa Theologiae*, 3a, 75, 1.
23. Aquinas, *Summa Theologiae*, 3a, 75, 4.
24. Richard Dawkins likens religion to a computer virus, see 'Is God a computer virus?' (*New Statesman and Society*, 18 December 1992/ 1 January 1993, pp. 42–5). Successful viruses are hard to detect, but there are typical symptoms: conviction without evidence or reason; feeling virtuous about this; thinking mystery a good thing. Catholics suffer from a particularly strong form of the virus, for they believe the 'Mystery of the Transubstantiation'. 'Any wimp in religion could believe that bread symbolically represents the body of Christ, but it takes a real, red-blooded Catholic to believe something as daft as the transubstantiation' (p. 44).

25. See G. Enger (P. J. Fitzpatrick), 'Some thoughts on the Eucharistic presence', in Herbert McCabe, *God Matters* (London: Geoffrey Chapman, 1987), pp. 130–45. See further P. J. Fitzpatrick, *In Breaking of Bread: The Eucharist and Ritual* (Cambridge: Cambridge University Press, 1993).
26. Jean-Luc Marion, *God Without Being: Hors Texte*, tr. Thomas A. Carlson, foreword by David Tracy (Chicago: University of Chicago Press, 1991), p. 164.
27. Karl Rahner and Herbert Vorgrimler, *Concise Theological Dictionary*, second edn (London: Burns & Oates, 1983), p. 510.
28. Gareth Moore, 'Transubstantiation for beginners', *New Blackfriars*, 67 (1986), pp. 530–7, p. 536. That Moore finds an analogy for transubstantiation in the order of monetary exchange cannot be considered accidental for a discussion that seeks to problematize ideas of 'gift' and 'exchange'. See further David Moss, 'Costly giving: on Jean-Luc Marion's theology of gift', *New Blackfriars*, 74 (1993), pp. 393–9. 'What is at stake for Marion . . . is the very possibility of our being delivered from the economic exchange of debt and account into "an entirely other exchange", characterised by "the play of donation, abandon and pardon"' (p. 394).
29. Moore, 'Transubstantiation for beginners', p. 537.
30. Marion, *God Without Being*, pp. 161–82.
31. Marion, *God Without Being*, p. 165.
32. Marion, *God Without Being*, pp. 165–6.
33. Marion, *God Without Being*, p. 167.
34. Marion, *God Without Being*, p. 167.
35. Marion, *God Without Being*, pp. 167–8. On the liturgical need for the 'deprioritisation of the psyche', see Pickstock, 'Sacred polis', p. 373.
36. Marion, *God Without Being*, p. 168.
37. Marion, *God Without Being*, p. 177.
38. Marion, *God Without Being*, p. 168.
39. Marion, *God Without Being*, p. 169.
40. Marion, *God Without Being*, p. 169.
41. McCabe, *God Matters*, p. 118.
42. McCabe, *God Matters*, p. 121.
43. McCabe, *God Matters*, p. 122.
44. McCabe, *God Matters*, p. 123.
45. McCabe, *God Matters*, p. 124.
46. McCabe, *God Matters*, p. 125.
47. McCabe, *God Matters*, p. 127.
48. McCabe, *God Matters*, p. 128. See Pickstock, 'Sacred polis', p. 377.
49. Much of Milbank's article, 'Can a gift be given?', is concerned to contest Marion's theology of charity beyond ontology, arguing for '*another* ontology, perhaps precisely an ontology of the gift, but all the same an ontology' (p. 137).
50. Marion, *God Without Being*, p. 170.
51. Marion, *God Without Being*, p. 170.
52. Marion, *God Without Being*, p. 171.

53. Marion, *God Without Being*, p. 171.
54. Marion, *God Without Being*, p. 171.
55. Marion, *God Without Being*, p. 172.
56. Marion, *God Without Being*, p. 172.
57. Marion, *God Without Being*, p. 172.
58. Marion, *God Without Being*, p. 172.
59. Marion, *God Without Being*, p. 173.
60. Marion, *God Without Being*, p. 174, quoting M. Proust, *A la recherche du temps perdu*, Pléiade, 2 (Paris, 1954), p. 639.
61. Marion, *God Without Being*, p. 175.
62. Marion, *God Without Being*, p. 176. See Pickstock, 'Sacred polis', pp. 379–81.
63. Marion, *God Without Being*, p. 175.
64. Marion, *God Without Being*, pp. 175–6.
65. Marion, *God Without Being*, p. 176.
66. Aquinas, *Summa Theologiae*, 1a, 38, 1.
67. Aquinas, *Summa Theologiae*, 1a, 38, 1, *responsio*.
68. Nicholas Lash, *Believing Three Ways in One God: A Reading of the Apostles' Creed* (London: SCM, 1992), pp. 92, 105. God's 'utterance' is of course the Word or Son. See further Jean-Luc Marion, 'Metaphysics and phenomenology: a relief for theology', tr. Thomas A. Carlson, *Critical Inquiry*, 20 (1994), pp. 572–91, pp. 587–9.
69. Aquinas, *Summa Theologiae*, 1a, 38, 2.
70. See further John D. Zizioulas, *Being as Communion: Studies in Personhood and the Church*, Contemporary Greek Thinkers 4 (Crestwood, NY: St Vladimir's Seminary Press, 1993).
71. Milbank, 'Can a gift be given?', p. 135.
72. Milbank makes this criticism of Marion; 'Can a gift be given?', pp. 133–4.
73. Milbank, 'Can a gift be given?', p. 134.
74. Milbank, 'Can a gift be given?', p. 135.
75. Milbank, 'Can a gift be given?', pp. 135–6.
76. Milbank, 'Can a gift be given?', p. 136.
77. Milbank, 'Can a gift be given?', p. 136.
78. This address is also published as the final chapter of my book *Telling God's Story* (Cambridge: Cambridge University Press, 1996).

8

Confession and Re-formation: Walter Hilton's Sacramental Theology

JOHN CLARK

Medieval theology of sacramental confession is often parodied as a crude magical act, more concerned with priestly power than with ensuring that true repentance accompanied the formal absolution. Certainly Aquinas' view of the priest's words as the 'form' of the sacrament and effective in themselves, provided no barrier was placed in their way, gave added impetus to such misconceptions. But even a century later the fourteenth-century English spiritual writer, Walter Hilton, was still assuming the older view, that the words of absolution were simply declaratory of a forgiveness already conferred by God. Some response, however, was required to contemporary Lollard objections. As John Clark observes, this was done by setting the sacrament in its wider context of the re-formation of the individual as a whole, within which baptism and eucharist also play their part. 'Mortal sin', for instance, was seen as a pattern of thought and behaviour rather than a single act. Might such stress on re-formation have weakened the force of the Reformation?

Personal re-formation in an unsettled age

The English mystic, Walter Hilton, is valued especially for the close integration of his teaching on prayer and on moral and spiritual growth with dogmatic belief and sacramental practice. He sets out explicitly matters which are taken for granted by the author of the *Cloud of Unknowing*, between whom and himself a close inter-connection may in fact be demonstrated.[1]

142

Hilton has a firm grasp of a rather conservative Augustinian theology cast in a scholastic mould, and is well grounded in a monastic theology which reaches back to the Desert Fathers and Cassian. He also draws heavily on Augustine, Gregory the Great, and Bernard and other early Cistercians, but it is significant in this respect that his higher training was in Canon Law rather than in theology as such. There is abundant circumstantial evidence that he studied at Cambridge;[2] he appears as a Bachelor of Civil Law at the Ely Consistory Court in 1375, but a manuscript tradition states that he was an Inceptor in Canon Law – that is, one who had qualified for the doctorate but had not actually taken it. The study of Civil Law could be a prelude to that of Canon Law. A Latin letter of Hilton's refers to his having renounced a promising legal career,[3] and his writings show a familiarity with Canon Law as well as an interest in moral theology.

Hilton was one of a circle of clerks and canonists associated with Thomas Arundel while Arundel was Bishop of Ely, and there is evidence that after Arundel was translated to York in 1378 this association continued, and that Hilton, with others, shared in Arundel's campaign for pastoral and spiritual orthodoxy in the northern Archdiocese. This campaign included a response to the 'enthusiastic' and potentially disruptive movements associated with followers of the great Yorkshire hermit Richard Rolle, and which emphasized Rolle's 'heat, sweetness and song' at the expense of other more sober and traditional elements in his teaching; it also provided an answer to the growing threat to church polity and to the accepted patterns and goals of spirituality which was posed by the Lollard movement; and, to judge especially from references in Hilton, it also had an eye to warding off any potential incursion of the antinomian 'Movement of the Free Spirit' which had proved so subversive on the mainland of Europe, and to which teachers such as Ruysbroeck had provided a clear-cut response.[4]

Hilton himself spent a period as a hermit, but a Latin letter reveals him as unfulfilled in this.[5] He was by inclination a pastor and also a man with a strong sense for living in community. Sensitive to the needs of others, and with his background in Canon Law, he was well equipped to deal with the situation of those living in the world as well as addressing vowed religious. He wrote a significant letter (in Latin) to a clerk of King Richard II who became a Carthusian of Beauvale,[6] but while his own writings were to be much respected by the Carthusians he himself joined the community of Augustinian Canons at Thurgarton near Nottingham about 1386; their 'mixed life' of practical action and of contemplation was clearly congenial to him. He died in 1396. It is during his years at Thurgarton that his major works were written, including especially the two books of the *Scale of Perfection*.[7]

The first Book is ostensibly at any rate addressed to an anchoress, and describes the way to contemplation through the renewal or 'reforming' of the image of God in man, occluded by the 'image of sin' in consequence of Adam's Fall. While the 'image of God' remains ineradicable in every human person, leaving open the possibility of responding to God's call to know and love him, the 'likeness' of God (cf. Gen. 1.26), conformity to God in virtue, has been lost, and has to be restored through responding to the grace of Christ[8] – through entering the narrow gate and taking up the Cross, as Christ bids us in the Gospel; Hilton repeats St Paul's injunction to 'mortification', to putting to death the old human nature in order that the life of Christ may grow in us.[9] The 'likeness' of Christ – his 'livery', with which, in Pauline terms, we have to be clothed – consists in the inter-related and inclusive virtues of humility and charity[10] through which the 'image of sin', rooted in pride and the related capital sins, is to be broken down.[11] The eminently wise and practical advice on sins and virtues in Book One ensured that this book was read widely by devout people living in the world as well as by the religious for whom it was intended. Closely related to this first Book and complementary to it, is the little book *Mixed Life*, addressed to a devout man of rank with social and family respon-sibilities living in the world.

The second Book of the *Scale*, which must have been com-pleted some time after the first Book, and can only have been finished shortly before Hilton's death, takes up the theme of 'reforming', basing this now explicitly on the teachings of St Paul: *Nolite conformari huic saeculo, sed reformamini in novitate sensus vestri* (Do not be conformed to this world, but be reformed in newness of your feeling, Rom. 12.2). Such a reforming is real and intrinsic to the soul, 'that you may be filled with knowledge of his will in all spiritual wisdom and understanding' (Col. 1.9 RSV); 'Be renewed in the spirit of your minds, and put on the new nature, created after the likeness of God in true righteousness and holiness' (Eph. 4.23–4 RSV).[12]

In this second Book, Hilton describes the progress of the spiri-tual life in terms of two basic stages: reforming in faith, where the inward renewal of the soul is believed to have taken place, on the authority of the Church, but where the inward renewal through the turning of the will to God is hardly perceptible, and the old habits and impulses to sin still press hard; and reforming in feeling, where this is no longer the case.[13] The reader has first simply to believe that renewal has taken place, and then, through grace, to live a just life as his faith requires. As purity of heart is recovered, reforming in faith alone gives place to reforming in feeling.[14]

Reforming in feeling is the disclosure of the supernatural work of grace in the soul, a 'lively feeling of grace'.[15] It is this deepened understanding of what constitutes contemplation, which now compels Hilton to say that 'reforming in feeling' is no 'optional extra' to the spiritual life, nor simply something that should be sought by vowed religious; but that it can and should be sought by every rational soul – every human soul that is made in the image of God[16] – precisely because this alone confers conformity to God's will in spontaneous obedience to the leading of the Holy Spirit: 'For all who are led by the Spirit of God are sons of God' (Rom. 8.14 RSV).[17]

Penance and the importance of intention

In this book, Hilton is at pains to relate the process of reforming especially to two sacraments of the Church through which 'reforming' is effected: baptism, and the sacrament of penance, which is seen as an extension of the baptismal process.

He makes the common distinction between the original sin of Adam, in which we are involved willy-nilly, and actual sin, the sins we knowingly and willingly commit. In line with the view commonly held in his day, he takes it that original sin entails the passing on not simply of an inherited weakness and tendency to sin through the loss of the intuitive awareness of God and of conformity to his will, but the guilt which Adam incurred. So Hilton, a generally sensitive and compassionate man, can say as a matter of course that an unbaptized child is a brand of hell. It is baptism which (in conveying the gift of faith in Christ's saving passion) cancels out the guilt of original sin, and in the case of an adult who is baptized – Hilton refers to the conversion of Jews and Moslems – cancels out also any actual sins committed before baptism.[18] Few modern Christians will share Hilton's ultra-Augustinian view of the status of the unbaptized, but most of Christendom continues rightly to affirm, as he does, that baptism is a real and effective sign of an inward and spiritual grace. No doubt there are points which a systematic theologian would want to add to his treatment – for instance, that baptism does confer a real gift of the Spirit – a gift of that Spirit whose work in the developed Christian life Hilton will later expound so powerfully.

Hilton's strongly ecclesial sense is exhibited in his expressed conviction that the soul is reformed from actual sins committed after baptism through the sacrament of penance. He gives a careful rationale for this, which is designed both to reassure those of orthodox persuasion who have tender consciences, and also to answer such as the Lollards who suppose that confession to God in the presence of a priest is superfluous. Any Christian, Hilton says, who has lost the likeness of God through mortal sin, if through grace he turns from his sin with contrition and purpose of amendment, and receives the sacrament of penance – or, if he cannot and has the will to do it – will have his person restored.[19]

Hilton accepts the common definition of venial sin as weakening the life of the soul, and of mortal sin as taking away the soul's life of communion with God.[20] It is interesting to compare him with St Thomas Aquinas (1225–74) who had taught that mortal sin, involving grave matter knowingly and wilfully committed against God, causes a sickness of the soul that is irreparable by any intrinsic principle – a fresh infusion of sanctifying grace is needed.[21] St Thomas' firm balance of act and intention caused him to qualify the bold passage in which one of his predecessors, William of St Thierry (1085–1148), had declared that in his denial of Christ, Peter did not lose charity. His fall was due to the infirmity of the flesh rather than to deliberate malice, William tells us, and so in spite of his action, his heart remained with Christ.[22] William's position is based on a primacy of intention, though a primacy less absolute than that advocated by his contemporary Peter Abelard (1079–1142), who held that all acts are in themselves morally neutral, and that intention alone constitutes merit or sin.[23]

Hilton like Thomas refuses to sunder intention and act. But in *Scale*, Book One,[24] building on what he has said earlier in a Latin letter,[25] he emphasizes the power of intention directed to God – an intention which he now explicitly identifies with God's gift of love for himself in the infused virtue of charity – to enable us to return readily to our course towards God after an involuntary fall.

When he comes elsewhere to define mortal sin, he characteristically looks behind the act to the intention. Some acts are so self-evidently evil to a healthy conscience and to the mind of the Church that to commit them must imply a previous disposition of mortal sin:

> The common grace, which is charity, stays whole whatever a man does, as long as his will and his intention is true to God, so that he does not wish to sin mortally – or else the deed that

he does wilfully is not forbidden as a mortal sin . . . It is mortal sin when his conscience deliberately testifies that it is mortal, and nevertheless he still does it; or else his conscience is so blind that he considers it no mortal sin, although he wilfully does a deed which as mortal sin is forbidden by God and by holy Church.[26]

'Mortal sin' is a term applied by Hilton less to individual acts considered by themselves than to a total condition of the soul – a condition of blindness and self-will which hinders a person from turning to the light that shines in the darkness.[27] If one must speak of individual acts of mortal sin, these are significant not so much for themselves as for their disclosure of the bad state of the will already existing. An act of mortal sin in gluttony is seen as the outcome of a condition of mortal sin in pride and envy.[28]

Absolution as declaratory of forgiveness

Hilton's emphasis on the priority of intention has a corollary in his theology of sacramental absolution. He assumes purity of intention in going to confession – sorrow for sin arising from love of God rather than from shame before the world or fear of hell.[29] In this context, absolution is seen as declaratory of a forgiveness already conferred by God. The act of going to confession and receiving absolution after being in mortal sin is an act of humility leading to reconciliation to the Church after one has already been forgiven by God through contrition, and also an act of satisfaction for the wrong that has been done:

> This is a great courtesy of our Lord's . . . , who so easily forgives all kinds of sin and so promptly gives abundant grace to a sinful soul that asks him for mercy. He does not wait for great penance to be done or for painful bodily suffering before he forgives it, but he asks for a loathing of sin and a full forsaking by the will of the soul, for love of him, and a turning to him of the heart: this he asks, because this he gives . . . The sin is forgiven, so that the soul shall not be damned. Nevertheless, the punishment due for the sin is not yet fully forgiven unless contrition and love are the greater; and therefore he is to go and show himself and make confession to his spiritual father, and receive the penance enjoined for his trespass.

> This is the just ordinance of holy Church . . . , that though the sin may be forgiven by virtue of contrition, nevertheless, in fulfilment of humility and to make complete satisfaction, he shall if

he can make plenary confession to his priest, for that is his
token and his warrant of forgiveness against all his enemies . . .
For since he has forfeited both to God and to holy Church, it
is proper for him to have forgiveness from the one and a warrant from the other.[30]

At this point Hilton is re-stating what he had earlier written in
a Latin letter to a layman who had experienced a religious conversion and was wishing to enter a religious Order – a course
from which Hilton did his best to dissuade him, since the man
was unsuited to the religious life. This layman was beset with
doubts and scruples, and Hilton expounds the 'declaratory' theology of sacramental absolution there at greater length to reassure
his reader that God has indeed forgiven him upon his repentance,
and that if there were any sins which he had forgotten to mention
in his confession, his general intention of repentance is sufficient.[31] Hilton will return later in Book Two, to the need for firm
faith in the reality of God's forgiveness, and to the rejection of
scruples as to any sins that one may have omitted inadvertently
to confess.[32]

Also in this Latin letter Hilton makes use of the traditional –
and very telling – illustration of the raising of Lazarus (John 11)
to illustrate the importance of sacramental absolution. This
illustration is already found in Gregory the Great, while its continuing popularity in the Middle Ages is illustrated through its
inclusion in Peter Lombard's *Sentences* and Gratian's *Decretum*.
Christ raises Lazarus from death – symbolizing the death of sin;
but he instructs the disciples – representing the ministers of the
Church – to loose his grave-clothes and let him go.[33]

The insistence on purity of intention in contrition is in line
with the teaching of Peter Lombard (d. 1160)[34] and the earlier
penitential tradition, with some such mitigation as we find in later
scholastics, including St Bonaventure (1221–74). The latter
accepts that one may approach the sacrament of penance with
mixed motives; equally, he takes it that 'perfect contrition' is a
prerequisite for forgiveness. So he assumes that the process of
confession and absolution – taken as a whole – may effect a real
and perceptible purification of intention.[35]

St Thomas, however, goes beyond the older 'declaratory'
understanding of absolution. Building on the teaching of St
Albert the Great (1193–1280), he sees the sacrament of penance,
of which the words of absolution are, in Aristotelian terminology,
the 'form', as an effective sign – like all the other sacraments –

conferring in a real sense the benefit which it represents.[36] Corresponding with this, St Thomas allows that one may approach this sacrament with less than perfect contrition, but says that this imperfect contrition suffices for justification, provided that one does not put obstacles in the way of grace.[37]

Hilton goes on to mention two further good reasons for going to confession. Absolution is a source of reassurance to those who are 'reformed in faith only', without as yet an experiential awareness of God's love and grace active in their souls. Second, it is in the course of this sacrament that many are led to proper repentance, and so to forgiveness, who else would not have felt sorrow for their sin.[38]

Although Hilton's theology of absolution is basically 'declaratory', he does see the sacrament in its totality as having a creative value. Just as baptism effects a hidden renewal in a child, just so a person who has been encumbered with mortal sin all his life, 'by the sacrament of penance, humbly and truly received . . . is reformed in his soul within – imperceptibly, except for the conversion of his will through a secret power and a gracious action of the Holy Spirit'.[39] Again, someone in mortal sin may be 'restored to life through the sacrament of penance'.[40]

Hilton says that if all men had been close to God in spirit, the Church might well not have ordained that all should go to confession. (He is referring to the decree *Omnis utriusque sexus* of the Fourth Lateran Council in 1215, enjoining confession before Easter each year.) But we do live in an imperfect world, so all are expected to use the sacrament.

Such is his answer to those who say that confession in the presence of a priest is unnecessary. This must be a reference to the Lollards.[41] Hilton takes it that the great mass of Christians who are 'reformed in faith' only, and yet who have no intention of committing mortal sin, will still want to go to confession and make an act of reparation for the lighter faults that they have committed.[42] Later in Book Two Hilton will be at pains to emphasize the essential importance of passing through the 'luminous darkness' of mortification, the passage from the false day of disordered self-love to the true day of love of God.[43] In this he is developing further what he has already said in Book One. But this is now given added point by the need to combat those who suppose that there is a short cut to contemplation, apart from the disciplines of the Church. Hilton readily grants that God may give his gifts of grace where he will,[44] but points to the pride and the divisive attitude of those who scorn the Church's laws, who claim that what they do is humility and obedience to the gospel, but whose exaltation of themselves and contempt of others gives the lie to their claim.[45] For Hilton, the sacrament of penance remains a powerful force for growth in humility and charity within the life of the Church.

Faith and feeling in the eucharist

While Hilton gives explicit and systematic teaching on the sacraments of baptism and penance, his teaching on the eucharist is almost incidental. No doubt this is because while in his day everyone attended the eucharist, the reception of the sacrament was infrequent. The eucharist was a focus of the devotion to the Real Presence of Christ and an expression of the unity of the Church, but the regular disciplines of prayer and meditation which Hilton enjoins were intended to take place on a daily basis – something which outstripped the actual reception of the sacrament.

Hilton affirms the need for a 'firm belief in all the articles of the faith and sacraments of holy Church', and for resisting any diabolical suggestion to doubt them.[46] Later in the same book, he describes the temptations that may assail the soul in times of spiritual aridity. It is a context heavily influenced by a work of the Augustinian friar William Flete (fl. 1358–80), *Remedies Against Temptations (De Remediis contra Tentationes)*, but Hilton is not following Flete, but rather reflecting contemporary difficulties with the Lollards, when he speaks of temptation to 'disbelief in articles of the faith, or in the sacrament of God's body . . . , or blasphemy toward our Lord or any of his saints'.[47]

There is another explicit eucharistic reference in *The Pricking of Love*, an English version of the popular *Stimulus Amoris*, a Latin work compiled by various hands on the basis of a book by the thirteenth-century Franciscan James of Milan. This English version, which contains a number of expansions for which there is no equivalent in the Latin, is attributed in some manuscripts to Hilton and may well, on internal evidence, be his, though his authorship is not beyond dispute. The *Pricking* follows the Latin in saying that if we feel no affection in receiving the eucharist, it is a sign of spiritual sickness, but then goes beyond the Latin to observe that this may be permitted by God in order that we may be humbled.[48] In *Scale*, Book Two, Hilton applies his distinction between 'faith' and 'feeling' especially to the progress towards an experiential realization of the grace covered in the sacraments of baptism and penance. This finds a certain parallel in the *Pricking*:

For though a man may not immediately feel sweetness and spiritual savour in this worthy sacrament, he shall not despair on that account, but await patiently the grace of God, and do what is in him to have it. For a sick man when he receives a medicine is not whole immediately, but he hopes through it to be whole.[49]

There is a further point in the *Scale* where Hilton does not explicitly refer to the eucharist but where he speaks of the oblation of the Christian life – of that oblation which is an extension of our participation in the offering of Christ in the eucharist:

> Whether you pray or meditate, or do anything else . . . , cast it all in the mortar of humility and pound it small with the pestle of the fear of God, throw the powder of all these things in the fire of desire, and offer it to God . . . St Paul taught us so when he said: . . . Whether you eat or drink, or whatever kind of work you do, do it all in the name of our Lord Jesus Christ (1 Cor. 10.31) . . .[50]

This stands close in intention to the words of Hilton's contemporary in *The Cloud of Unknowing* – words which suggest the *Sursum corda* of the eucharist: 'Lift up your heart to God with a humble impulse of love'.[51]

Notes

1. *Walter Hilton: The Scale of Perfection*, ed. J. P. H. Clark and R. Dorward (New York: Mahwah, Paulist Press, 1991), pp. 25–6. All references to the text of the *Scale of Perfection* are to this edition.
2. Hilton, *Scale*, pp. 13ff.
3. *Walter Hilton's Latin Writings*, ed. J. P. H. Clark, *Analecta Cartusiana* 124, 2 vols (Salzburg: Institut für Anglistik und Amerikanistik, 1987), p. 262.
4. Hilton, *Scale*, pp. 28ff.
5. Hilton, *Latin Writings*, pp. 90–1.
6. Hilton, *Epistola de Utilitate et Prerogativis Religionis*, *Latin Writings*, pp. 103–72.
7. Hilton, *Scale*, pp. 15–21, discusses the chronology and canon of Hilton's writings, and the relation to the *Scale* of the other writings.
8. Hilton, *Scale*, 1, 42–3, pp. 112–15; 45, pp. 117–18; *Scale*, 2, 1–2, pp. 93–196.
9. Hilton, *Scale*, 1, 42, p. 113.

10. Hilton, *Scale*, 1, 51, p. 123: cf. 1, 62, pp. 133–4; etc.
11. Hilton, *Scale*, 1, 52–6, pp. 123–7; 63–4, pp. 134–5; 69, p. 139; 71, pp. 142–4; 73, pp. 146–7; 76, p. 148; 84–8, pp. 154–8.
12. Hilton, *Scale*, 2, 31, pp. 257–8.
13. Hilton, *Scale*, 2, 5, pp. 199–200.
14. Hilton, *Scale*, 2, 11, pp. 210–11.
15. Hilton, *Scale*, 2, 40, p. 284.
16. Hilton, *Scale*, 2, 41, pp. 287–8.
17. Hilton, *Scale*, 2, 35, p. 268.
18. Hilton, *Scale*, 2, 6, pp. 200–1 with notes.
19. Hilton, *Scale*, 2, 7, p. 201.
20. Hilton, *Scale*, 1, 87, pp. 156–7. Hilton's moral and sacramental theology is discussed in more detail by J. P. H. Clark, 'Intention in Walter Hilton', *Downside Review*, 97 (1979), pp. 69–80.
21. Thomas Aquinas, *Summa Theologiae* 1–2, q, 72 a 5; q. 88 a1–a2.
22. Aquinas, *Summa Theologiae* 2–2, q. 4 a 12. William's teaching is found in *De Natura et Dignitate Amoris*, Patrologia Latina 184, 389–90.
23. Peter Abelard, *Scito Teipsum*, 3, 5, 7 (Patrologia Latina 178, 640; 644; 647F; 650F); cf. D. E. Luscombe, *The School of Peter Abelard* (Cambridge: Cambridge University Press, 1969), p. 139.
24. Hilton, *Scale*, 1, 22, pp. 95–6.
25. Hilton, *Latin Writings*, p. 234.
26. Hilton, *Scale*, 2, 41, pp. 288–9.
27. Hilton, *Scale*, 2, 16, p. 218.
28. Hilton, *Scale*, 1, 72, p. 145; cf. 1.82, p. 152.
29. Hilton, *Scale*, 2, 10, p. 206.
30. Hilton, *Scale*, 2, 7, pp. 201–2.
31. Hilton, *Latin Writings*, pp. 265–78.
32. Hilton, *Scale*, 2, 22, p. 231.
33. Hilton, *Latin Writings*, p. 268, with notes.
34. In Peter Lombard, for the demand of perfect contrition, see *Sententiae* 4, d. 15, c. 1; for the 'declaratory' understanding of absolution, d. 17 c. 1; d. 18, cc. 4–7.
35. Bonaventure, *In Sent.* 4, d. 17, p. 2, a 2, q. 3. St Bonaventure goes on to speak of the role of the priest as praying with and for the penitent, as well as exercising a juridical function – *In Sent.* d. 18, p. 1, a 2, q. 1.
36. Aquinas, *Summa Theologiae*, tr. Reginald Masterson and T. C. O'Brien (London: Eyre & Spottiswoode, 1965), 3a, 84, 3, with 62, 1. For St Albert's teaching, see *Dictionnaire de Théologie Catholique*, art. 'Pénitence', cols 958–9.
37. Aquinas, *Summa Theologiae*, Supplementum 18, 1 (= *In Sent.* 4, d. 18 q. 1 a 3 qa. 1).
38. Hilton, *Scale*, 2, 7, p. 202.
39. Hilton, *Scale*, 2, 8, p. 203.
40. Hilton, *Scale*, 2, 17, p. 220.
41. Hilton, *Scale*, 2, 7, pp. 202–3.

42. Hilton, *Scale*, 2, 10, p. 205.
43. Hilton, *Scale*, 2, 24, pp. 234–8.
44. Hilton, *Scale*, 2, 26, pp. 240–1.
45. Hilton, *Scale*, 1, 21, p. 94.
46. Hilton, *Scale*, 1, 37, p. 108, with notes.
47. Walter Hilton, *The Prickynge of Love*, ed. H. Kane (Salzburg: Institut für Anglistik und Amerikanistik, 1983) 2 vols, ch. 22, p. 122. Discussed by J. P. H. Clark, 'Walter Hilton and the "Stimulus Amoris"', *Downside Review*, 102 (1984), p. 92.
48. Hilton, *Prickynge*, p. 122; discussed by Clark, 'Walter Hilton'.
49. Hilton, *Scale*, 1, 23, pp. 96–7.
50. *The Cloud of Unknowing*, ed. J. Walsh (New York: Mahwah, Paulist Press, 1981), ch. 3, p. 119.

PART THREE
WORDS MEDIATING THE WORD

Word and sacrament are often contrasted, and indeed in some liturgies the eucharist is seen as a two-stage process: first, the ministry of the word and then the ministry of the sacrament. Though right and proper in its place, there is also something to be said on the other side. Two factors in particular merit consideration. First, language is itself a system of symbols; like water or bread and wine a means of conveying something other than itself. Second, as we have already noted, the most explicit use of incarnational language in the New Testament makes use of the image of language: 'And the Word was made flesh, and dwelt among us' (John 1.14). The notion of language as more than declaration or preaching would thus seem embedded in the very foundations of the Christian faith. Like the themes of the two previous sections, incarnation and sacrament, the richness of language and its metaphors may therefore be said to exercise an intimate, mediating role, in which in some sense the symbols participate in the reality they are seeking to convey. But how?

Perhaps the most obvious way in which this issue raises itself is in the liturgy itself. Clearly it is not only the symbolic actions which mediate Christ; words also play a role. But how important is this? What sort of images should be used, and how familiar should they be? Stephen Sykes in his contribution argues for the indispensability of repetition.

But in an age in which we are bombarded by words as never before, whether printed or in the constantly playing television or radio, there is a temptation to long for a silent mediation of the divine that bypasses such channels. This finds its most obvious

focus in nature, and no doubt explains the rise of various movements in our own day both in and outside the Church. Nonetheless,
our last three essays throw up some warning signals. John Riches
observes that though the Swiss theologian, Hans Urs von Balthasar,
was keen to offer a form of sacramentalism based on creation, in
the end he thought this only possible if mediated through literature, in particular the poetry of Gerard Manley Hopkins. David
Fuller takes a specific aspect of nature, sexual love, and observes
the way in which the sixteenth-century Anglican poet, Edmund
Spenser, uses the language of his poetry to wrestle with the question of whether or not such love might be described as sacramental,
and if so, in what sense. Finally, Peter Phillips, taking a poet and a
theologian as his examples, illustrates the way in which the
Romantic tradition has always seen the need for such mediation,
in decisive moments of disclosure, whether it be through poetry
(as in Wordsworth) or through art (as with Tillich). The powerful
metaphor or visual image helps us to focus upon what is already
there.

9

Ritual and the Sacrament of the Word

STEPHEN SYKES

The free availability of numerous versions of Scripture and a parallel diversity in forms of liturgy has meant, Stephen Sykes argues, the loss of something very important: the sacramental imprinting upon our consciousness of key phrases that can act as a resource for us in time of need. Protestantism has traditionally been suspicious of ritual, but its emergence in both word and deed is inevitable; so what matters is the avoidance of meaningless repetition, rather than repetition itself. Contemporary historians and philosophers have alike made us acutely aware of the issue of power. The essay therefore ends by asking how agreed patterns of repetition can avoid the accusation of being the alien impositions of an élite. For the author the answer is to be found in treating the biblical narrative as normative.

The sacramentality of repetition

In this essay I shall argue that among the neglected resources at the Church's disposal are rituals and the practice of repeating the same things frequently. My reason for mounting the argument is because rituals and repetitions are undervalued or under attack, sometimes for no better reason than that it is a strand in our culture to want variety. Variety is the vehicle of novelty, and of novelty we cannot have enough.

My domestic target here is implicitly the Church of England's 1980 Alternative Service Book, which is the most conspicuous local monument to liturgical variety. In practice, of course, a given parish church adopts its own version of the liturgy and repeats that. So in the end not too much harm is done. But the message of that book is, clearly, that hardly anyone should be denied a variant if they can mount a plausible argument in its favour. The great bishop Hensley Henson once observed that a rubric saying that something shall be done seemed to a certain type of Anglican cleric a provocative challenge to his authority. So now we have a book of variants which perfectly corresponds to the inclinations of a liturgically literate élite, and equally perfectly mirrors that élite's lack of self-confidence.

But within my sights explicitly is another, more considerable target, which is the question of who is authorized to determine the rituals and repetitions of the liturgy. If, as I shall suggest, this is among the most far-reaching decisions any church can make, then it is not enough to point to its legally competent decision-making body. Imposing a liturgy is, on my assumption, a very considerable act of power, locating the worshippers in a particular social space, constructing the horizons of their world, and prompting them to, or dissuading them from, certain courses of action. It is, in short, an archetypal mode of domination, all the more insidious for working subliminally. Who is entitled to do that? The answer I propose at the close of my discussion will, I believe, take us to the heart of the ecumenical issue. Liturgies, I shall argue, need to stand as close as possible to the narrative and metaphors of God's self-revelation if they are to achieve this strong sense of being authorized. Otherwise, the danger of their being an arbitrary and dominating imposition is very great. There is more here than one single essay can achieve. But my hope is that at least the portion I delineate will be clear.

I once went to visit an old man in mental hospital. I was a young priest, and he an old one, retired after a lifetime of distinguished service to the Church, a man of deep and sincere piety upon whom the terrors of a senile depression, probably of organic origin, had fallen. He sat in his dog-collar beside his bed, wrapped in misery. He refused to look his visitors in the eye, and when addressed either turned away or repeated over and over again that when certain (imaginary) facts about his life were publicly known, his good name and that of his family would be destroyed. I attempted to reason with him without avail. I talked brightly of other things, and he stared fixedly away, insisting that God had abandoned him. I put out my hand to hold his, and he withdrew it as if it were leprous. Finally in desperation I seized a prayer book, and opening it at random read from the Psalms 'The Lord is full of compassion and mercy', and immediately he replied with the other half verse 'Longsuffering, and of great goodness' (Ps. 103.8 BCP). A moment later he added, sadly, 'But that is not for me'.

The immediacy of the recall of that sentence, however, convinced me that something good had happened. Of course, part of his spiritual discipline as an Anglican priest had been the reading of the Psalms. He was not accustomed, I knew, to a daily eucharist. His piety was strongly focused on the study of the Bible. He was scholar enough to be clear that the Authorised Version contained obscurities and even mistakes, but that and Coverdale's psalms had been for more than sixty years his meat and drink. So he knew them, if not by heart, then to the point where a prompt could trigger immediate recollection of the context.

Now this, I believe, is worth reflecting on, since memory is a function of the brain, and the brain is a physical entity. An incarnational and sacramental religion like Christianity makes much of the fact of this bodiliness, and rightly. It is, according to William Temple, the most materialistic of all religions. Yet evangelical piety, though insistent on the doctrine of the incarnation of the divine Word, and on belief in a bodily resurrection, sometimes distances itself from the physicality of sacramentalism, preferring to speak of obedience to the divine Word in Scripture and proclamation. Christians of that persuasion would not naturally rely on the objectivity of the sacrament under conditions of doubt and distress. Rather they would look for reassurance from the interiorization of an objective promise of faith. The interesting feature of my experience with the elderly priest is precisely the discovery that what has been committed to memory is physically within us, and has become as much part of us as the physical reception of the host at the eucharist. It is indeed the Word made flesh tabernacling among us.

Further, if we take seriously the thought that the priest I had visited had within his memory a veritable bank of resonances and recollections drawn from his knowledge of the Authorised Version and Coverdale's psalms, then the act of citing one verse may have had further repercussions. From the psalm I had quoted come the following verses:

He will not always be chiding: neither keepeth he his anger for ever. He hath not dealt with us after our sins: nor rewardeth us according to our wickednesses. For look how high the heaven is in comparison of the earth: so great is his mercy also toward them that fear him. Look how wide also the east is from the west: so far hath he set our sins from us. (Ps. 103, 9–12 BCP)

Or again we might consider the word 'compassion', in the frequency of its use in the Authorised Version in relation to Jesus' ministry itself: 'Jesus, moved with compassion, put forth his hand, and touched him, and saith unto him, I will; be thou clean' (Mark 1.41). Here is the Lord, full of compassion and mercy, touching and healing a leprous hand. That the human mind has this capacity for combinations and connections, and delights in them, is, together with rhythm and rhyme, the power and attraction of poetry. One does not need oneself to be a creative poet, to enjoy and be nourished by these associations, through the subliminal activity of our unconscious minds.

Protestantism and 'vain repetition'

A story of this kind puts in some perspective the recent history of biblical translation and liturgical change. Such gains as have been made in the freshness and impact of new versions and forms of worship have come at the expense of our capacity to learn passages of Scripture by heart. Is that just nostalgic illusion? I think not. A chaplain in a mental hospital tells the story of an elderly woman, with the ward reputation for being very withdrawn and difficult, who recited for him by heart the whole of the prayer of consecration. That is something which many priests now cannot do. One does not learn what one does not repeat or hear in precisely the same words, time after time. And these resources of memory matter to us, not just for the extraordinary circumstances I have described, but for ordinary recall with all the supportive associations of familiarity, comfort and above all hope. The nervous flitting from text to text, which sometimes goes under the euphemistic heading of 'enrichment', is an all-too-faithful reflection of the superficiality of our culture and its obsessive fear of boredom. The losses entailed have until recently rarely been given adequate attention.

But there is also, of course, to be taken into account nonsense and vain repetition. 'But when ye pray,' says Jesus to his disciples, 'use not vain repetitions, as the heathen do: for they think they shall be heard for their much speaking . . . After this manner therefore pray ye: Our Father which art in heaven . . .' (Matt. 6.7–9 AV). It is ironic that the most frequently repeated prayer of all in the Christian tradition should follow an injunction against vain repetition. Whatever may have been meant by this prohibition, it has not prevented classical Christianity from developing standard forms of prayer. It seems that we shall be in need of a distinction between repetition and vain repetition, much as Mary

Douglas in her classic discussion of ritual found that she needed a distinction between ritual and 'ritualized' ritual: 'It is fair enough that "ritualised" ritual should fall into contempt. But it is illogical to despise all ritual, all symbolic actions as such. To use the word ritual to mean empty symbols of conformity, leaving us with no word to stand for symbols of genuine conformity, is seriously disabling to the sociology of religion.'[1]

Here I wish to recall with some affection the actions of my strictly Protestant and Calvinist father, in the church of which he was priest-in-charge. At the end of the office of Matins or Evensong, and before the sermon, he would go to the vestry with his senior church warden, take off his surplice and scarf, and put on his Cambridge MA gown and hood; and thus arrayed in the garments of the learned teaching ministry he would walk to the pulpit. I used the words 'go' and 'walk', but it was of course a procession, without exception in the same order. If challenged, of course, he would most strenuously have denied that he was engaged in a ritual. A ritual for him would have been precisely an empty symbol of conformity; and this was no empty symbol. The churchwarden helped him into his hood and gown, and prayed with him before he left the vestry. There was no pride or pomposity in the movements; they were plain, orderly and practical. But they were also invariable and full of significance, a ritual but no 'ritualized' ritual. Although the Reformation is, in Mary Douglas' account, largely responsible for anti-ritualism in Christianity, in practice it is enormously difficult to be consistently anti-ritualistic, not least in Protestantism. Even so-called extempore prayer quickly falls into established patterns. Turns of phrase which embody a theology satisfactory to the intercessor tend to recur, as do movements and bodily postures. Knees may be less flexible than hands, but there is still a limitation to what the joints will stand. I can see no sensible distinction as ritual between jigglings and genuflexions, corybantic hand waving and crossing oneself. One is not sincerer than the other; both may become empty forms.

The distinction between ritual and ritualized ritual, or between repetition and vain repetition has to do with meanings and the internalizing of religious experience. Drawing on Douglas again, we may note three phases in the move away from ritualism. First is contempt of external ritual forms; second is the private internalizing of religious experience; and third, the move towards humanist philanthropy. Of these it is the second which ought to occupy our attention.

The emphasis on interiority is unmistakeable in the

Reformation. Luther classically developed a separation between physical or external, and spiritual or internal Christianity. It turns out to be more obscure than it appears at first sight, but the intention is clear.[2] Externals belong to the realm of works. Justification by faith alone is the secret work of God upon the heart of humankind. Externals of all kind are of the devil unless preceded by the life-changing, interior transformation of one's standing before God. Once it is established that worship, including sacramental worship, is not offered in the hope that it will appear meritorious in God's sight, it ceases to be vain. Calvin's commentary on 'vain repetition' makes precisely this point:

> Christ is checking the folly of those who, to persuade God, and to win Him over, pour out a great flood of speech. This is not opposed to the teaching that persistence in prayer wins frequent approval in Scripture. When we come to pray with serious intention, the tongue does not outrun the heart, nor is God's favour secured by an empty flow of words, but rather, the longings which the devout heart sends out like arrowshoots are those that reach to heaven. This condemns, of course, the superstition of those who trust they will win merit with God for long mutterings . . .[3]

The general Reformation tradition of attending to intention leaves undecided the status of the external act. On the one hand, it might be taught that it was unsafe to develop rituals and repetitions, and quite unlawful (as being contrary to Christian freedom) to enforce them. On the other hand it could be argued that, since forms of repetition and ritual were unavoidable it would be preferable to determine what these forms should be than to leave them to the vagaries of local custom or individual whim. The latter is, indeed, the position for which I propose to argue, but to do so in the context of an account which fully recognizes the power of such a liturgy, and the radical objection to enforcing it.

Foucault and the question of power

We need first to address the question of the power of ritual and repetition. The psychological context of public worship is that of heightened sensibility and focused attention. It deals with the range of human emotion, from a sense of sorrow for the intolerable burden of sin, to the joy of a liberated and transformed prisoner. To worship is to focus the attention. As Simone Weil said, prayer is 'attention in its pure form', and is aided by studies which are 'a form of gymnastics of the attention'.[4] In Christian worship, the being of God the Holy Trinity provides a focal unity-in-plurality, sustaining a great variety and richness. It is this richness which has classically given rise to spiritualities of both breadth and inti- macy, capable of combining the externality of creation with the interior depths of consciousness. This astonishing range needs to be remembered when we offer the view that the power of ritual and repetition derives from the structuring of this variety, its incorporation into a single, albeit complex, narrative whole. It is within a single narrative that we learn both of the glory and mis- ery of humanity, of creation, fall and redemption, of an old order groaning for its liberation, and of community already enjoying by anticipation elements of the banquet of the last days. The narra- tive implies not merely a temporal pilgrimage, but an interior journey through a spiritual landscape, a geography of the heart, which has unfathomable depths, and yearnings for unseen heights.

It is in the context of this narrative that the Church proposes to set the life-history of the believer, from the earliest dawning of consciousness to the last breath, and to be there as the major life-transitions are negotiated, to provide familiar words for those who rejoice and those who mourn. The narrative is loosely enough drawn to be open to creative addition or subtraction. It provides resonances as well as repetitions. It does not merely illuminate and inform; it casts doubts and raises problems, and has given rise to a formidable tradition of philosophical interpre- tation and speculation. The narrative lends itself to being subtly recast, by the emphasizing of now one, now another feature. It is not univocal, but multivocal. The liturgical framework for the narrative is provided by a memorable creed, which briefly high- lights certain leading features, and establishes certain language habits as normative. The ritual specifies what shall be done when the congregation assembles and meets together. It thus transmits a specific culture, and in so doing acculturates the participants to its way of seeing the world. Moreover it locates the worshipper in a specific world of meaning as sinner or saint, denier or believer, insider or outsider, lost or saved. All the transactions of worship are laid across the alternatives in such a way as to provide a route from one to the other. Conversion or transformation of status is the constantly reiterated opportunity. It is a conformation to the baptismal promise of moving from death to life, of 'continually mortifying all our evil and corrupt affections, and daily proceed- ing in all virtue and godliness of living'.[5]

To describe the power of ritual and repetition in such a way is to become aware of resistances. It is ordinary experience that some of those who are most assiduous about religious observances are strangely unaffected by them, to the point where suspicion arises that participation in the rituals serves completely other ends. Human motives are exceptionally obscure, and self-deception is an everyday occurrence. It must be the case that the act of gathering one's distracted gaze to focus upon God is by no means easy; the conforming of one's conflicting desires and intentions to a single pattern of faith, hope and love an elusive project.

But, precisely as one attempts to do justice to the capacity of Christian liturgy to locate a person in a particular landscape and journey, a more radical objection springs to mind. The French philosopher Michel Foucault gives a disturbing analysis of the genesis of modern individuality. He argues that knowledge bestows power. Power 'produces reality; it produces domains of objects and rituals of truth. The individual and the knowledge that may be gained of him belong to this production.'[6] He goes on to say that discipline operates through the anterior acceptance of what is normal. Bentham's *Panopticon* (the nineteenth-century 'model' penitentiary, where the inmates are housed on wings radiating from a central block, from which the governor can see them all as they supposedly reflect upon their offences) is, Foucault suggests, the architectural figure of a type of surveillance which induces the individual person, as 'prisoner', to make the constraints of power 'play spontaneously upon himself . . . he becomes principal of his own subjection'.[7] Under the universal reign of the normative, teachers, doctors, educators, social workers (and, one must add, priests) create what Foucault calls 'a carceral network', in which souls are at once manufactured and imprisoned.

In Foucault's account, Christian rituals are not directly in view, except in so far as monasticism provides the scholastic background for modern educational disciplines. But it is not possible to read his account of panopticism without recalling that God is, in the Christian tradition, the only one 'unto whom all hearts are open, all desires known, and from whom no secrets are hid'.[8]

Foucault's analysis of how power and knowledge work is by no means beyond question on historical grounds, and has been most effectively criticized in detail. He himself seems to have felt the oddity of being an educator, a professor at the Collège de France. His own attempts to tell a kind of truth about modernity are not immune from the corrupting mutual impact of the mechanisms of power and knowledge; nor do his books explode once read, as he disarmingly suggested was his preference. But even when we have made these observations about Foucault himself, and the ambiguities of his own position, we may still owe to his work the realization that those who determine the content of Christian liturgy exercise a power of constriction, not just of text, but of the life of a whole community, for good or ill. This point deserves serious attention.

Power and liturgical uniformity

I should add, as an Anglican, that the question of who imposed the various versions of the Book of Common Prayer through the successive Acts of Uniformity is now historically unavoidable, because of the work of the Reformation historian, Dr Eamon Duffy.[9] Far from sweeping away the last dregs of a debased and hypocritical religion of works, he has shown that the early English Reformation destroyed a delicate and nuanced pattern of lay piety which was devoutly believed in, as well as practised. The Reformation only 'worked' because it was ruthlessly imposed by force. In an apt metaphor a well placed observer said in 1553 that the new religion 'is not yet printed in the stomachs of eleven of twelve parts of the realm'.[10] The imposition of the Prayer Book was an instrument, in due course largely successful, of the transformation of consciousness. But behind the priest holding the book was the monarch holding the sword. Is therefore the interiorization of this liturgy the principle of the individual's subjection?

I have raised, but do not intend to answer the question historically with reference to the English reformations, because the issue is capable of more general formulation. Indeed, as Foucault has presented the matter, there would be no essential distinction between the power of an army, or of a pontiff threatening excommunication, or of a literate élite with access to the relevant committees. Each would be a case of domination, and the means would amount to variants on a single theme. Startling though it has been to consider them in this light, the processes of consultation by which modern liturgies have been used 'experimentally' have lent themselves to sociological description as the manipulative activities of élites. It is an appropriate question whether the commissions and committees which prescribe the form of worship for the Christian churches are entitled so to do, bearing in mind what it is that they do. Is this an instance of domination, or could it be a form of freedom?

Two types of theological answer might be given to such a question. The first would relate to the theological status of the body which made the decision, whether this was the Papacy, the episcopate, or some form of synodical government. Church polities are a proper subject for theology, and since churches are bound to have decision-making powers, the legitimacy and theological appropriateness of the structure making the decisions about liturgies are a proper subject of theology. But such theologies vary and would need separate and more extensive discussion.

A second type of answer might exist, which would concern the specific form of the liturgy so authorized. In other words, it might be argued that a given body, though legally entitled to decide as it saw fit, would be constrained theologically by the very content of what it was deciding. In my view the force of Foucault's objection to the strategies of domination could only be resisted if the specific content of Christian liturgies were themselves subject to constraints which decision-making bodies would be obliged to observe. The argument would run somewhat as follows: the Christian Church is authorized and empowered only to proclaim a specific gospel of God-with-us, a public self-revelation of a God who loves the world he oversees, and has shown himself in Jesus Christ. This gospel is inseparable from a specific narrative and specific metaphors. It is this narrative which is liberative not dominative, because its content is the God who gives himself freely to humankind without reserve. The truth of the narrative thus is inseparable from that life and those deeds; and the lives which are the result of discipleship themselves interpret the revelation. The Christian Church is not, therefore, empowered to decide on any liturgy, ritual or structures which seemed good to it, but only those which reproduce and embody the narrative from the gospel. Liturgies which departed from this tradition would be dominative, precisely because they had no other authorization than the knowledge or wills of those who formulated them. Liturgies which retained the narrative and metaphors of the gospel would be liberative because of their content, rather than by reason of the decision-making channels through which they were formulated.

I recognize, of course, that this is the kind of argument an Anglican would be likely to formulate, since the Prayer Book tradition itself gave rise to the literary phenomenon in English culture of what has been called 'scripturalism'. Many of the reformers' liturgical compositions amount to catenae of scriptural references and allusions. The biblical metaphor of the 'heart', already astonishingly vital within English literature, plays a major role in the interiorization of ritual characteristic of the Anglican reformers. But the argument of this essay is intended to look beyond Anglicanism to an ecumenical future, not of ever-more precise doctrinal formulations, still less of legitimated structures of authority, but of liturgies which belong to the family of narratives and metaphors in which the gospel is proclaimed, and through which men and wcmen are nourished in the faith. It matters more than anything in the world that the narrative of God's dealings with humankind should be imprinted on the physic and chemistry of the human brain. Prayer books are not, of course, the only available instrument in the process. Hymn books have the same function, and so do well trained and disciplined preachers. Architecture and art, ceremony and self-imposed asceticism have long pedigrees as assisting in the same formation. There is plenty of opportunity for variety, but at this stage of our nervous and distracted culture we have every reason to emphasize repetition and common rituals as vehicles of that freedom which is promised in the gospel.

Notes

1. M. Douglas, *Natural Symbols* (London: Barrie & Rockliff, 1970), p. 21.
2. B. Lohse, *Martin Luther* (Philadelphia: Fortress, 1986), p. 179.
3. J. Calvin, *Commentaries. A Harmony of the Gospels. Matthew, Mark and Luke* (Edinburgh: St Andrew Press, 1972), 1, p. 203.
4. S. Weil, *Gravity and Grace* (London: Routledge & Kegan Paul, 1963), pp. 108–9.
5. Book of Common Prayer, end of the service for The Ministration of Publick Baptism of Infants.
6. M. Foucault, *Discipline and Punish* (Harmondsworth: Penguin, 1982), p. 194.
7. Foucault, *Discipline and Punish*, pp. 202–3.
8. Book of Common Prayer, Holy Communion Service, opening collect.
9. E. Duffy, *The Stripping of the Altars* (Yale: Yale University Press, 1992).
10. Lord William Paget, cited in A. G. Dickens, *The English Reformation* (Glasgow: Fontana, 1967), p. 351.

10

Balthasar's Sacramental Spirituality and Hopkins' Poetry of Nature: The Sacrifice Imprinted upon Nature

JOHN RICHES

Despite the eucharistic imagery of chapter 6, many (including Bultmann) have found John's doctrine of creation elusive. John was Balthasar's favourite gospel, and that tension between two different readings is also reflected in his writings, and explains why Barth found so much accord with him in his doctrine of grace. Yet, though denying that 'a piece of pure nature' is anywhere to be found, Balthasar remains insistent that there is sufficient analogy between creation and divine being to justify the appropriate metaphysic. However, in the end the connection is made through literature, in particular the Ignatian spirituality of Gerard Manley Hopkins. The synergism of God and poet enable us to read the world correctly, not as nature set apart from God but infused from the beginning with the sacrifice of his Son.

A spirituality of nature or redemption?

A central question which the sacramentalist must face is this: in what sense is the notion of sacramental spirituality, the view, that is, that the Spirit may use matter to express itself ('matter as a symbol or instrument of the spirit') compatible with central Christian insights about grace and redemption? To that question those coming from a Protestant or prophetic tradition might reply with a firm negative while those for whom the eucharist is the centre of their worship might find nothing exceptional in the extension of this spiritualizing of matter into a Teilhardian *Messe sur le Monde*[1] or into Orthodox veneration of icons and holy places. Allied to this would presumably be a sense of God's beauty being revealed in nature and in works of Christian and non-Christian art, in architecture and in myths.

Here I shall make my focus more narrow and consider all this with specific reference to Hans Urs von Balthasar (1905–88), the great twentieth-century Swiss theologian. Let me advance what may seem an extreme thesis, and see how these issues apply with respect to his work, and where it is to be found – or not, as the case may be.

The thesis is this. For von Balthasar the revelation of God in physical creation – matter as opposed to spirit – is not the main focus of his attention. He is primarily attracted to the central mystery of the revelation in Christ which is the place of the encounter of the loving God with sinful men and women: *Glaubhaft ist nur Liebe* (only love is believable).[2] The fundamental analogy for him is the loving encounter between two people; and in his writing this is worked out in terms of the drama of the Son's self-emptying and entering into the world of sin and radical opposition to God – bearing that sin and willing men and women round through the costly drama of the *Triduum Mortis* (the concluding three days of Holy Week).[3]

Nevertheless, it is of course equally a distinctive and vital part of his work that there is an analogy to be perceived and exploited between the manner in which the Son takes flesh and reveals himself to the world and the way in which the Spirit manifests and hides itself in and through the world of matter and the flesh. And, by extension, there is an analogy between the way the artist creates a work of art and the way God creates his world. By the same token von Balthasar wants also to assert that there is analogy, continuity but even greater discontinuity, between the perception of the divine, mysterious and glorious, in the myths – in Homer, Virgil, Goethe and Hölderlin – and the Christian vision of God's beauty in Christ.[4]

It is important to stress the sheer intellectual effort which von Balthasar expended on restoring the aesthetic analogy to its rightful place in theology, if for no other reason than to counter the extreme Christocentricism of his more zealous neo-conservative supporters. There is however little doubt that he actually spends little time developing his own theology of creation or of God's revelation in nature.

What he does is first, to engage in discussion of the *analogia entis* (analogy of being) and the Catholic doctrine of nature in Karl Barth,[5] and second, to develop a theological aesthetic in *The*

Glory of the Lord, vol. I which exploits the analogy between perception of the beautiful and the Christian vision of the revelation *Gestalt* (configuration), in the course of which he gives a brief account of the disclosing and concealment of the divine in nature and in creation.[6] Most importantly, he discusses the work of Christian poets, notably that of Hopkins (in *Glory*, vol. III), and gives considerable attention to the physical manifestation of God's glory in the patriarchal visions of glory in his discussion of the Old Covenant (in *Glory*, vol. VI). By contrast the vision of glory in the New Covenant is focused on the kenosis of the Word made flesh and the fruit which that self-emptying bears in the life of believers.

The question then is: does this give us grounds for – even the means for developing – a sacramental spirituality, for construing Christianity as a religion of the material? Or does, even on von Balthasar's view, Christianity emerge as a form of life which is ultimately about the love between Christ and his Church? Let me put it another way. If, to speak with John, 'without him was not anything made that was made' (John 1.3 RSV) then we may take it that matter is not in itself opposed to God; but then, if we further assert with John that its life is 'in the Logos', that it is the Logos alone that provides light to the created world, then we may certainly ask questions about how far the natural world declares his glory (Ps. 22) or whether it is merely the recipient of light; just as we may ask what it is about the relationship between the Word and his creatures, his 'own', that enables them to glorify him and the Father. And John does speak not only of the Son glorifying the Father, as the Father and the Spirit glorify the Son (16.14; 17.1–5); but of the Father and the Son being glorified in the disciples (15.8: in bearing much fruit; 17.10: in their being his, the Son's). Certainly for John the key to such creative glorifying lies in the incarnation, seen, however, principally as the obedience of the one whom the Father sent and gave, and who came to his own: 'my food is to do the will of him who sent me' (4.34 RSV); to accomplish his work (cf. 17.4); just as it is in the disciples' cleaving to him, loving him, fulfilling his commandments, bearing fruit that the Father is glorified in them.

I start with these Johannine reflections partly because John is the theologian of the East, where the sense of matter as transformed and radiant of Spirit has been strong; partly because he is the Evangelist from whom both von Balthasar and his soulmate Adrienne von Speyr[7] have drawn their deepest inspiration; not least because of the elusiveness of John's doctrine of creation and redemption. Does he, when he speaks of the cosmos ('he was in the world, and the world knew him not'): even have the world of created matter in mind at all?[8] Does his doctrine of realized eschatology not demythologize Christian hopes for the final transformation of the world of matter – Paul's creation groaning and travailing – in favour of a purely spiritual communion between the believer and the Son and thereby with the Father? 'It is the spirit that gives life, the flesh is of no avail' (John 6.63 RSV). The point of such questions is to make us look the more closely at the Christology which underlines John's profound and dialectical meditations, to focus precisely on the preceding claims: 'the bread which I shall give for the life of the world is my flesh' – 'He who eats my flesh and drinks my blood abides in me, and I in him' (John 6.51, 56 RSV), where creation is portrayed as finding its fulfilment, its true life, in union with the Logos, with 'my flesh'. True life is realized as Christ unites men and women with God as they commune with his flesh. For 'his flesh' is the very moment of union between the divine, the Logos, and the sphere of the transitory, 'flesh' which now however finds its true meaning in being taken up into the divine life.

Balthasar's tendency to ascribe all to grace

So too with von Balthasar there is, as Noel O'Donoghue has pointed out in a wonderfully perceptive critical and sympathetic review of the first volume of *The Glory of the Lord*,[9] a deep tension within his understanding of the relation between created nature and the redeeming God. In a crucial discussion of von Balthasar's claim that it is in the in-forming of the believer with the form of Christ that she is both judged and saved, O'Donoghue argues that we can discern in von Balthasar two very different views of the divine–human relation.

The passage to which O'Donoghue refers is the following:

> The form which inscribes itself in the living centre of my being becomes my salvation by becoming my judgment . . . The metamorphosis of which Paul speaks (Rom 12.2; 2 Cor 3.18; Phil 3.21) is above all an assumption of form, the receiving of Christ's form in us (Gal 4.19), the character and the impress in us of the only valid image of God. This occurs the more im-pressively, in the literal sense, the less resistance the impress the divine image encounters. Mary's *Ecce Ancilla* [Behold the handmaid] is the supreme instance . . . Allowing the Word its way in me is not an action, and is not, therefore, an accomplishment and a work; it is contemplative obedience

that of its own passes over into the Passion in accordance with the law of the image which leaves its impress on it.[10]

Such a passage, so O'Donoghue maintains, seems to point in two ways. It allows both a reading which stresses the 'human initiative, e.g., in Mary's *ecce ancilla domini* (theology from below, building on the human)' but 'on closer reading shows an undertow of the kind of theology in which man is passively receptive and does not in any real sense work out his own salvation'.[11] Such a way of conceiving the working of divine grace (monergism as opposed to synergism) is mechanical, portraying 'the living process of salvation' as the dead process of the meeting of God's grace with the *massa damnata*, or 'condemned humanity', of fallen nature. Thus the Church is portrayed as the receptacle of Christ's fullness – 'nothing other than Christ's fullness' – and 'can claim for herself and for the world no other figure than the figure of Christ which leaves its stamp in her and shapes her through and through as the soul shapes the body'.[12]

Such a theology threatens to exclude the very stuff of human life – its 'misery, pathos and individual human countenance' from the life of grace. 'Surely', asks O'Donoghue, 'the human heart and mind have something to say, something to give, really to give as they respond to the Father's love?'[13] And indeed this element too is present in von Balthasar's work – drawing on his debt to Scheeben, Karl Adam, Guardini and Przywara – and informs part of the excitement of his theology as the tension between monergism and synergism is worked out.

All of this is to give some meaning to the pair of terms 'symbol or instrument' when we seek to speak of matter as the symbol or instrument of the spirit. It is admittedly to focus the issue of the relation between matter and the spirit by way of the question of the relation between the believer and her Lord. But this, if we are to see the taking of the flesh by the eternal Word as the key to the relation of Spirit and matter seems wholly appropriate.

So at least it would seem to Barth, who drew from von Balthasar one of the sharpest and most sympathetic commentaries in his *The Theology of Karl Barth*. As O'Donoghue says, we can see much of Barth's influence in the 'monergism' of *The Glory of the Lord*, its insistence that the response of faith is no work, no action but contemplative obedience. We can indeed also see in that passage his siding with Barth against Bultmann's denial of the objective – 'objectifying' – aspects of faith: its aesthetic dimension, the beholding of the glory, which for Bultmann becomes a sightless act of obedience whereby Christ becomes revealed for us really as we accept him and thereby all our goals are turned upside down and we receive new life – a transformed self-understanding:[14] not though objective knowledge of Christ to which we become conformed. But von Balthasar did not merely agree with Barth: he challenged him precisely over his understanding of analogy and nature. It was not, in the end, enough to try to derive one's doctrine of creation from Christology. This would lead to a christological *stretto* (*Engführung* – narrow direction), a squeezing of the doctrine of creation through the straits of Christology, whereas at this point theology needs to be in dialogue with philosophy.[15] Von Balthasar is here keen to avoid any charge that Christian theology can simply be predetermined by a prior doctrine of being and nature. Such provides only an analogy where the dissimilarity is always much greater than the similarity to the truth and goodness and beauty of the divine being which is revealed in and through Christ. But without such an analogy we would be unable to comprehend the truth and beauty and goodness revealed in Christ.

'Pure nature' as a basis for something more

This insistence on the need for a philosophy of being, of truth, beauty and goodness, is met in Balthasar's own theology by his setting alongside his biblical theology of glory, his treatment of the great tradition of metaphysics in volumes IV and V of *The Glory of the Lord*. But how do they relate? It is not clearly resolved in his earlier discussion of the Catholic doctrine of nature in *Karl Barth*,[16] for here he has to engage with the doctrine of *natura pura* which was designed to defend the notion of the gratuity of grace. In brief: if natural kinds are defined in terms of their ends (the end of a wing is to fly) then in order to be what they properly are certain conditions must be met: (there must be air). Now if the end of humankind is to see God, then the necessary conditions of such vision must as a right be satisfied: grace, that is to say, becomes a *debitum* (something owed), not something freely given. To avoid such consequences it was then necessary to develop a doctrine of *natura pura* asserting that men and women in their basic nature have natural, as distinct from supernatural, goals which do not include the vision of God, such as peace, tranquility, the common good. De Lubac and de Rondet and the school of the *nouvelle théologie* at Lyons sought to counter this sharp separation between natural and supernatural by invoking the Fathers and insisting that man in *puris naturalibus* was indeed capable of the vision of God. Von Balthasar's position is again delicately balanced. He insists on the one hand that 'nowhere is there a piece of pure nature'. God's prevenient grace is always active in the world, granting glimpses of his glory; the notion of pure nature is a purely theoretical one, nowhere actually instantiated. On the other hand, in his article on Christian universalism (where again he takes issue with Barth's treatment of that theme under the heading of Election) he asserts the steadfastness of God's will to bring all things into union with him. In the purposes of God, if not in the nature of things, all things have their end in him.[17] Where does this take us? Does such an account of the relationship of nature and creation indicate to what extent matter itself may become the vehicle of divine revelation? Tentatively two conclusions may be drawn: but this is still only a prelude to his major work.

Balthasar's 'nowhere is there a piece of pure nature' may be seen at one level as merely an astute compromise in politically fraught circumstances brought about by the condemnation of certain propositions of the Lyons school in *Humani Generis* (1950). The distinction between nature and supernature is allowed to stand while the place of all nature within God's saving gracious purposes is affirmed. But we might go further: the retention of the doctrine of *natura pura* – albeit within such qualification – is still an affirmation of its own integrity, of the particularities and goals, hopes and fears of such nature, that which, as O'Donoghue would say, it may bring as a gift into the union with God, which God establishes by his initiative of grace.

But more, as von Balthasar's preface to the second edition makes clear, his insistence on the *analogia entis* (that there is an analogy, however tenuous, between creaturely being and divine being), provides the basis for a plea for a philosophical metaphysic.[18] Precisely because the creature participates in being – a being analogous to the Being of God – however tenuously, then there is that on which we can reflect, that which can teach us something of the mysteries of being, of what there is. In this sense then, and it is no small point, matter may be the object of our philosophical reflection. Yet though von Balthasar pleads strongly for a (Christian) philosophy which would inform our Christian theology, it is clear from his subsequent work that it is not here that his heart (or indeed his real gifts) ultimately lies. What most evidently cuts across the monergism of his Barthian-Kierkegaardian 'undertow' is the controlling force of the analogy of beauty which runs through the first part of his trilogy and is sustained in the second by the notion of drama.

The artistic analogy

Again, as with all fertile analogies and metaphors, this may work variously. In the first place Balthasar wants to stress the indissolubility of spirit and medium in the work of art and beauty. That which is beautiful is not something other than, separable from, the individual parts or elements which together are beautiful. The *splendour* of a work of art is only to be grasped in and through its parts. They are not as it were signs which point to a meaning, a reality other than the work of art.[19] They point to the spiritual depth which is revealed and concealed in and through the 'body' of the work of art. Thus the parts do indeed make their contribution to the whole, to the *splendour* of the work. The form is not just, as it were, impressed on the artist's medium: there is an interaction between the freedom of the artist's spirit and his chosen media, through which he expresses himself: What is created is specific, unique with its own necessity and rightness; the parts have a proportion and measure, which means that the work has to be seen as a whole.

This is a rich analogy which is suggestive and fertile in many areas of von Balthasar's theology: in his reading of biblical theology; in his 'sighting of the revelation form', as that which gives shape and wholeness and unity to the complex and diverse history of revelation; in his extended exploration of the drama of salvation in the second part of his trilogy; and in the exploration of the relation between the believer and Christ which is a constant theme of *The Glory of the Lord* and which is certainly (somewhat against O'Donoghue's emphasis) richly exploited in these aesthetic terms. True, the Christian life for von Balthasar (and Adrienne von Speyr) is one fundamentally of obedience, of openness to the revelation, of acceptance of the charge or mission (*Auftrag*) given. But in this obedience the Christian is drawn into a life of discipleship which bears fruit in a myriad of ways. The conforming of Christians to the life of Christ is not simply the impression of a certain stamp; it is being drawn into a particular *Lebensform* (form of life) in which individuality can be expressed.[20] Such a *Lebensform* will of course be deeply marked by its character of discipleship of the Lord who has taken upon himself the condition of sinful humanity and entered into the darkness of death in the descent into hell. Whatever we bring will be transformed, will find its new life and *Gestalt* in relation to this life. But that is not to say that it is simply *used*.

What does all this tell us about physical creation, its ability to speak to us of God and indeed of his grace? As I have already suggested, von Balthasar is in the end less at home in the world of natural theology than in that of literature and biblical meditation. Thus we should not expect to find formal treatments. Rather, as is characteristic of his work, much is stated through the work of others, his chosen poets, writers and theologians, both inside and outside the Christian tradition: Homer and Virgil, Dante, Péguy and Claudel. Here his chapter on Hopkins is exemplary.[21]

Through Hopkins a true appreciation of nature's role

Gerard Manley Hopkins (1844–89), though like von Balthasar schooled in the Jesuit tradition of Ignatian spirituality, nevertheless did not look Ignatius full in the face. In the end it is to Scotus that he turned for his inspiration in developing a speculative metaphysics, an account of the nature of things which would do justice to his poet's eye for the individuality, the uniqueness of things. What fascinates Hopkins – and here von Balthasar sees the English tradition at work which resists the flight into the abstract – is the particularity, the distinctiveness of things: what Scotus attempted to explore as *haeccitas* (thisness) von Balthasar gives a sympathetic account of through Hopkins' notion of *in-stress*: the energy, life of things which unites us with them as we recognize in them the same dynamic force of being and not being that we experience in ourselves; and *in-scape*: the creative springing up of things within them which gives them their individual form which holds them and which it is the poet's task to read and to discern, for it is here that we discern, directly as it were, the creative work of God.

According to von Balthasar such aesthetic vision is, however indirectly, the product of Hopkins' schooling in the Ignatian tradition. For it is the emphasis on the believer's decision which ultimately allows the uniqueness of the individual to emerge most fully. Of the *Spiritual Exercises* von Balthasar writes:

> [Here] for the first time in the history of Christian spirituality everything is placed on the knife edge of the mutual election that takes place between God and man, behind which retreats any consideration of 'perfection in general'. Here are dissolved all the confusing clouds of the mythical in order to uncover the absolute, hard reality in which alone the true glory of being shines forth. The impatience of this breaking through to the uniquely true glory determines Hopkins' whole ethos . . .[22]

This passage in von Balthasar is revealing. It makes clear, I think, that for him there is at the very least a hierarchy of revelations

of the divine: the incomprehensibility of worldly images to which
the majesty of God's oneness bears witness; the spirituality of the
Exercises with its relentless focus on the acceptance of divine election, 'the knife edge of the mutual election that takes place
between God and man'.

Hopkins' poetry – and here we find von Balthasar closest to
our theme as he writes of his 'Sacramental Poetry' – is an attempt
to discern 'the way the mystery of God takes form in the worm'
and for this von Balthasar writes 'the conception of the sacramental is at hand, which certainly contains within itself the power
of the "symbol", while it goes far beyond it; the form of the image
is a likeness to the primordial form in that it has the "stress" of
the latter in itself: *sacramenta continent quae significant*' [sacraments
contain what they signify]:[23]

> So it is the mystery of the sonnet, 'The Windhover' – dedicated
> to 'Christ our Lord' – to draw out the image in an immense,
> ascending intensity, which starts by spiritualising the bold
> soaring of the wild bird in order then to interpret the utmost,
> now motionless, suspension at the highest point, with out-
> stretched wings, as the final unfolding of power from which the
> embers drop down: a sacramental image of the Cross. At the
> natural level the image is overstretched, but as a whole it is not;
> it accomplishes no *metabasis*, no allegory; Christ's Cross is
> indeed not one historical fact among others to which a natural
> process can more or less arbitrarily be related: it is the funda-
> mental, ontological presupposition of all natural processes that
> all, knowingly or not, intrinsically signify or intend by pointing
> beyond themselves. The 'Windhover' allows this connection to
> appear expressly only in the dedication; in the poem itself the
> image must say all. But there are other ways in which this
> connection can manifest itself in a poem.[24]

Here Hopkins/Balthasar is drawing on Scotus with his belief
that 'the Sacrifice of the Son is God's first thought of the world'[25]
– 'the lamb slain before the foundation of the world' (Rev. 13.8)
which for von Balthasar is the divine decision which accompanies
the act of creation of the world. This then stamps all creation and
finds its fullest expression in the cross which is as it were written
into history.

It is thus that Hopkins' poetry can work at different levels: on
the one level it is an exploration of the creative power and the
glory of God:

'Glory be to God for dappled things . . .
for Whatever is fickle, freckled (who knows how?)
. . . He fathers-forth whose beauty is past change:
Praise him.'[26]

But there is also to be discerned in nature the sense in which it is grounded in Christ.

Nature's glory in Christ's sacrifice

'The image that should interpret the mystery of Christ is, in itself as an image of nature, utterly overtaxed, but in so far as it is grounded in Christ as the presupposition of nature, it is allowed to say by grace of the archetype what it cannot say of itself.'[27] For von Balthasar, however, it is the poems of Hopkins which explore the outworking of our eternal election to be brothers and sisters, members of Christ, which ultimately hold his attention. There are resonances of earlier discussions of pure nature when he writes that the 'core of our personal "pitch"' (Hopkins' word for our specific orientation, aim, according to von Balthasar) 'lies in the supernatural and thus our self-choice can only be perfected concretely within the grace of God.'[28] Now Hopkins wrote illuminatingly – and as a pastor – on the outworkings of divine grace. Here indeed perhaps we have the most eloquent commentary on von Balthasar's 'nowhere is there a piece of pure nature'. It is God's prevenient grace accompanying us, drawing us, recognizing our inclination towards him that precedes and leads to the full affirmation (of the *Exercises*), the Yes or No to the great sacrifice.

Man lives that list, that leaning in the will
No wisdom can forecast by gauge or guess,
The selfless self of self, most strange, most still
Past furled and all foredrawn to No or Yes![29]

So the poet seeks to discern this love in men and women 'in their homecoming as sinners, to God, in the bursting forth from him of love in all its cunning'.[30] The images are forged from the life of ordinary men and women, neighbours; images of the underlying love and grace of God.

For von Balthasar it is, though, in the great shipwreck poems that Hopkins' work reaches its height; for here 'the foundering and shattering of all worldly images and symbols yield a final picture of the sacrament of the world: perishing and ascending to God – death as Resurrection: Resurrection not beyond death but in death . . . The wreck is as a harvest . . . , the beach as a goal . . . ;

everything alive was washed away . . .' Foundering in God: nothing is left to cling on to, only God '*Ipse*, the only one'. The poet here has achieved his goal of interpreting 'the formless and unformable chaos of the night as form and in the senselessness of pure question to know the who and the why':

> Ah! there was heart right!
> There was single eye!
> Read the unshapeable shock night
> And knew the who and the why . . .[31]

Where does this leave us? With, I suppose, a nice dialectic; a sense that precisely because of its christological ground, physical nature is patient of expressing God's glory most fully when its breaking, its grounding in the great sacrifice is glimpsed. Nature finds its fulfilment, its true meaning in the imaging – but precisely through the breaking of its images – of the cross, of the great sacrifice. But what it images is here more than the glory of the creative force and beauty of God; it is the costly election of men and women which leads to the kenosis of the Son and the Yes and No of those called.

It is indeed a delicate balance: it is too easy for the overzealous to press too quickly to the foundation of things; to scorn the sheer glory of nature or the subtle and half perceived drawings of grace. It requires the poet's – or the mystic's – eye sensitive to the extra-ordinary richness of creation and the cunning of grace in history to continue to sustain a vision of the glory of the world as it is.

Notes

1. P. Teilhard de Chardin, 'The Mass on the World', a meditation suggested in the desert where it was impossible for him to celebrate mass: *Hymn of the Universe* (London: Fontana, 1970), pp. 19–35.
2. Published in English as H. U. von Balthasar, *Love Alone: the Way of Revelation* (London: Sheed & Ward, 1968).
3. See H. U. von Balthasar, *Mysterium Paschale* (Edinburgh: T. & T. Clark, 1990).
4. H. U. von Balthasar, *The Glory of God: A Theological Aesthetics* (Edinburgh: T. & T. Clark, 1982) 7 volumes.
5. See H. U. von Balthasar, *The Theology of Karl Barth* (New York: Holt, Rinehart & Winston 1971).
6. Balthasar, *Glory*, I, pp. 441–7.
7. See e.g. H. U. von Balthasar, *First Glance at Adrienne von Speyr* (San Francisco: Ignatius Press, 1981).

8. See e.g. R. Bultmann, *The Gospel of John* (Oxford: Oxford University Press, 1971), p. 54.

9. N. O'Donoghue, 'A Theology of Beauty', in *The Analogy of Beauty*, ed. J. Riches (Edinburgh: T. & T. Clark, 1986), pp. 1–10.

10. Balthasar, *Glory*, I, pp. 485f.

11. O'Donoghue, 'A Theology of Beauty', 3.

12. Balthasar, *Glory*, I, pp. 558f.

13. O'Donoghue, 'A Theology of Beauty', p. 4.

14. Bultmann, *The Gospel of John*, pp. 68f.

15. Balthasar, *Theology of Karl Barth*, pp. 221–7.

16. Balthasar, *Theology of Karl Barth*, pp. 247–70.

17. H. U. von Balthasar, 'Christlicher Universalismus' in *Verbum Caro* (Einsiedeln: Johannesverlag, 1960), pp. 260–75.

18. Balthasar seriously misunderstands Barth's rejoinder in *Church Dogmatics* IV/1, p. 768 which sharply distinguishes created being and the being which is bestowed by God and participation in his being.

19. Balthasar, *Glory*, I, pp. 17–23.

20. See the introduction of this notion at the beginning of Balthasar, *Glory*, I, pp. 23ff.

21. Balthasar, *Glory*, III, pp. 353–99.

22. Balthasar, *Glory*, III, p. 357.

23. Balthasar, *Glory*, III, p. 393f.

24. Balthasar, *Glory*, III, p. 394.

25. Balthasar, *Glory*, III, p. 380.

26. Balthasar, *Glory*, III, p. 395 quoting G. M. Hopkins, 'Pied Beauty'.

27. Balthasar, *Glory*, III, p. 394.

28. Balthasar, *Glory*, III, p. 378.

29. Balthasar, *Glory*, III, p. 384.

30. Balthasar, *Glory*, III, p. 398, referring to 'Felix Randall'.

31. Balthasar, *Glory*, III, p. 399.

11

The World, the Flesh and the Spirit: Love as Sacramental in Spenser and Other Poets

DAVID FULLER

How are sexual love and physical beauty to be regarded? Do they inhibit spiritual perception? Or should they be seen as an important vehicle towards a higher reality? Or do they themselves mediate that reality? (the sacramental position). Taking the Four Hymns *of the sixteenth-century poet Edmund Spenser as a case study, David Fuller exhibits the considerable tensions within Christianity between these three positions. Drawing parallels and contrasts with a wide range of other English and European poets, his conclusion is that despite his equivocations Spenser wanted a richer vein of sacramentalism than orthodox Christ-ianity has traditionally offered.*

'To what serves mortal beauty?'

How does love between human beings relate to love of God? How does perceiving the beauty of creation – including human beauty – relate to a vision of the divine? Throughout his work, and above all in his *Four Hymns*, the great Renaissance poet Edmund Spenser is concerned with these subjects. Augustine gives the orthodox views. With love we must distinguish between charity and cupidity – love directed (ultimately) towards God, and love directed towards oneself. With beauty we must not stop at the beauty of the created object but see in it the beauty of the Creator.[1] The difficulties and dangers which these orthodoxies negotiate are well implied by Gerard Manley Hopkins.

To what serves mortal beauty – dangerous; does set danc-
Ing blood – the O-seal-that-so face, prouder flung the form
Than Purcell tune lets tread to? See, it does this: keeps warm
Men's wits to the things that are; what good means – where
                    a glance
Master more may than gaze, gaze out of countenance.
Those lovely lads once, wet-fresh windfalls of war's storm,
How then should Gregory, a father, have gleaned else from
                    swarm-
Ed Rome? But God to a nation dealt that day's dear chance.
To man, that once would worship block or barren stone,
Our law says: Love what are love's worthiest, were all known;
World's loveliest – men's selves. Self flashes off frame and face.
What do then? How meet beauty? Merely meet it; own,
Home at heart, heaven's sweet gift; then leave, let that alone.
Yea, wish that though, wish all, God's better beauty, grace.

Hopkins' constant subjects are the presence of God in creation,
and art as a form of revelation: as he puts it, praising Purcell, 'he
has . . . uttered in notes the very make and species of man as
created both in him and in all men generally'. Hopkins also
throws up doubts about such views both of art and of human
beauty. When he joined the Jesuits Hopkins destroyed his own
poetry, seeing it as his religious duty to do so. In 'To what serves
. . .' human beauty is dangerous because it provokes the passions.
It is also of great spiritual value: that the beauty of the young
Englishmen in the Roman slave market led to England's becoming part of Christendom is paradigmatic.

There are three basic attitudes to this subject, seen in
Buddhism, Neoplatonism and Sufism. For Buddhism everything
is on fire: you have entirely to divest yourself of this fire (desire of
any material kind) to approach the highest spiritual states. With
Neoplatonism desire directed towards the material is a stage which
you move through, and are expected to move wholly beyond. In
the mystical ecstasies of Sufism desire is not at odds with the spiritual: it is a permanent aspect of full spiritual being. Christianity
has taken all three attitudes. They can be seen respectively in St
John of the Cross, Dante and Milton. In *Four Hymns* Spenser
pretends to be a lapsed Neoplatonist who has (as it were) become
a follower of St John of the Cross. In reality his position is more
Miltonic. The hymns present an open contest of perspectives,
Catholic (Neoplatonist, syncretist) versus Puritan: Spenser is
conducting that quarrel with himself out of which Yeats claimed
poetry is properly made.[2] The poems are open dialogues with

each other within which Spenser the Puritan intervenes to tell the reader which of his fragmented selves to take for the whole. In each pair of poems the speaker is a version of Spenser who presents one part of his view as its whole. Though each speaker presents his view as complete, each is finally characterized as less dispassionately wise than he at first pretends. The poet's total view is to be understood from the four poems taken together.

The *Four Hymns* state opposite positions: *A Hymn in Honour of Love* (*HL*) and *A Hymn in Honour of Beauty* (*HB*) claim that earthly and heavenly love are continuous; *A Hymn of Heavenly Love* (*HHL*) and *A Hymn of Heavenly Beauty* (*HHB*) that they are at odds. This division reflects a double view in Spenser's classical sources: the mythic sources, as Spenser uses them, show earthly and heavenly love as analogous; the Neoplatonic sources treat them as distant, and finally separate. The division also reflects a divided view in Christian tradition itself in its attitude to the material world. The Old and New Testaments can be seen as at odds over this – in the Old Testament association of the chosen people and the land, sometimes manifested as assertive nationalism emphasizing racial purity (the Pentateuch; Ezra-Nehemiah), as against the internationalism of the New Testament (but Isaiah, for example, is an internationalist); or in related contrasting attitudes to the temple, in the Old Testament as cultic centre symbolizing God's choice of Israel as his own people, again contradicted by the internationalism of the New Testament with its move away from Jerusalem as no longer central to the new religion. That is, in the New Testament there is not, as there is in much of the Old, a material location of holiness – in a people, or place, or building. Other elements of Christian tradition can be seen as similarly contradictory in their attitude to the material. The symbolism of the eucharist, the insistence that resurrection is in some sense bodily, and above all the incarnation, all suggest the potentially redeemable nature of matter. In this context of hymns to love and beauty, the attitude to sexuality shown by the exaltation of the Virgin and St Paul's ascetic hierarchizing of celibacy and marriage (1 Cor. 7.6–7) are manifestations of more negative attitudes to the material and the sensuous.

These are elements not just potentially at odds in the traditions with which Spenser is dealing, but also in his own sensibility. His partly Catholic inheritance tends to an acceptance of the fulness of human capacities in art, and so to a refined but full version of the sensuous world as coterminous with religious feeling; also that revelation is various, and can include aspects of Hellenistic culture. At odds with this is a version of Christianity, intense and admirable in its way, which is narrowed by a Hebraic and exclusive moral rigidity – in contemporary terms, Puritanism, which tended to a radical distrust of the sensuous. These tensions already present in Spenser's Christianity are heightened by his typically Renaissance syncretism, which leads him to combine with this already divided Christian inheritance diverse classical sources. Of these the myths concerned with Venus and Cupid have always been treated by Christianity with (to say the least) unease. And even the Neoplatonic sources, which already had a long-evolved relationship with Christianity, came to Spenser, not through the Fathers, but through the great Renaissance translator of and commentator on Plato and Plotinus, Marsilio Ficino (1433–99) – that is, with their Platonic bases, and so their potential problems for Christianity, refreshed.

This divided feeling in Spenser is not simply a muddle resulting from a clash of traditions (the intrusion of the Puritan into the Catholic), or an ambitious syncretism (an attempt to harmonize philosophies and myths that are inevitably at odds). It reflects a genuine problem about the potential sacramentality of the material world. It is possible to resolve the divided view Spenser presents, in the terms he offers, by distinguishing 'love' (so-called) which contains the impurity of purely physical desire from love in which physical being is important wholly as a vehicle of spirit. In this form human love is analogous with, and so a help to understanding, the heavenly. This resolution is actually implied by the unity of the four hymns as a group – despite Spenser's overt denial of such a unity. I want also to reflect on the whole issue by comparing Spenser's divided view with the similar division in Petrarch; and by examining other treatments – those of Dante and Milton – which deal with the issue in contrasting ways.

Dante and Petrarch: worship or idolatry?

St John of the Cross presents a purely negative view of the relation of earthly love to the divine:

> The reason for which it is necessary for the soul, in order to attain to Divine union with God, to pass through this dark night of mortification of the desires and denial of pleasures in all things, is because all the affections which it has for creatures are pure darkness in the eyes of God, and, when the soul is clothed in these affections, it has no capacity for being enlightened and possessed by the pure and simple light of God.[3]

One might question how far this fiercely ascetic doctrine is qualified by the analogies drawn from erotic feeling by which, in his poetry, St John attempts to describe mystical experience. St John himself insists on discontinuity. Mystical experience is quite distinctive: analogies from the already known are remote; the gap between the mystical and all other experience is finally unbridgeable. T. S. Eliot takes a passage from *The Ascent of Mount Carmel* as an epigraph to his *Sweeney Agonistes*. But Eliot himself allows a more inclusive view. In *Four Quartets* 'the way up and the way down are the same' (an epigraph from Heraclitus), and 'The fire and the rose are one' (the final line of the final poem): the way of desiccation and the way of plenitude, the way of evacuation of sense and the way of visionary knowledge which is sensuous in origin, lead finally to the same point.

A divided view – both that love can be genuinely religious, and that it can be idolatrous – is found in many of the great Christian love poets. It is present in a limited way in Dante.[4] In the *Vita Nuova*, for all the intensity of feeling, Beatrice herself is etherialized beyond erotic response. But in the *Commedia* there are traces of sublimated erotic feeling in the language of religious vision, and at crucial moments of ascent in the *Paradiso* Dante is inspired both by his love for Beatrice and by a vision of the divine reflected in her beauty. Nevertheless, the reader is almost always conscious of Beatrice as, in the allegory, the Church. Because of this, and because Beatrice is so often lecturing the pilgrim on theology or cosmology, for much of the poem the allegorical function overwhelms the sense of personal feeling. The *Commedia* as a whole, though, does not take a purely negative attitude to erotic love. The most famous people in hell may be the lovers, Paolo and Francesca. The most surprising people in Paradise are Solomon and Cunizza da Romano – Solomon, as famous for wives as for wisdom, Cunizza, as famous for four husbands and two lovers as for freeing the slaves of her father and brothers. Why is Solomon (supposed damned by no less an authority than Augustine) in Paradise? He wrote the Song of Songs. Why is Cunizza, dead only twenty-one years, not at least in Purgatory? She freed her slaves. With both, their virtues imply the generous impulse underlying their sin.

More directly related to Spenser is Petrarch. Petrarch's most direct statement on the subject comes in his *Secretum*, a private work, ostensibly not written for publication, in which Petrarch is in dialogue with St Augustine. Augustine is not so much an external interlocutor as an alter ego: we know from the poetry that he expresses Petrarch's own doubts. In their dialogue on love (Book III) Petrarch claims that love of Laura led to love of God. Augustine responds by convicting Petrarch of self-deception: obsession with Laura was idolatry; it caused forgetfulness of God. In the *Canzoniere* (*Love-lyrics*, which Spenser knew: he translated one of the most notable [323]) Petrarch takes both these views: Laura is, like Beatrice, a manifestation of divine beauty (248), 'lume che 'l cielo in terra mostra' ('light that shows heaven on earth', 192); after her death she is, like Beatrice, a spiritual guide (359). But also, in the penitential 'Padre del Ciel' ('Father of Heaven'), and elsewhere, love and beauty are dangerous to the soul (62; cf. 214). The positive view, which is present in the poems of the first part, is dominant in the poems written after Laura's death; but the penultimate poem, 'I' vo piangendo i miei passati tempi' ('I go weeping for my past time'), is a lament for time wasted on love; and in the final poem Laura is repudiated and the Virgin enthroned in her place. The narrative order, which allows this pious view eventually to predominate, is not unimportant. But it has never been felt decisive: for all the serious doubts throughout the *Canzoniere* the weight of the poetry is against it. Like Spenser, therefore, Petrarch offers opposite views on the relation of human beauty and love to knowledge and love of God. And, as I shall argue of Spenser, Petrarch too offers a resolution in which nothing is resolved.

The themes of Spenser's *Four Hymns*

The myths of *A Hymn in Honour of Love*, myths of Venus and of Cupid, show love as a power basic to the origin of creation, and continually sustaining it. The Venus myth does not separate the erotic from other kinds of love. Venus is a single figure. There is no division (as there is with Aphrodite in Plato's *Symposium*) into Venus earthly and heavenly. Nor is the distinction Spenser makes between lust, which sinks the lover spiritually, and love, which raises him, a simple pietistic division between physical and non-physical: it is a distinction between feeling which seeks only the satisfaction of the body, and feeling which is for, and is expressed through, the whole being, including the body. The true lover who is successful enjoys a paradise like *The Faerie Queene*'s Garden of Adonis (III.vi), a paradise

> Of all delight, and joyous happy rest,
> Where they do feed on nectar heavenly-wise,
> With *Hercules* and *Hebe*, and the rest

Of *Venus'* darlings, through her bounty blessed,
And lie like gods in ivory beds arrayed,
With rose and lilies over them displayed.

There with thy daughter, *Pleasure*, they do play
Their hurtless sports, without rebuke or blame,
And in her snowy bosom boldly lay
Their quiet heads, devoid of guilty shame,
After full joyance of their gentle game.[5]

A Hymn in Honour of Love has a unitary myth of Venus, but two myths of the birth of Cupid. Cupid is the eldest of the gods; before creation he 'long time securely slept/ In Venus' lap': love and beauty can rest satisfied together. Cupid is also the child of Plenty and Penury: love can be based on a feeling of insufficiency which yearns for plenitude – a view of love which can be connected either with Neoplatonism or with Petrarch and his followers. Spenser draws on both traditions, but very much in his own way. Where, for the Neoplatonist, response to beauty is the starting point on an ultimately ascetic quest, for Spenser the intimation of the divine which beauty gives explains the intensity of human love and desire. Man,

having yet in his deducted spright   *weakened spirit*
Some sparks remaining of that heavenly fire,
He is illumined with that goodly light
Unto like goodly semblant to aspire:
Therefore in choice of love he doth desire
That seems on earth most heavenly to embrace:
That same is Beauty, born of heavenly race.

For sure, of all that in this mortal frame
Contained is, nought more divine doth seem,
Or that resembleth more th'immortal flame
Of heavenly light, than Beauty's glorious beam.
What wonder then if with such rage extreme
Frail men, whose eyes seek heavenly things to see,
At sight thereof so much enravished be?
                    (106–19)

Earthly love can be an aspect of the heavenly. It also has the potential merely to intensify earthly obsessions. The negative effect of love may be a potential development of the positive (106–33). It may be an inevitable obverse (190–203): the excellent moral consequences of aspiration can be bound up with a negative psychological effect – obsession caused by the feeling of lack. If the possibility of completion and plenitude sensed in love is fallacious – and the speaker confesses that his knowledge is belief, not experience – then the reality of human love may be a craving which inherently seeks more than it can ever find. The poem celebrates a faith, but it also at times registers an undercurrent at odds with its predominant argument. Its play on the ambiguity of 'fain' and its derivatives,[6] its classical examples of love, all of which are tragic (231–7), the speaker's admission that he has no experience of the paradisal state he hopes for, and above all the image of the lover as Tantalus, pining amidst satiety – all these undermine the poem's apparently confident statement.

The main issue of *A Hymn in Honour of Beauty* is the interrelation Spenser asserts between physical and spiritual beauty. It is this that gives beauty its sacramental function. Spenser accepts that the potential connection is not always actual – because of the recalcitrance of matter to the shaping power of spirit; and because, when spirit has successfully shaped matter, material form itself offers, as well as inspiration for spiritual ascent, temptation to spiritual decline. But though spirit may not achieve its ideal material form, it is always a force shaping matter. Spenser finds explanations for the manifest fact that spiritual and physical beauty are not always conjoined, but these explanations are ways of continuing to insist that in their ideal forms physical and spiritual beauty can be united, and physical beauty is therefore always potentially of spiritual value. The proper form of human love is not physical attraction: what may appear as that to a false understanding is in fact spiritual affinity, the fulfilment of which is assisted by physical attraction. Always there is this connection between the physical and the spiritual in their ideal forms. The ultimate form of the beloved's beauty is a matter both of something perceived and something bestowed. It is in part the perceived spiritual form of the loved one – which may not wholly succeed in manifesting itself physically. It is also bestowed by the spiritual ideal sought by the lover, for which the beloved acts as purifying and intensifying focus.

A great deal of this argument is Neoplatonic, with sources in Plato and Ficino, most obviously the argument basic to each pair of hymns that love is the desire for beauty, which Spenser found in *The Symposium* and in Ficino's *Commentary*. But Spenser's Neoplatonism is severely qualified, first, because he intensifies the connection of the spiritual and the physical by combining his Neoplatonic frame of reference with less rarefied attitudes sanctioned by the respected example of refined passion in Petrarchan love poetry. Then, though Neoplatonic ideas give the framework

Spenser wants for understanding love, he does not accept the evaluation of the physical implied by the Neoplatonic ladder – the scale described by Diotima in *The Symposium* (211) – by which the lover ascends through and beyond contemplation of individual to contemplation of universal beauty. Spenser's attention at the end of the hymn returns to the individual beloved, and to his desire for complete union with her – spiritual, and, therefore, physical. It is this unusual combination of Neoplatonic claims about love and beauty as vehicles of divine knowledge with the praise of Venus that produces a sacramental view of the sensuous world denied by orthodox Neoplatonism. As Enid Welsford puts it, for Spenser 'physical beauty is sacramental, and the true lover is like a Catholic whose belief in transubstantiation only increases his reverence for the outward and visible vehicles of an inward and spiritual grace'.[7]

A Hymn of Heavenly Love reverses the direction of the previous hymns. Most of the poem is a straightforward account of the central elements of the Christian scheme – the fall of the angels, the creation and fall of man, the nativity, the summary of the law, the institution of the eucharist, and the crucifixion. Spenser's subject is now not the love of man for God but of God for man as this is manifested by the two great evidences of heavenly love, the creation and the incarnation. With this all but overwhelming perspective in view the proper Christian response can only be to attempt that unreserved dedication to God from which human nature will always lapse, while Spenser's meditation on the sufferings of the Incarnate Christ mean that any response which is oblique and involves pleasure – proper as such a response may be to God's love manifested in creation – naturally seems inadequate. 'Rouse thyself' (we are told),

> out of thy soil,   *dirt*
> In which thou wallowest like to filthy swine,
> And dost thy mind in dirty pleasures moyle.   *defile*
>   (218–20)

Far from being sacramental, physical being is now 'sinful flesh', 'fleshly slime', 'clay, base, vile, and next to nought'. The antithesis to the previous hymns could scarcely be more marked.

A Hymn of Heavenly Beauty at first ignores this *volte-face* and endorses the earlier poems. Spenser returns to oblique responses. By contemplating earthly beauty we may ascend to knowledge of the divine (22–8). In a context of heavenly 'forms' this seems to be the Platonic argument of an ascent through human beauty to divine wisdom, but Spenser illustrates from the beauty of creation,

and when the argument is restated it is given a specifically
Christian turn: through the beauty of creation we can learn to
look towards the Creator (127–33). There is no contradiction.
Plato is absorbed into Spenser's heavenly scheme (the realm of
Ideas is above the heaven we can see, but below that of the hier-
archies of angels [78 ff.]). The goodness of God is shown forth by
the beauty of creation because 'all that's good is beautiful and
fair' (*HHB*, 133) – which is precisely the (Neoplatonic) argument
of *A Hymn in Honour of Beauty* (139). Spenser's Platonism and
his Christianity are at one. In different but not incompatible ways
created beauty may lead to a knowledge of God. The last section
of the hymn, however, shows a complete disdain for the material
creation. Venus, the power behind creation in *A Hymn in Honour
of Beauty*, is superseded by Sapience, Eternal Wisdom. Venus is
now an 'Idol',[8] the product of 'fabling wits'. Love of Sapience
transports us 'from flesh into the spright [spirit]'. The poem
repeats the conclusion of *A Hymn of Heavenly Love* (274–80): to
those granted an unmediated vision of Eternal Wisdom, earthly
love and beauty,

> that fair lamp, which useth to enflame
> The hearts of men with self-consuming fire,
> Thenceforth seems foul, and full of sinful blame.
> (274–6)

The Faerie Queene *and* Paradise Lost

Before attempting to bring the contradictions of the four hymns
into their implied relationships I want to look at how love and
sexual desire are treated elsewhere in Spenser, particularly in his
most important poem, *The Faerie Queene*. In one place – in
Amoretti, sonnet 72 – Spenser describes human love as a decided
barrier to divine love. But the *Amoretti* is a work showing a spiritual progress (through courtship to marriage), and the concluding
marriage poem, *Epithalamion*, is quite different in its attitude. In
The Faerie Queene the effect of love as ennobling is constantly
emphasized, and emphasized in relation to the most important
characters – Britomart, the knight of Chastity (by which Spenser
means not celibacy but faithful love); and Prince Arthur,
Magnificence, the figure in whom are summed up all the knight-
ly virtues.[9] In *The Faerie Queene* love, 'of honour and all virtue is/
The root' (IV, poem, 2): love is the desire for beauty, and beauty
an index of virtue. And, as in the earthly hymns, sexual love is
carefully distinguished from purely physical desire. In Book II,

the book of Temperance, the climactic Bower of Bliss episode, while vividly admitting the powerful attractions of sexual desire, condemns sexual feeling which is purely physical pleasure. Acrasia, the enchantress who presides over the Bower, is a Circe figure: men who accept the pleasures she offers are transformed into animals. But sexual *love* is treated quite differently. Venus is a central figure of Book III, the book of Chastity, and of Book IV, the book of Friendship. In Book III the central positive myth is that of the Garden of Adonis, a paradise over which Venus presides, and which, in the structure of *The Faerie Queene* as a whole, is the antithesis of the Bower of Bliss: the Garden shows the true form of those forces which the Bower corrupts by parody. All living things originate from the Garden, and, as in the hymns, Spenser presents this creativity by a syncretism of classical and Christian sources – the myth of Venus, the Platonic idea of a pre-existent state, and a Christian injunction: procreation in the garden obeys the behest 'of th'Almighty Lord,/That bade them to increase and multiply' (III.vi.34). Venus is not subdued by these more austere associations. The episode's account of creative forces includes a thoroughly unpuritanical celebration of sexual love (III.vi.41).

The same attitude to sexual love is shown in the Temple of Venus episode of Book IV, and in the hero Calidore's vision of the Graces in Book VI. In Book IV Venus again embodies universal fecundity. She is praised in a prayer which paraphrases the opening of Lucretius's *De rerum natura* (IV.x.44–7). The prayer is spoken by a votary in Venus's temple, not in Spenser's own voice: but, though Spenser puts the view dramatically, it is not identified as inadequate as is the comparable (but sexually corrupt) Song of the Rose in the Bower of Bliss (II.xii.74–5). As C. S. Lewis notices,[10] Venus in Book IV is both the planetary goddess who arouses the feelings which replenish the world, and the *Paradigma* of creation, the eternal pattern of beauty described by Plato in the *Timaeus* (29). The same is true of Venus in the Garden of Adonis. There 'her heavenly house, /The house of goodly forms and fair aspects', is the source

> Whence all the world derives the glorious
> Features of beauties, and all shapes select,
> With which high God his workmanship hath decked.
>   (III.vi.12)

In Book VI it is as a result of Calidore's love for Pastorella – a love in which the physical fulfilment of desire is delicately

acknowledged (x.38) – that he has his vision of the Graces, dancing naked on Mount Acidale, an earthly paradise, the favoured
resort of Venus. The source of Venus's power, and of the power of
poetry (they are the inspiration of the poet-piper, Colin Clout),
the Graces are also the well-spring of the book's central virtue,
Courtesy – which is not, for Spenser, a narrow issue of manners,
but a quasi-religious virtue fundamental to truly civilized living.
So that in both Book IV and Book VI of *The Faerie Queene* love of
beauty and sexual love are central to the poem's eclectic portrait
of Christian virtue.

The last of my non-Spenserian perspectives is the positive view
of sexual love in *Paradise Lost*. Here Milton may have been influenced by Spenser, whom he pronounced (citing specifically the
moral implications of the Bower of Bliss) 'a better teacher than
Scotus or Aquinas'.[11] His own view is first shown in *Paradise Lost*
by the hymn to marriage (IV.741–59). The archangel Raphael
explains the place of human love in relation to knowledge of
God:

> love refines
> The thoughts, and heart enlarges, hath his seat
> In reason, and is judicious, is the scale
> By which to heav'nly love thou may'st ascend.[12]

Taken in isolation this might sound like the Platonic ladder:
taken with the hymn in praise of marriage it is clearly not Platonic.
Like Spenser, Milton distinguishes love which is expressed physically from simple physical desire, but he goes further in presenting
love's bodily expression as splendidly holy. It is an attribute not
only of men but of angels. 'Love not the heav'nly Spirits', Adam
asks Raphael,

> and how their love
> Express they, by looks only, or do they mix
> Irradiance, virtual or immediate touch?'
>   To whom the Angel, with a smile that glowed
> Celestial rosy red, love's proper hue,
> Answered: 'Let it suffice thee that thou know'st
> Us happy, and without love no happiness.
> Whatever pure thou in the body enjoy'st
> (And pure thou wert created) we enjoy
> In eminence, and obstacle find none
> Of membrane, joint, or limb, exclusive bars;
> Easier than air with air, if Spirits embrace,
> Total they mix, union of pure with pure

Desiring; nor restrained conveyance need
As flesh to mix with flesh, or soul with soul.
                    (VIII.615–29)

As Douglas Bush remarks (somewhat drily in the circumstances),
'Milton here goes beyond traditional angelology'.[13] Milton 'goes
beyond' because he has a heterodox view of creation. This is
implied in *Paradise Lost* (V.469–500; VII.168–73), and stated in
the private notebook in which Milton worked out his theology
while writing the epic (*De doctrina christiana*, I.vii). Milton did
not accept the idea of *creatio ex nihilo*. His alternative was to see
creation as emanation from God, a view which gives a peculiar
sanctity to matter. It is on this that his very high valuation of
love involving the whole physical-spiritual being depends.
Milton's is the Spenserian view – that is, the view of *The Faerie
Queene*, the *Epithalamion*, and the earthly hymns – but set in a more
exclusively Christian frame of reference: instead of Spenser's
heterodox syncretism Milton draws on a heterodox theology.

Never trust the poet: trust the poem

Vouchsafe then, O thou most almighty Spright,   *Spirit*
From whom all gifts of wit and knowledge flow,
To shed into my breast some sparkling light
Of thine eternal Truth, that I may show
Some little beams to mortal eyes below,
Of that immortal beauty, there with thee,
Which in my weak distraughted mind I see.   *distracted*
                (*A Hymn of Heavenly Beauty*, 8–14)

No reader should fail to take seriously Spenser's serious prayer
to the Holy Spirit. But neither should we fail to take seriously the
parallel prayer to Venus at the beginning of *A Hymn in Honour of
Beauty* (15–21). Not that Spenser believed in Venus in the sense
in which he believed in the Holy Spirit, but for Spenser Venus is
a supreme fiction: what the mother of love and beauty personifies
is as real to him, as important and as valuable, as any force in
creation below the Holy Spirit, and may, indeed – so the rest of
Spenser's work implies – finally be understood as an aspect of
the divine which the ethics and myths of Christianity have not
adequately acknowledged.

Spenser offers his own simple solution to the contradiction
between his earthly and heavenly hymns: he did not mean what
is said in the earthly ones. The dedication sets out this view – not
without some internal self-contradiction – claiming that the

earthly hymns were writtten when the poet was young, that they
can corrupt, and that they have only been published because,
already distributed in manuscript, they could not be called in.[14]
There are no extant manuscripts of either hymn. There are no
stylistic differences between the two sets of hymns. Broad and
detailed structural correspondences between the two pairs suggest
that they were conceived as a group.[15] In any case, the corrupting
effect of the earthly hymns is said to depend, not on the poems
themselves, but on the corruption of readers who suck 'poison to
their strong passions' where they might suck 'honey to their
honest delight'. And the women to whom the poems are dedicated
are praised as examples 'of all true love and beauty, both in the
one and the other kind' – that is, they exemplify the qualities of
all four poems: evidently Spenser was not meaning to insult them
as examples of 'gross dunghill' qualities. The claim that the earthly
hymns are youthful compositions is fictional, an apology which
veils their heterodox implications.

A Hymn of Heavenly Love begins with a statement of re-direction, and it is this apparent re-direction that is the great stumbling
block to reading the four poems as a unity:

> Love, lift me up upon thy golden wings,
> From this base world unto the heaven's height,
> Where I may see those admirable things,
> Which there thou workest by thy sovereign might,
> Far above feeble reach of earthly sight,
> That I thereof an heavenly hymn may sing
> Unto the God of Love, high heaven's king.

> Many lewd layes (ah woe is me the more)   *poems*
> In praise of that mad fit which fools call love,
> I have in th'heat of youth made heretofore,
> That in light wits did loose affection move.
> But all those follies now I do reprove,
> And turnèd have the tenor of my string,
> The heavenly praises of true love to sing.

Though this is apparently intended as a repudiation of the two
previous hymns clearly it misrepresents them: on no possible view
are they in any sense 'lewd' (they are neither sensually provocative nor ignorant and unphilosophical), nor are they poems that
might move loose affection, even in light wits: no reader could
find them erotically titillating. They are both philosophical and
(in Spenser's usual sense) chaste. What these opening stanzas
imply positively about a new object of love is endorsed by the

visionary poetry of the end of the hymn. The question is how far the terms of this repudiation and of that vision imply a fundamental and complete change of direction, or how far this statement of re-direction represents only part of Spenser's mind – an orthodoxy at odds with the more heterodox meaning of *Four Hymns* as a whole.

The main reason for insisting that *A Hymn of Heavenly Love* is partial is not literary but religious. In its concentration on Christ's sufferings and man's guilt it is a poem for Lent. It is no more a full representation of Spenser's Christianity, and therefore of his whole view on love, than Jeremiah is the prophet for Advent. The hymn's matter is decisive about its partiality, but this view can be enforced by more purely literary arguments.

The main literary argument is about the structure of *Four Hymns* as a whole – the many parallels between the first and second pairs. Each hymn has a broadly similar structure: invocation, account of creation, vision of paradise. Within each pair of hymns there is a contrast: creation is construction according to a pre-existing pattern (*HL, HHL*); creation is a process of development (*HB, HHB*). The contrast within each pair forms a parallel between the two pairs. These are not geometric correspondences: they are skewed Gothic symmetries. Their effect is to complicate the statement of clear-cut contrasts and a progress from Error to Truth with a set of more complex complementary interrelationships. The biblical account of creation in *A Hymn of Heavenly Love*, for example, could be seen either as superseding or as complementing the Platonic account of *A Hymn in Honour of Love*. In both the motive power is love, but love that operates in different ways. In *A Hymn in Honour of Love* Love is a gravitational force drawing separate things into ordered relationships – a force drawing inwards. In *A Hymn of Heavenly Love* Love is a force impelled outwards, creativity of which the characteristic expression is self-less generosity. Despite *A Hymn of Heavenly Love*'s opening repudiation, these forces are shown by the other hymns not as incompatible but as complementary. One basis of the earlier account of creation is Platonic (*HB*, 29) – the Demiurge of the *Timaeus*. Spenser explicitly unites Christian and Platonic ideas of heaven in *A Hymn of Heavenly Beauty*, where he also uses the Platonic notion of the Form to distinguish the spiritual world that poetry inspired by the Holy Spirit reveals from what the mind unaided by such grace can know (*HHB*, 78–84, 19). Evidently he saw Christian and Platonic ideas as compatible. He took the usual Renaissance view: like other highly regarded classical writers, Plato had understood correctly as far as reason unaided by revelation can. On a Catholic view revelation completes reason: it does not contradict it. The two accounts of creation are not in conflict. The effect of love in creation identified in the earthly hymn is complementary to that of the heavenly – as it is in *Colin Clout's Come Home Again*. There Spenser speaks in praise of love through a *persona*, Colin, a 'priest' of Cupid, who both is and is not the poet. In Colin's hymn a myth of Cupid as creator, a myth which expresses the Neoplatonic view of love as the power which unites and moves the world, is combined with an account of creation based on Genesis.[16]

Other aspects of structure and language in *Four Hymns* give a similar effect of cross-reference, and so complication of idea, between the two pairs of poems. In the final lines of *A Hymn of Heavenly Love* Spenser uses the Neoplatonic notion of the Idea to distinguish knowledge of the Jesus of history from knowledge of the ascended Christ. This draws *A Hymn of Heavenly Love* into a structural pattern which relates it to the previous hymns in which an ideal form is extrapolated by the lover from the beloved's physical beauty to infer her spiritual state (*HHL*, 193; *HHB*, 214). Though we are told there is an abyss between the two kinds of love, the parallel Platonic ways of conceiving inference from the earthly to the heavenly connect the two: the frameworks and language by which the loving mind understands its experiences cannot be irrelevant to what is understood. There is here a problem inherent in the language of religious vision: any poet seeking a language for the ineffable must struggle with the sense of an unbridgeable gap between experience and any possible embodiment of it, as Spenser does in this hymn (40–9). That said, the language of the end of *A Hymn of Heavenly Love* harks back specifically to the language of erotic experience which the plain sense repudiates.[17] In so doing, like the parallel Platonic frames of reference, it undermines the apparent insistence on discontinuity between *eros* and *agape*, erotic and heavenly love.[18]

At the close of *A Hymn of Heavenly Love* Spenser returns to the repudiation of earthly love as that 'with which the world doth blind/ Weak fancies, and stir up affections base'. By distinguishing between desire ('love', so-called, which 'stir[s] up affections base') and true love the previous hymns precisely deny that *all* love does this. The close of *A Hymn of Heavenly Love* does not reject this argument: it ignores it. It is as though the earlier distinction – one generally accepted by Renaissance Christian Neoplatonists – had never been made. The hymn ends with the view of St John of the Cross, a view incompatible with Spenser's *Epithalamion* on his own marriage (published the year before the

Four Hymns) and with the treatment of love in *The Faerie Queene* (Books IV–VI of which were published in the same year as *Four Hymns*). One can only make some consistent sense of this by noticing that, at the end of *A Hymn of Heavenly Beauty* (as at the end of *A Hymn in Honour of Love*), the positives from which this repudiation springs are not put in terms of achieved experience: they are postulates drawn from the deflected desires of a disappointed lover who is cheering himself up (288–94). The speaker who considers all earthly love as incompatible with the love of God has not realized the ideals of the first two hymns and passed beyond them: he is finding in the love of God consolation for an emptiness in human love at odds with the earthly hymns' no less partial but still eloquent affirmation.

Thus, at any rate, an argument for the unity of the *Four Hymns* may run, though it may be necessary finally to admit that such an argument cannot confidently be sustained in terms of intention, but only in terms of saving the poet from his own Puritan censor. This censor mistook the beautiful extensions of Neoplatonism in the earthly hymns for lewd lays, but publication, with whatever excuse, allowed the earthly hymns to stand. And stand they do, as philosophical and – in terms recognized by *The Faerie Queene* – religious poems.

On such an account neither of the heavenly hymns gives a conclusive view. *A Hymn of Heavenly Love* is disqualified by its Lenten subject matter, its narrow (albeit powerful) perspective, its structural relation to the preceding hymns, and its earthly-love vocabulary of religious vision. In *A Hymn of Heavenly Beauty* the speaker's denigrations and aspirations are not unconditioned ideals but deflected disappointments. The final statement about love of the four hymns taken altogether can therefore be inferred by seeing them, not as the epistle and the opening of *A Hymn of Heavenly Love* suggest, as progressing from error to truth, but as complementary and cumulative – that is, by extrapolating, where their ethics clash, an overview which subsumes the apparent contradictions. Both pairs of hymns are true. It is not Lent all the year round. Only a neurotically ascetic recoil from sexual love and human beauty sees them as inescapably of the flesh and the world, and conventionally triadic with the Devil. As elsewhere in Spenser's work, on this view human love and human beauty are, properly considered, of the Spirit, forms of revelation, types and shadows of the divine.

'Literary criticism should be completed by criticism from a definite ethical and theological standpoint.'[19] Thus T. S. Eliot, and I agree. But the danger of this lies in enlisting poetry to subserve one's own ethical or theological views. I regard the view of love I have extrapolated from the *Four Hymns* as splendidly humane, if it can be realized. I do not, though, intend to project my own ethics on to Spenser. My own view is that sexual expression in love is proper only when the desire (which is, finally, spiritual) to be as fully as possible conscious of the beloved exceeds – and in so doing quells – the powerful egotism of physical desire. Which it rarely does. I have two misgivings about this. First, that it may be based on a puritanical inability to accept physical pleasure except in terms that are unrealistically idealized – though pleasure, so long as it is not exploitative, has a valid moral function: it makes people kind to one another. Then, if you do not take the simple view of complete separation between physical and spiritual, and human and divine love, you are forced to make difficult judgements about the quality of your own feelings. A mind seeking to purify the egotism of physical desire by an adequate regard for the loved one's otherness may be too willing to find this difficult selflessness fully accomplished in its least manifestation. My own views are present in this argument to this extent: it seems to me that, unqualified by their earthly counterparts, Spenser's heavenly hymns endorse attitudes which are too negatively puritanical towards noble-minded delights. Human love and beauty can be sacramental. And so the earthly hymns – and all the rest of Spenser's work – say.

Of the range of views, from St John of the Cross to Milton, on this one aspect of the issue of matter as symbol or vehicle of spirit perhaps the most widely shared is some version of that evinced by the Hopkins sonnet: a doubt about the danger of sensual impurity, or the more insidious danger of idolatry; but a conviction too that one can see in human love and beauty – without approaching it ascetically: *in* it, not (as in the Platonic scheme) *through* it – a valid intimation of the divine. The presence of Venus in Spenser's poetry, especially in *The Faerie Queene*, suggests that Spenser felt it necessary to go outside Christianity for an adequate myth of the creative sexual forces in the world. That myth carries with it attitudes to sexuality not obviously present in mainstream Christianity with which Spenser complements his Christian views on love – not obviously present, except perhaps in the Song of Songs, of which, indicatively, Spenser made his own (lost) translation. I do not imagine he felt that the usual allegorization about Christ's love for the Church exhausted its meaning.

Notes

1. Augustine, *De doctrina christiana*, III.x.16; *De libero arbitrio*, II.xvi. 42.
2. W. B. Yeats, 'Per Amica Silentia Lunae' (1917), *Mythologies* (London: Macmillan, 1959), p. 331.
3. St John of the Cross, *The Ascent of Mount Carmel*, I. iv. *The Complete Works of Saint John of the Cross*, tr. E. Allison Peers, 3 vols (London: Burns & Oates, 1943), I. 24.
4. It is not certain what Spenser knew of Dante. He read Italian (Ariosto and Tasso were important influences on *The Faerie Queene*), and the *Commedia* was available in England and known among Spenser's closest associates, including Sir Philip Sidney and Gabriel Harvey.
5. *HL*, 281–91. Quotations from Spenser are from *Spenser's 'Faerie Queene'*, ed. J. C. Smith, 2 vols (Oxford: Clarendon Press, 1909); and *Spenser's Minor Poems*, ed. Ernest de Selincourt (Oxford: Clarendon Press, 1910). Spelling and punctuation are modernized; Spenser's archaic vocabulary is glossed where necessary.
6. Fayning / fayned – words connected with both desire and illusion: *Oxford English Dictionary* (*OED*), 'fain', *v.* 3, 'longing, wistful' (which cites *HL*, 216 – cited by the Osgood concordance to Spenser under 'feign'); *OED*, 'feign', II (a range of meanings connected with illusion and deceit). Especially doubtful uses are *HL*, 216, 254, and *HHB*, 223 (where it is combined with 'Idol', cf. note 8).
7. Enid Welsford, *Spenser. 'Fowre Hymnes'. 'Epithalamion'. A Study of Edmund Spenser's Doctrine of Love* (Oxford: Blackwell, 1967), pp. 46–7.
8. The word is not necessarily negative: it can mean 'counterpart, likeness' (*OED*, II.3.b, citing *Faerie Queene*, II.ii.41), an earthly embodiment of the divine – a sense Spenser also uses in *Amoretti*, 61 ('The glorious image of the maker's beauty, /My sovereign saint, the idol of my thought').
9. III.iii.1–2 (of Britomart); III.v.1–2 (of Prince Arthur).
10. C. S. Lewis, *Spenser's Images of Life*, ed. Alistair Fowler (Cambridge: Cambridge University Press, 1967), pp. 43–4.
11. *Areopagitica*, *The Works of John Milton* (New York: Columbia University Press, 1931), 18 vols., IV, 311.
12. *Paradise Lost*, VIII. 589–93. Quotations from Milton are from *Milton. Poetical Works*, ed. Douglas Bush (London: Oxford University Press, 1966).
13. Bush, *Milton. Poetical Works*, p. 369.
14. The stance of the dedication may have been influenced by the predispositions of the dedicatees, who were daughters of a notable Protestant family. Their father, Francis Russell, had been (with his father) a signatory to the deed by which Edward VI settled the crown on Lady Jane Grey. Imprisoned under Mary I, he escaped to Geneva and was involved in the Wyatt rebellion initiated in

response to Mary Tudor's marriage to Philip of Spain. He remained
active in church/state affairs during the reign of Elizabeth I. The
husband of Anne (Spenser's 'Marie') was Ambrose Dudley.
Brother-in-law to Lady Jane Grey, he was, even more deeply than
Russell, involved in the attempt to have her succeed Edward VI.
That the Protestant controversialist 'Martin Marprelate' found
occasion to admire his conduct in a dispute with the Archbishop of
Canterbury over the placing of a priest is probably indicative of
Puritan sympathies. (Martin Marprelate, *The Epistle*, ed. Edward
Arber, Westminster: Constable & Co., 1895, pp. 28–9.) In this con-
text Spenser cannot but have felt that the dedication of his earthly
hymns required careful handling. For a discussion of Spenser and
the Countess of Warwick see 'Spenserus', *Essays by Rosemund Tuve:
Spenser, Herbert, Milton*, ed. Thomas P. Roche Jr. (Princeton:
Princeton University Press, 1970), pp. 139–63; and of Spenser and
the Countess of Cumberland see Jon A. Quitslund, 'Spenser and
the Patronesses of the *Fowre Hymnes*: "Ornaments of All True Love
and Beautie"', in *Silent but for the Word*, ed. Margaret Patterson
Hannay (Kent, OH: Kent State University Press, 1985), pp.
184–202.

15.   These parallels can be interpreted in different ways. Interpreting
them as contrasts Einar Bjorvand attributes to *Four Hymns* mean-
ings at odds with the treatment of love in the rest of Spenser's work.
See 'Spenser's defence of poetry: some structural aspects of the
Fowre Hymnes', in *Fair Forms*, ed. Maren-Sofie Røstvig (Cambridge:
D. S. Brewer, 1975), pp. 13–51.

16.   Written in 1591, *Colin Clout's Come Home Again* (*CCHA*) was
revised before publication in 1595. Robert Ellrodt argues (on stylistic grounds) that the more Neoplatonic sections of Colin's hymn
are part of this revision (*Neoplatonism in the Poetry of Spenser*,
Travaux de Humanisme et Renaissance, 35, Geneva: Droz, 1960,
pp. 19–22). The poem is at points particularly close to *A Hymn in
Honour of Love*: see *CCCHA*, 839–54, and *HL*, 57–98; *CCCHA*,
871–4, and *HL*, 104–12. Not saying in what sense he believed
them, Spenser elsewhere entertains myths far more difficult to
reconcile with Christian doctrine than this combination of Genesis
and Neoplatonism. The Garden of Adonis subscribes to an idea of
reincarnation (III.vi.33); *A Hymn in Honour of Beauty* accepts a
related, and equally unorthodox, idea of the soul's heavenly pre-
existence (201–3).

17.   Flame/inflame (*HL*, 8, 102, 115, 124, 152; *HHL*, 270); kindle (*HL*,
28, 65, 124; *HB*, 5, 58, 100, 180; *HHL*, 287; *HHB*, 5, 297); ravisht/
enravisht (*HL*, 119; *HB*, 12; *HHL*, 268, 281; *HHB*, 1); rage/
enragement (*HL*, 117; *HB*, 4, 73; *HHL*, 286; *HHB*, 1).

18.   If one accepts the numerological analysis (Bjorvand, 'Spenser's
defence of poetry', 41) which remarks that Sapience enters *Four
Hymns* in their 153rd stanza – 153 being the sum of the numbers
from 1 to 17; 17 being the number symbolizing the unity of the Old

and New Testaments (10 Commandments, 7 Gifts of the Spirit) – this, too, implies a contradiction of the dedication's disclaiming of the earthly hymns, and that the poems form an elaborate unity. But numerological analysis of Spenser needs to be treated with care. Spenser at times composed numerologically, as in the simply patterned introduction into *The Faerie Queene* of the arithmetically named brothers, Priamond, Diamond and Triamond (IV.ii.42). Such an obvious simple use of numbers is not evidence of secret complex uses – rather the reverse. The attribution of esoteric meanings (by definition those the many could not be expected to see) is a charter for fancifulness unless accompanied by responsible scepticism. Without this, eager exegetes can too readily devise the patterns they suppose themselves to reveal. (See Enid Welsford's discussion of A. Kent Hieatt's numerological analysis of Spenser's *Epithalamion*, Welsford, *Spenser's Doctrine of Love*, appendix II.)

19. T. S. Eliot, 'Religion and Literature', *Selected Essays*, 3rd edn (London: Faber & Faber, 1951), p. 388.

12

The Romantic Tradition and the Sacrament of the Present Moment: Wordsworth and Tillich

PETER PHILLIPS

In contrast to the Platonic tradition which he sees as enjoining an escape from materiality, Peter Phillips identifies Romanticism as thoroughly sacramental. To illustrate this, he compares the thought of the poet William Wordsworth and the theologian Paul Tillich. Despite the century which separates them, both abandon a universal objectivity to focus upon a disclosure in a significant moment and experience. Often mediated by art (as in Tillich's case by German expressionist painting or by Cézanne), such kairoi (decisive moments) enable us to penetrate beyond nature to God as its ground. In arguing thus, Tillich had been anticipated by Wordsworth's notion of 'spots of time' and by Kant's claim in The Critique of Judgement *that reflection on experience can generate legitimate, though non-provable, principles.*

The Platonic temptation

Plato sought to banish the artist from his Republic. As 'an image-maker whose images are phantoms far removed from reality',[1] the artist poses a threat. The problem, of course, for Plato was not that such images are poor, inaccurate representations, but that they are too good. Rather than visible embodiments which challenge us into striving for what is real, these images become phantoms which seduce us into resting in the image itself. Having escaped from the shadows, it is all too easy to seek to remain in the warm security of the cave and bask in the cosy and dangerous comfort of the fire with its flickering fantasies. Such fantasies are invariably of our own making.² Plato calls on us to forsake images and to risk the tortuous and costly journey to gaze at the light of truth itself. It is tempting to interpret this journey as one depicting the soul's escape from the trammels of materiality and many have succumbed to the temptation. Christianity, however, must remain resistant to this temptation, attractive though the lure of Plato's vision has seemed to many in the course of the history of Christian thought.

St Thomas Aquinas alerts us to this in his reaffirmation of the fact that the beginning of all knowledge is to be found in the senses.³ Materiality forms the conceptual matrix of our thinking: this is what it means to be human. We are beings embodied in an unfolding, physical universe. Though we are intellects capable of apprehending that which is intelligible, we are open only to an intelligibility involved in matter. For Thomas, as well as for the Welsh poet and visionary, David Jones, the human being is by nature a borderer, 'the sole inhabitant of a tract of country where matter marches with spirit'.⁴ This view of what it means to be human represents a careful balance of extremes. It denotes not only a rejection of attempts to reduce intellectual activity to a variety of sensation but also challenges attempts to dispense altogether with sensation, conceding to the intellect a direct access to an intelligibility of forms somehow isolated from matter. In other words, we find ourselves at home in a sacramental universe. The mind might delight in the subtle play of metaphor and symbol, but these are no luxury. It is in the nature of being human that we simply cannot escape their necessity. St Thomas reminds us that when it comes to talk of the divine we can proceed in no other way: 'poetry employs metaphors for the sake of representation, in which we are born to take delight. Holy teaching, on the other hand, adopts them for their indispensable usefulness'.⁵ This leads to an ambiguity which belongs to the heart of all theological discourse: there remains an element of risk, something inevitably precarious in the enterprise. God reveals himself through the stuff of creation but at the same time his nature remains hidden and beyond our grasp.

The Romantic alternative

This theme becomes particularly acute for the poets, artists and philosophers who shaped that revolution in thinking and feeling which is generally termed Romanticism, and which in so many ways still provides that context for our own way of experiencing the world. Our discussion might be developed fruitfully by taking

two representatives of this multifaceted tradition, one from its
first flowering, and another from its later development: the poet
William Wordsworth, and the philosophical theologian Paul
Tillich. The writings of both of these thinkers are strongly autobiographical and can be identified by that sense of passionate
engagement which was so much a feature of the Romantics. Both
Tillich and Wordsworth can be placed in very specific contexts,
but the vision which such contexts engender allows us to understand more richly the texture of our own humanity.

Romanticism has its own myths of the fall of souls and the
journey towards enlightenment but these myths are significantly
different from those of Plato. Wordsworth's 'Intimations of Immortality from Recollections of Early Childhood', published in 1807,
provides such a myth in its exploration of the fall from the undifferentiated experience of dreaming innocence and our journey
towards enlightenment. Wordsworth was as aware as Plato had
been of the earthly temptations to 'endless imitation'[6] but to read
this poem as a wistful yearning for, and recreation of, lost innocence is seriously to misread it. Here is no sentimental nostalgia
offering the comfort of fireside tales. Wordsworth's journey towards
the light of truth is as demanding as Plato's journey out of the
Cave, but for Wordsworth the path is necessarily indirect, a
journey made by way of metaphor and symbol. The 'philoso-
phic mind' wrestles with a meaning which can only be attained
sacramentally:

> To me the meanest flower that blows can give
> Thoughts that do often lie too deep for tears.[7]

It is in this context that we can best understand the particular
significance and originality of Tillich's lecture 'On the Idea of a
Theology of Culture', delivered to the Kant Society in Berlin, in
April 1919. This is a revolutionary work, an attempt to offer a new
way forward after the certainties of pre-war theological reflection
had been so completely shattered in the devastation of war.
Tillich intended his work to be a manifesto and it has all the
enthusiasms and inconsistencies that we associate with such a
document.

Wordsworth's *Prelude* offers a striking parallel. Both *The Prelude*
and 'On the Idea of a Theology of Culture' are works of relatively
young men whose radical thinking would, in later years, become
rather more circumspect. Sadly, they were both somewhat tem-
pered by success. Although great masters of the past such as
Spenser and Milton contribute considerably to shape the thought
and vocabulary of the poem, Wordsworth, in the opening sections

of that work, carefully rejects as unsatisfactory the received tradition of historical, or biblical, theme and determines on the autobiographical. Tillich, likewise, claimed to reject the received tradition of doing theology, but is as indebted to his predecessors as Wordsworth proved to be. Tillich was caught up in a general crisis of both thought and self-confidence in the aftermath of the First World War in a strikingly similar manner to the English poet in the crisis provoked by the French Revolution. As Wordsworth had found his true poetic voice in the years following the French Revolution, so Tillich found his theological voice as he came to terms with the experience of the First World War. Far more significant than all these biographical similarities, however, is a strong similarity of theme. Like Tillich, the early Wordsworth makes a strong case both for the grounding of human recollection in the Absolute and for acknowledging the inevitable singularity of individual experience:

> Points have we all of us within our souls,
> Where all stand single, this I feel, and make
> Breathings for incommunicable powers.
> Yet each man is a memory to himself.[8]

For Wordsworth, autobiographical reflection is not merely a matter of style, important though this might be, but is a feature of what he was attempting to say. The argument Tillich invokes throughout 'On the Idea of a Theology of Culture' is also a peculiarly personal one.

The 'significant moment' in Tillich and Wordsworth

Tillich opens his paper by distinguishing between the empirical sciences and the systematic cultural sciences. The former he defines as situations in which error can be discovered by external, objective testing, concerning matters of historical or scientific fact. Historical and textual criticism of the Bible belong to this sphere; already we may note Tillich's strong unease regarding the methods and results of liberal scholarship. Faith, for Tillich, is too important an experience to leave to the vagaries of historical research. The systematic cultural sciences, which we might suggest necessarily includes such diverse activities as engaging in quantum physics or systematic theology, Tillich sees as situations in which 'the standpoint of the thinker belongs to the thing itself'.[9] For Tillich, the concept of the standpoint is fundamental. Here we begin to understand what Tillich means by sacrament which he regards as that point which marks the intersection of time and eternity. This is a theme which surely has its origin in Kierkegaard's discussion of the 'category of the moment', a category which emerges as soon as spirit is posited: 'the moment is that ambiguity in which time and eternity touch each other, and with this the concept of *temporality* is posited, whereby time constantly intersects eternity and eternity constantly pervades time'.[10] This is the context which provides the possibility of revelatory experience.

And so it was for Wordsworth: there are striking and resonant similarities in the powerful account of our access to the Unconditional which underlies *The Prelude*. This is what Wordsworth experienced one night rowing beneath the Lakeland hills,[11] which left a 'darkness', a 'solitude, Or blank desertion': an experience which posed for him the question of the mystery of being. It was something he discovered at the sight of a blind beggar in the overflowing streets of the great city.[12] Wordsworth constantly reflects on this most powerful visionary insight into the ordinary,[13] the product of recollection and reflection in which the spirit is as much actively constructing as passively receiving. This is clear from the passage reflecting on the significant and revelatory moments which he calls 'spots of time':

This efficacious spirit chiefly lurks
Among those passages of life in which
We have the deepest feeling that the mind
Is lord and master, and that outward sense
Is but the obedient servant of her will.
Such moments worthy of all gratitude,
Are scattered everywhere . . .[14]

The standpoint signifies, as one commentator puts it, 'the envisioning of a world from its creative centre'.[15] This is the point at which the world confronts us and we, in turn, are able to grasp the world as sacrament, as medium of revelation. Here is a thoroughgoing and consistent reworking of the idea of the concrete universal, the symbol as it is disclosed in the individual historical context of an existing person or community: 'it is a moment in the history of the development of culture; it is a definite concrete historical realisation of a cultural idea; it is not only cognisant of culture but also creative of it'.[16]

Tillich returns frequently in his writings to a discussion of the fact that sacraments belong both to individuals and to a community, although, for the sake of this essay, it will be appropriate to explore merely their individual dimension. Sacraments, for Tillich, are conditioned inevitably by history. They offer us fleeting moments of engagement, caught up as we are within the dynamics of history. Here we are in touch with the underlying sensitivity to history that is a central feature of Romanticism. This is something new. The Romantic consciousness appreciated the fragility and elusiveness of the passing moment in a way unknown before. It had to come to terms with a sense of change, a sense of history's irreversible and relentless flow.

Tillich seems to be suggesting that it is not only the act of artistic creation that allows a sacramental encounter, but also the individual's engagement with great works of art. This is one of the functions of all great art. Such highly privileged moments of human understanding yield an insight into the most ordinary and mundane encounters with the world around us; 'turn but a stone and start a wing', as Francis Thompson reminds us.[17] Tillich's engagement with the works of the German Expressionists invites us to follow him in accepting that the form and content of such paintings give way to a revelatory substance: the 'how' and 'what' of the painting gives way to the 'why', its power of prophetic social challenge.[18] The autobiographical tenor of Tillich's response to Expressionism leaves his account unfortunately more imprecise and idiosyncratic than we would wish. It is a pity that Tillich does not discuss individual examples. Nevertheless what he says can be applied particularly well to Kirchner's disturbing Berlin street scenes of 1913 and 1914. One is moved not simply by the paintings themselves but by the questions they raise. As Tillich himself comments: 'Nature has been stripped of her appearance. One looks to the ground of nature. But, says Schelling, dread dwells at the ground of all living things, and this dread sweeps over us from the pictures of the Expressionists . . . This dread seems to me also to be deepened by a feeling of guilt, which is to be interpreted not in a strictly ethical sense, but in a cosmic sense, the guilt of mere existence.'[19]

These powerful and profoundly disturbing pictures of the first decades of the present century are expressions of what George Steiner was later to characterize as that 'absent "thereness" . . . which is articulate in the master-texts of our age'.[20] In every momentary encounter with that which is other than ourselves can be discovered not merely the form and content of that which confronts us, but a deeper import which is our encounter with the mystery of being, challenging, disturbing – and perhaps ultimately bringing healing. Spiritual creativity, Tillich reminds us, is that to which religious language gives the symbol 'grace', that 'state of being filled with the divine'.[21] Again it is Steiner who might help us grasp the implications of this. Like Tillich, Steiner suggests

that in our striving to do justice 'to the unbounded diversities of
the modes of our meeting with the other',[22] it is not inappropriate
to argue that we have to do with transcendence: 'I am wagering,
both in a Cartesian and a Pascalian vein on the informing pressure
of a real presence in the semantic markers which generate Oedipus
the King, or Madame Bovary; in the pigments or incisions which
externalise Grünewald's Issenheim triptych or Brancusi's *Bird*;
in the notes, crotchets, markings of tempo and volume which
actualise Schubert's posthumous Quintet.'[23]

The philosophical background

Tillich develops the idea at length in various works: *The System of
the Sciences* of 1923 is a good example. Here Tillich insists that
'truth is not a system of abstract validities in relation to which
knowledge of the truth is either correct or incorrect. Truth is a
function that is realised only concretely and is realised correctly
in every creation.'[24] I think that there can be little doubt that the
underlying theme of Tillich's argument has its origin in Kant's
discussion of aesthetic judgement which is to be found in *The
Critique of Judgement*. Kant distinguishes between determinative
judgement and reflective judgement. The former represents our
ability to make sense of the world by working from the general to
the particular in order to identify and define what a thing is. This
is what we mean by conceptual thinking. Aesthetic judgements,
on the other hand, represent a response to the unique, the incom-
parable. Inevitably our response to the beautiful in nature, or our
delight in a great work of art, remains subjective yet Kant argues
that our response to the beautiful can lay claim to a sort of objectivity in so far as the beautiful is represented as the object of a
universal delight:

> Since the delight is not based on any inclination of the Subject
> . . . but the Subject feels himself completely *free* in respect to
> the liking which he accords the object, he can find as reason for
> his delight no personal conditions to which his own subjective
> self might alone be party. Hence he must regard it as resting on
> what he may also presuppose in every other person; and
> therefore he must believe that he has reason for demanding a
> similar delight from every one.[25]

Kant goes on to argue that, while the presence of such a principle
cannot be proved, it must none the less be assumed if thought of
particulars and of the nexus of phenomena in nature itself is to
be acknowledged as a possibility.

If it is the case that Tillich's argument rests on *The Critique of Judgement*, it is appropriate to turn to Tillich's own discussion of aesthetics to elucidate the matter further.[26] Tillich argues that if the truth of science is to be judged by a criterion of correctness, the truth of art is found in its power of expression. The great work of art, and our own engagement with it, illustrates the fact that we are dependent on 'an existential import' of reality: here we have to do with the realm of spirit, a category which is as independent of subjective feeling as it is of rational form: 'the existential import of things that it attempts to grasp is the revelation of pure being, of the unconditioned import within the particular form of things'.[27] This is not something which can become an object to be grasped directly, but is rather that which allows a grasp of anything at all. Indeed understanding would be an impossibility if we were not able to posit this existential import. It is something constitutive of understanding: 'the unconditioned form does not exist as a reality that can be grasped. The spiritual act can be directed to the universal only when it intuits the universal in a concrete norm, in an individual realisation of the universal'.[28]

Tillich's concept of norm is central here. Functioning in the same way as Kant's reflective judgement it 'can only be a law from and to itself'.[29] The norm functions as one of the ways in which Tillich articulates his notion of sacrament. A norm, like the sacrament, reflects the fact that thinking begins in concrete experience[30] and is established on the plane of conviction. In other words, a norm, or sacrament, is created rather than given, yet it is not brought to the situation, but discovered in that situation. 'The norm is a product of a particular moment; thus it is not universal', claims Tillich, but 'universally valid':[31] as such it becomes the source of meaning, as well as the foundation for personal existence. The works of the Expressionists provide the best example of what Tillich means in so far as the power of these works combines a response to an object combined inextricably with creative interpretation: here we can identify a creation of the spirit, which in turn is the presupposition of creation. One might suggest also the new insight into the world hinted at in the finest poetry. Wallace Stevens' superb poem 'Anecdote of the Jar' is an example:[32] the artefact placed in the landscape gives a glimpse of something new, a new view of the world, a new insight into oneself. We are brought up against the grain of things. As Tillich had remarked in his lecture 'On the Idea of a Theology of Culture': 'the individual becomes a person by having such ideas, that is, by originating them for himself and by fashioning and interpreting his own existence in terms of them, for the basic function of

norms is to set goals for the conduct of life lived within the framework of the envisioned world, that is lived meaningfully.'[33]

This insight into the significance of the present moment can be
developed most usefully by turning to a theme explored by Frank
Kermode in his fascinating study of the literary significance of
apocalyptic, *The Sense of an Ending: Studies in the Theory of Fiction.*
His argument deserves careful study. Kermode sees the world of
the twentieth century as a world which no longer possesses points
of reference by which we might give coherence to our lives: there
are no longer clear ends or beginnings. In such a world we need
to create our own horizons, our own sense of coherence. Such
horizons are fictions but, as Wallace Stevens would insist, they are
necessary fictions: we cannot live without them. Kermode is
surely correct in suggesting that the concept of *kairos*, the sudden
recognition of the significant moment, functions as just such a
fiction. Such moments give coherence to the endless flux of time
and allow us to establish patterns which enable us to carry on
living.[34]

There is much to reflect upon in this little book, but it is
Kermode's application of this idea to the poetry of Wordsworth
which is of particular value for our own purposes. Kermode
explores the theme in relation to Wordsworth's 'Resolution and
Independence' in which the poet reflects on an earlier encounter
with a leech-gatherer in the darkening of the day on the hills
above Ambleside: this was for Wordsworth a sacramental and
revelatory moment, an orientating point through which *kairos*
(the significant moment) intervenes and gives direction to the
undifferentiated unfolding of *chronos* (ordinary time). The poem
is not about the leech-gatherer, the old and broken man whom
Wordsworth meets: the man and the meeting point provide
merely the context for an exploration and celebration of a
moment of Wordsworth's own subjectivity. Kermode's discussion
of the text is worthy of note:

> this poem mimes, as it were, that movement . . . out of the
> objective world of myth into the subjective consciousness
> working in time. That the old world is still represented in it –
> that you can still find a simple plot in the poem – is testimony
> to the strength, perhaps to the indispensability of the para-
> digms. But they are transfigured; one of the forces that go to
> make this change is certainly Wordsworth's sense of the past,
> the need to find power in temporal 'hiding-places'. The growth
> of a poet's mind, for him the true subject of an epic, is no
> longer a process of grasping the spatial relations of a six-days

world, turning oneself into a curious and universal scholar, but the process of finding oneself, by some peculiar grace, in lost time.[35]

This digression, taken to explore somewhat too briefly Wordsworth's fine and moving poem, was made because it offers us a most striking parallel to what Tillich is intending in his own account of *kairos*. Here Tillich is seeking tentatively to establish a theological grammar by which we might give a renewed sense to the notion of salvation, not as something set over against us, but as something discovered in subjectivity in the depths of our own experience of encountering our world. It is articulated in the sacrament of the significant moment. Tillich's position is effectively Wordsworthian. Like Wordsworth, and perhaps even more so, Tillich recognizes that to speak thus is no easy task. Good theology, like good poetry, demands engagement. It cannot be achieved by recounting the lessons of the past, even the past of the person of Jesus. This was at the root of Tillich's criticism of the Ritschlian theology which flourished in Germany in the period before the First World War. The theologian Albrecht Ritschl (1822–89) led the way to the greatest achievements of liberal theology which also generated its greatest weakness: its dry objectivity. It also saw in the moral imperative the only escape from our finitude.[36] But neither objectivity nor morality soothes the unhappy consciousness of which Hegel speaks.[37] For Tillich, as for Wordsworth, there can be no solution in turning oneself into Kermode's 'curious and universal scholar'. We cannot escape that sense of overpowering estrangement and yet in spite of that we are called to the struggle to make sense of our world in a way which demands a passionate engagement. We have no other option.

Implications for contemporary theology

Tillich's lifelong attempt was to continue to wrestle with this hard truth in the way of Wordsworth and his fellow Romantics. It is a path followed in this present century by poets such as Yeats and Wallace Stevens. Any attempt to reflect theologically in this style can only be fragmentary and fleeting after the manner of Coleridge's last great fragments. This is its nature. The task of the theologian standing in this tradition is to seek to fashion not a finished, objective work but, with the poet, to struggle hesitatingly to articulate both for himself and for those who accompany him on the way something that will suffice. It is no longer the poem itself but:

The poem of the mind in the act of finding
What will suffice.

Stevens' poem, 'Of Modern Poetry',[38] of which these words form
the opening lines, might offer a vision for the task ahead. We are
called to be aware of the possibilities of transcendence inherent
in the ritual of the common gesture: the man skating, the woman
dancing, or combing her hair. No longer can we seek to repeat
what is in the script, we have to learn the speech of the place. It is
here alone that we find the context in which to do our theologizing.

Although Paul Tillich has surprisingly little to say of sacraments
as they are traditionally understood in Christian discourse, a concern to explore the implications of an understanding of the world
itself as a vehicle of sacramental encounter pervades his writings.
There is no doubt that his thought is richly sacramental; this is
one of the aspects of his work that allies him closely with the
Romantic tradition, a theme I have attempted to tease out in this
essay. Unlike Plato, Tillich refuses to oppose matter to spirit. He
remains sensitive to the dangers inherent in such a dualism: the
human being, for Tillich, must be understood as a psychosomatic
unity.[39] Tillich's attempt to establish the sacramental standpoint
suggests that it is incorrect to charge him with subjectivism.
Nevertheless we are left with a sense of unease. Tillich claimed
that a belief-filled realism (*gläubiger Realismus*)[40] determined his
epistemology, but his thought, for all its sensitivity to the contingency of the present moment, remains idealist none the less.
This is a vein which emerges, sometimes more clearly, sometimes
less so, throughout Romanticism. Stevens' 'Of Modern Poetry'
remains a 'poem of the mind'. Similarly, as we have seen, Wordsworth could dispense with the person of the leech-gatherer: the
poem does not reveal his concern with what might become of
him in his increasing disability and poverty. The fact of the
encounter serves to generate a sacramental 'fiction', necessary
and creative though the encounter might prove to be.

Cézanne, whose 'Still Lives' Tillich so much admired, leads us
to encounter the reality of the apples and pears which he offers to
our gaze. For Cézanne, the important thing is our engagement
with the fruit as it lies before us. Tillich's concern is different. For
Tillich and his fellow Romantics the importance of the fruit is
that it leads to that which lies beyond: the 'thereness' of the
apples is nevertheless inescapable as the only way of mediating
what lies beyond, opening our minds towards it. It is our lot as
human beings to inhabit a sacramental world. This world is a
world of indirect communication making present the ground of

being by way of word and symbol. The artist, whether poet, painter, or theologian, is one who creates the landmarks which guide us on this journey.

Notes

1. Plato, *The Republic*, tr. F. M. Cornford (London: Oxford University Press, 1948), Bk 10, 604e.
2. See Iris Murdoch's rich and thought-provoking commentary on Plato's parable of the Cave, in *The Sovereignty of Good* (London: Routledge & Kegan Paul, 1970), pp. 77–104.
3. Thomas Aquinas, *Summa Theologiae*, tr. Paul T. Durbin (London: Eyre & Spottiswoode, 1968), 1a, 84, 6.
4. See Peter Phillips, 'Bonebound Spirituality', *New Blackfriars* (June 1990), pp. 297–303.
5. Aquinas, *Summa Theologiae*, 1a, 1, 9, tr. Thomas Gilbey (London: Eyre & Spottiswoode, 1963).
6. Wordsworth, 'Intimations of Immortality from Recollections of Early Childhood', line 106.
7. Wordsworth, 'Intimations', lines 206–7.
8. Wordsworth, *The Prelude* (1805 edition), Bk 3, 186–9.
9. Paul Tillich, 'On the Idea of a Theology of Culture', in *Visionary Science*, tr. and introduced, Victor Nuovo (Detroit: Wayne State University, 1987), p. 19.
10. Søren Kierkegaard, *The Concept of Anxiety* (Princeton: Princeton University Press, 1980), p. 88.
11. Wordsworth, *The Prelude* (1805 edition), Bk 1, 372–427.
12. Wordsworth, *The Prelude* (1805 edition), Bk 7, 589–632.
13. Wordsworth, *The Prelude* (1805 edition), Bk 3, 121–67.
14. Wordsworth, *The Prelude* (1805 edition), Bk 11, 269–74.
15. Nuovo, *Visionary Science*, p. 56. One wonders whether Nuovo was aware of the particularly appropriate allusion in the title of his study of Tillich's 'On the Idea of a Theology of Culture': 'visionary' is a word which plays a central role in the thought of Wordsworth.
16. Nuovo, *Visionary Science*, p. 19.
17. Francis Thompson, 'In No Strange Land'.
18. Nuovo, *Visionary Science*, p. 21.
19. Nuovo, *Visionary Science*, p. 30. He suggests (pp. 120f.) that the reference Tillich has in mind here is to Schelling's *Of Human Freedom*. I suspect it is better identified as a reference to Schelling's discussion of contradiction: 'All that comes to be can only do so in discontent; and as dread is the basic feeling of each living creature, so is everything that lives conceived and born only in violent conflict' (Schelling, *The Ages of the World* [322], tr. Frederick de Wolfe Bolman, New York: AMS Press, 1967, p. 211).

20. George Steiner, *Real Presences* (London: Faber & Faber, 1989), p. 230.
21. Paul Tillich, *System of the Sciences* (Luxembourg: Bucknell University Press, 1981), p. 142.
22. Steiner, *Real Presences*, p. 138.
23. Steiner, *Real Presences*, p. 215.
24. Tillich, *System of the Sciences*, p. 143.
25. I. Kant, *The Critique of Judgement*, tr. J. C. Meredith (Oxford: Oxford University Press, 1973), p. 50.
26. See Tillich, *System of the Sciences*, pp. 178–81.
27. Tillich, *System of the Sciences*, p. 180.
28. Tillich, *System of the Sciences*, p. 144; See also, Nuovo, *Visionary Science*, p. 21.
29. Kant, *The Critique of Judgement*, p. 19.
30. Tillich discusses this in detail in *The System of the Sciences* where he argues that 'norms are born in the creative spiritual process. They have reality only in the process. They do not exist in an ideal sphere, as do the pure forms of the thought sciences; nor do they have immediate reality, as do the structures of the empirical sciences. They have the peculiar reality that the creative spiritual process gives them. They enter the process, emerge from it newly formed, and reenter it. They originate from spiritual creation, and the latter is directed to them. They are individual when they are posited by the creative process; they represent the universal when creation is directed to them' (p. 148).
31. Tillich, *System of the Sciences*, p. 171.
32. Wallace Stevens, *Collected Poems* (London: Faber & Faber, 1984), p. 76. See the discussion in Steiner, *Real Presences*, pp. 161f.
33. Nuovo, *Visionary Science*, p. 30.
34. See Frank Kermode, *The Sense of an Ending* (Oxford: Oxford University Press, 1981), p. 58.
35. Kermode, *The Sense of an Ending*, p. 172.
36. See Paul Tillich, *History of Christian Thought* (New York: Simon & Schuster, 1972), pp. 512f.
37. For a fine discussion of the significance of this 'ritual flight from reality' into a world of political and religious kitsch, see Andrew Shanks, *Hegel's Political Theology* (Cambridge: Cambridge University Press, 1991).
38. Stevens, *Collected Poems*, p. 239.
39. See, for example, Tillich's article, 'Philosophy of Religion', reprinted in *What is Religion?*, ed. J. L. Adams (New York: Harper Torchbooks, 1973): 'Matter is not something to be understood in opposition to spirit but remains an expression of the basic originative, creative principle found in everything real, and reach(ing) even into the sphere of the spirit-bearing *Gestalten*' (p. 64).
40. See Tillich's paper, '*Über Gläubiger Realismus*', of 1928. This appeared in an English version as 'Realism and Faith', in Paul Tillich, *The Protestant Era* (London: Nisbet, 1951), pp. 74–92.